# DRAGONSCALES

## 3-Octave Scales and Arpeggios
## In Slow to Fast Rhythms
## In All Keys

### Nick Revel

Design by Kelly DiBernardo Rupert

ISBN 979-8-9875124-2-5

# Introduction

Welcome to DragonScales! This book contains a complete set of scales and arpeggios notated in slow to fast rhythms in all keys. Each key, starting with C, contains six scales (Major, Minor, Whole Tone, two Diminished, and Chromatic) and two sets of arpeggios progressing through eight harmonies. Each scale or arpeggio starts in a slow rhythm and progresses through faster rhythms. A set of audio play-alongs matching the notation is meant to accompany this book and can be streamed on YouTube via the QR code links found on each title page.

## The Notation

What makes DragonScales unique is that the standard rhythmic progression from slow to fast is made explicit in the notation, making it easy for students of all levels to read and understand the rhythmic content of their scale playing. Visual transitions from one rhythm to the next reinforce metric relationships and pulse within an overall tempo.

The notation is intentionally written without fingering or slurring suggestions so as to be more adaptable to students' and teachers' needs. A good place to begin is maintaining a consistent pulse by slurring in two-beat groups throughout the rhythmic progression (half note, two quarter notes, three quarter-note triplets, etc.). Then, you can experiment with different slur groupings and other variables including dynamics, tone, and articulations.

## The Audio Play-Alongs

While the notation does work as a stand-alone system, the addition of the DragonScales audio play-alongs transforms it into a powerful practice tool that keeps you grounded in pulse, rhythm, and pitch at every moment. Unlike traditional metronomes and static drones, DragonScales audio play-alongs accompany the notation exactly, offering a perfect reference for rhythm and pitch at all times, even in the fastest rhythms.

The play-alongs are found on YouTube in playlists organized by key. To stream, simply point your phone's camera at the QR code on the title page of the key in which you wish to play and allow your phone to open the YouTube app or web browser when prompted. You can then easily select your desired scale or arpeggio. Play-alongs are also available for purchase to enable offline use (www.nickrevel.com/dragonscales)

## The Rhythmic Progression

You can find the guide to the rhythmic progression used throughout DragonScales on the next page. These rhythms correspond to both the audio play-alongs and the fully notated scales in this book. For all the scales, each bar in the guide represents one full play-through of the 3-octave scale. The first play-through is all half notes, the second play-through is all quarter notes, and so on. Major and minor scales, the whole tone scale, diminished scales, and the chromatic scale all have their own rhythmic progression. In Arpeggios Version 1, the first bar in each two bar segment represents the rhythm for the first eight chords in the progression (3-note chords), and the second bar represents the rhythm for the final two (4-note chords). In other words, the first two-bar segment in the rhythm guide represents one full play-through of all the chords. Arpeggios Version 2 is opposite, where each chord moves through its full rhythmic progression one at a time.

# Rhythmic Progression

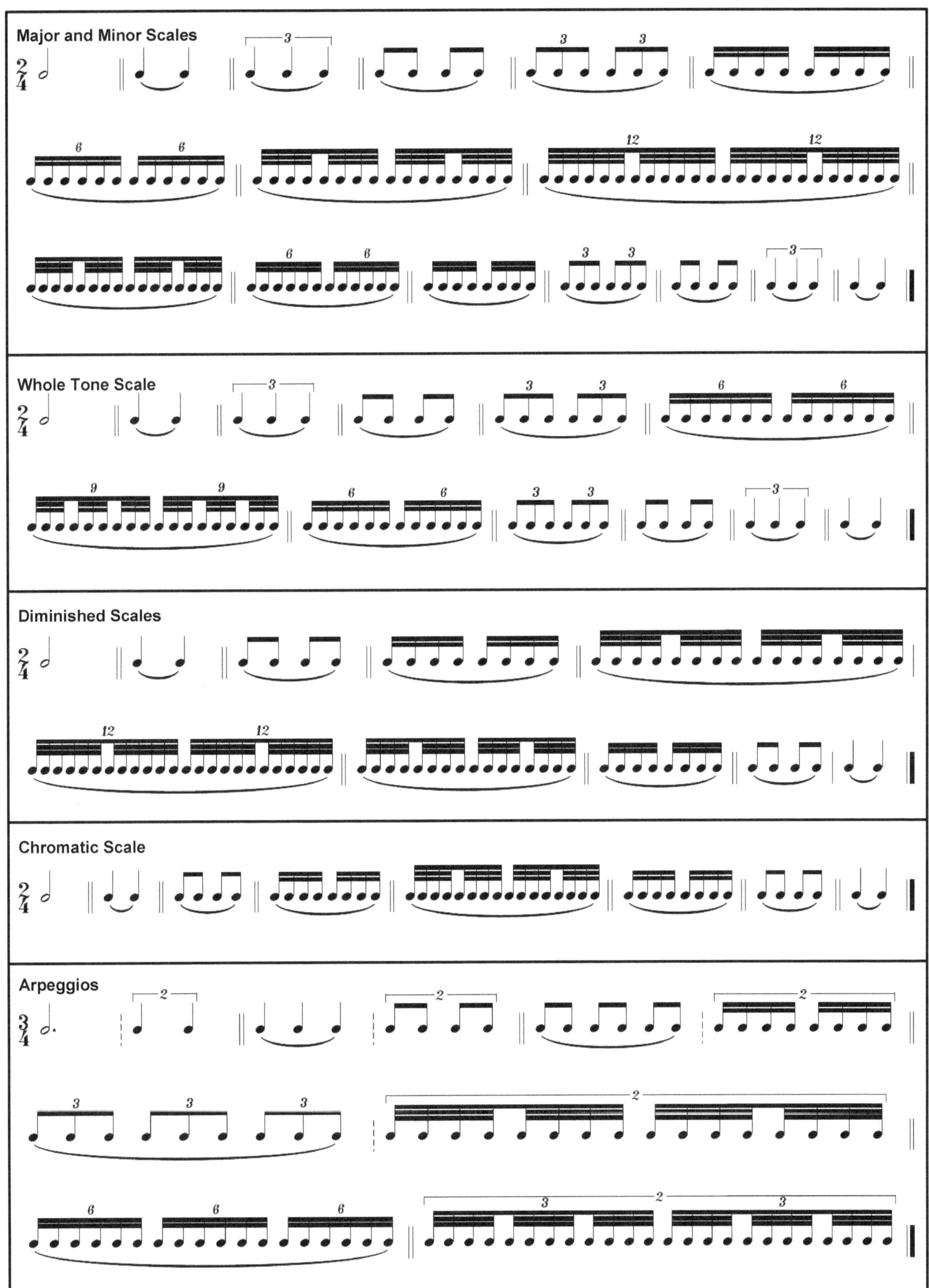

# DRAGONSCALES

3-Octave Scales and Arpeggios
In Slow to Fast Rhythms
In All Keys

Nick Revel

G

# DragonScales
## The Complete Set in G

Nick Revel

**Major**

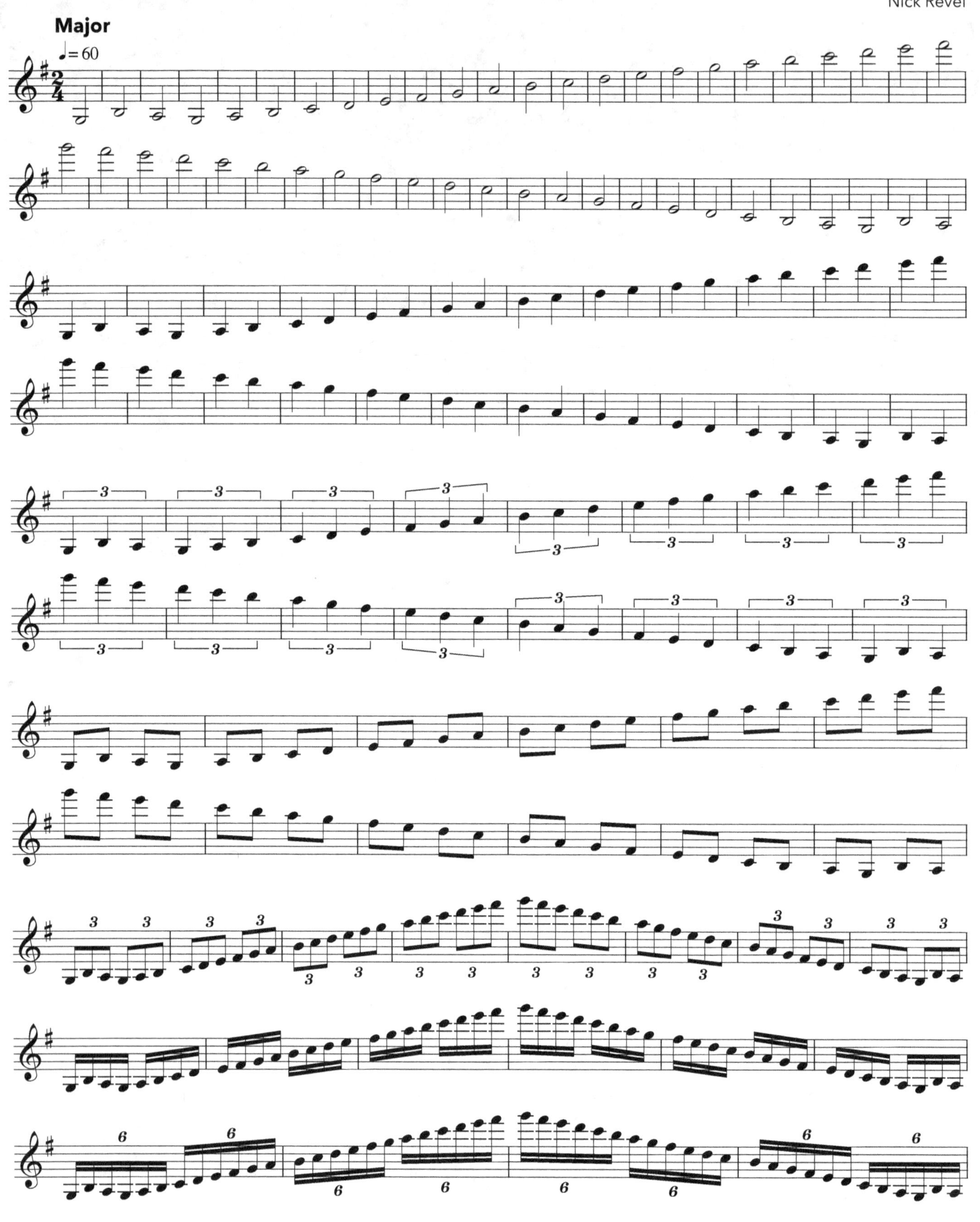


© Nick Revel 2018

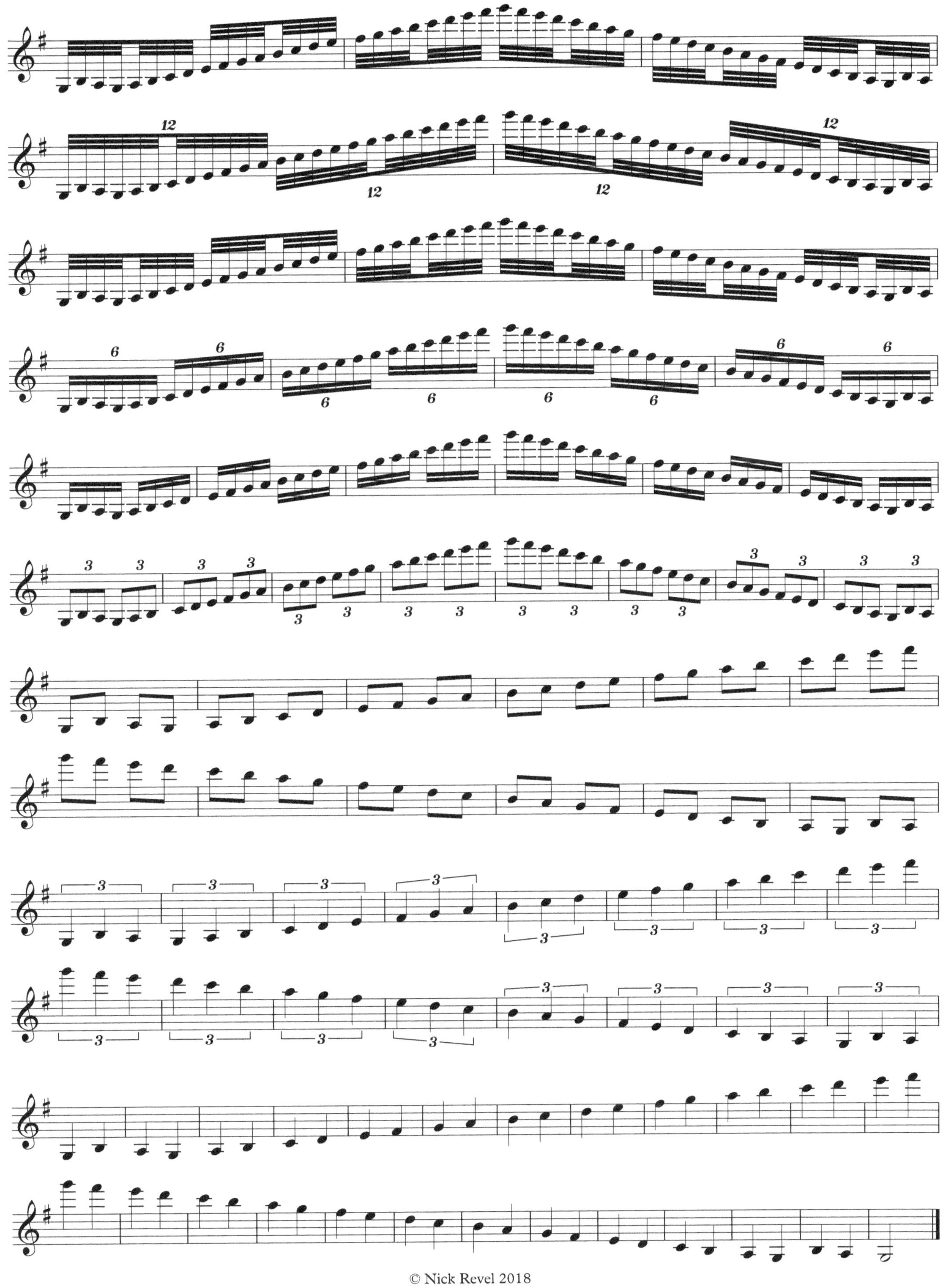

© Nick Revel 2018

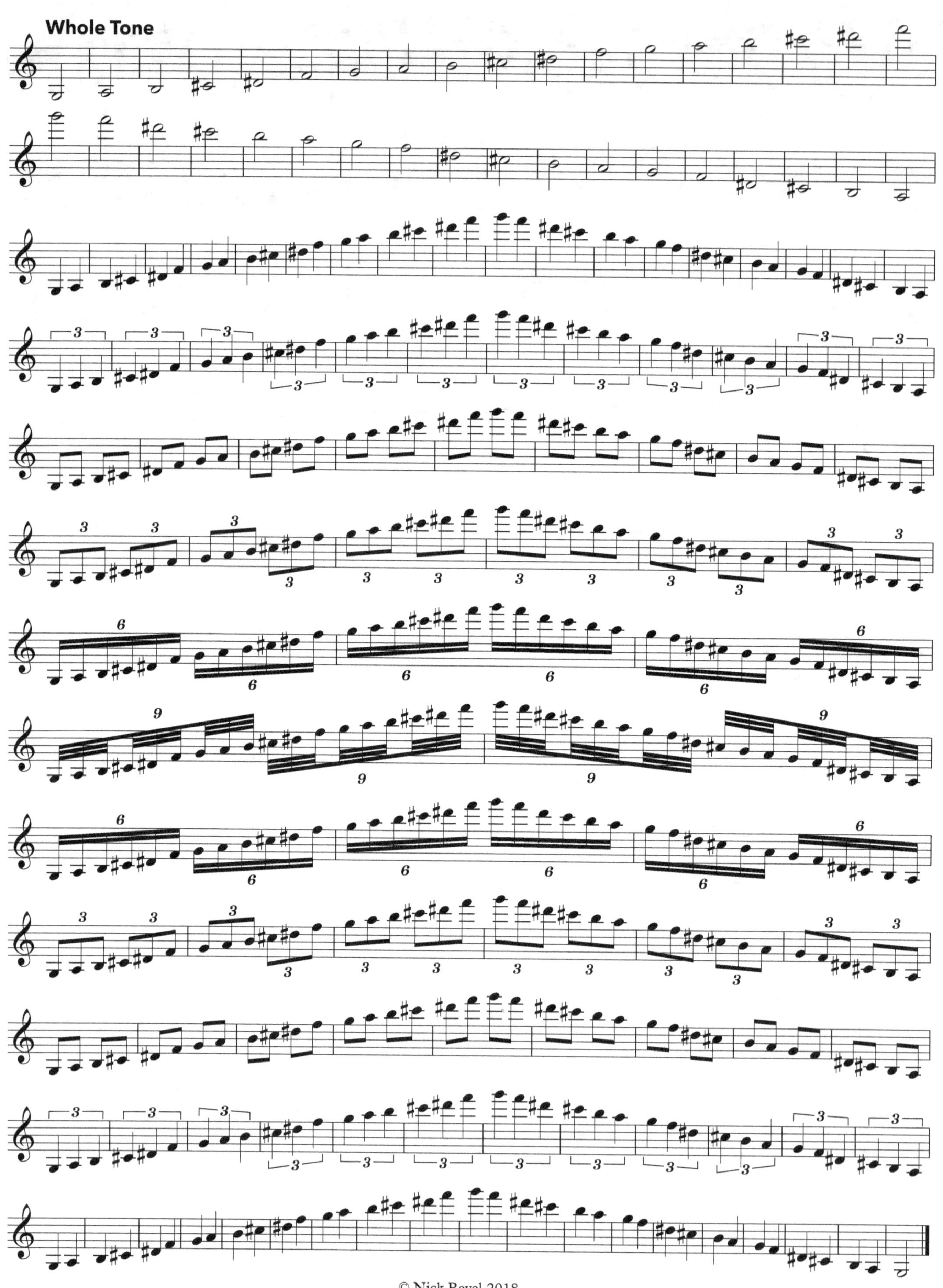

© Nick Revel 2018

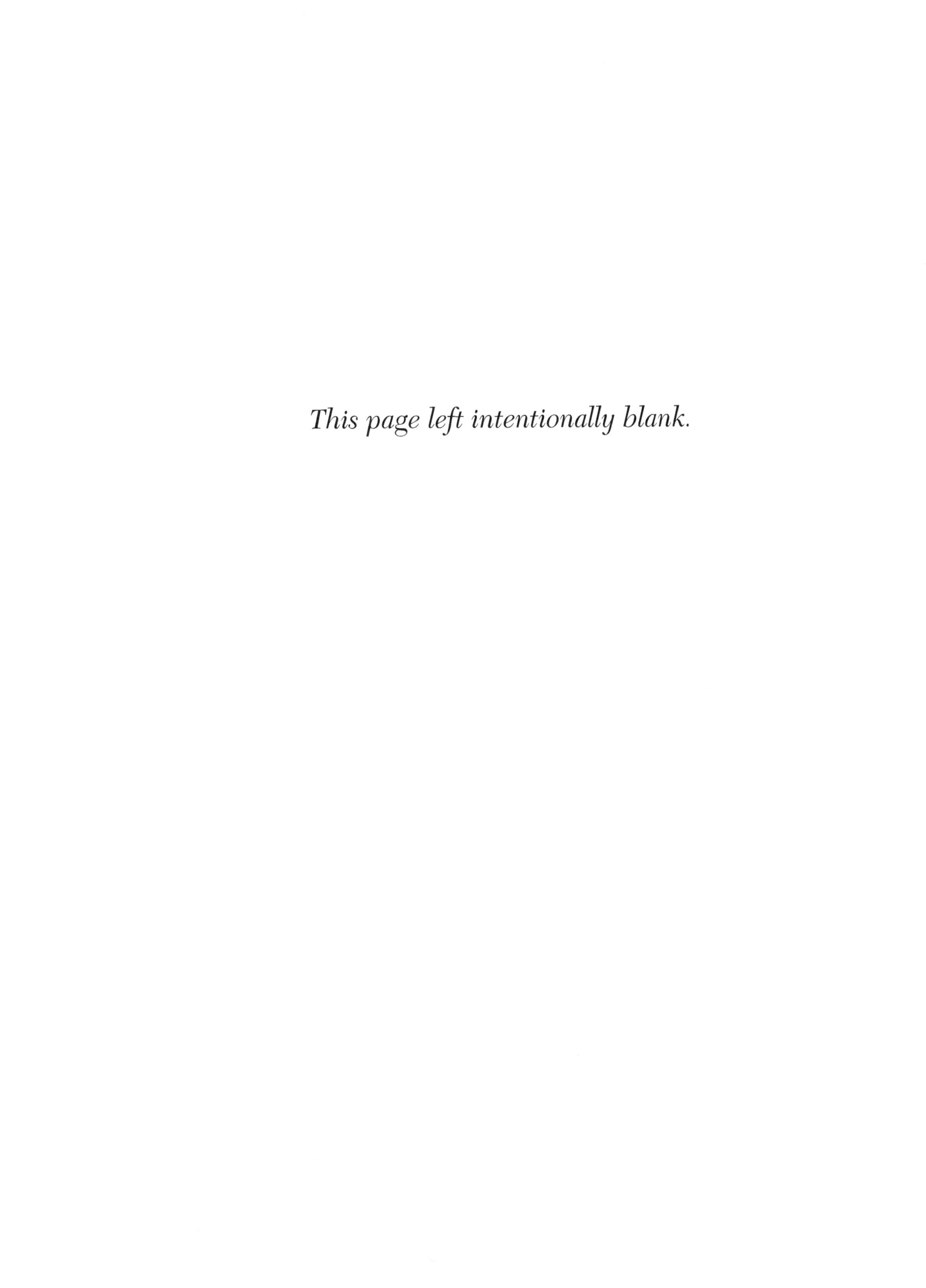

This page left intentionally blank.

# Diminished Scale Version 1

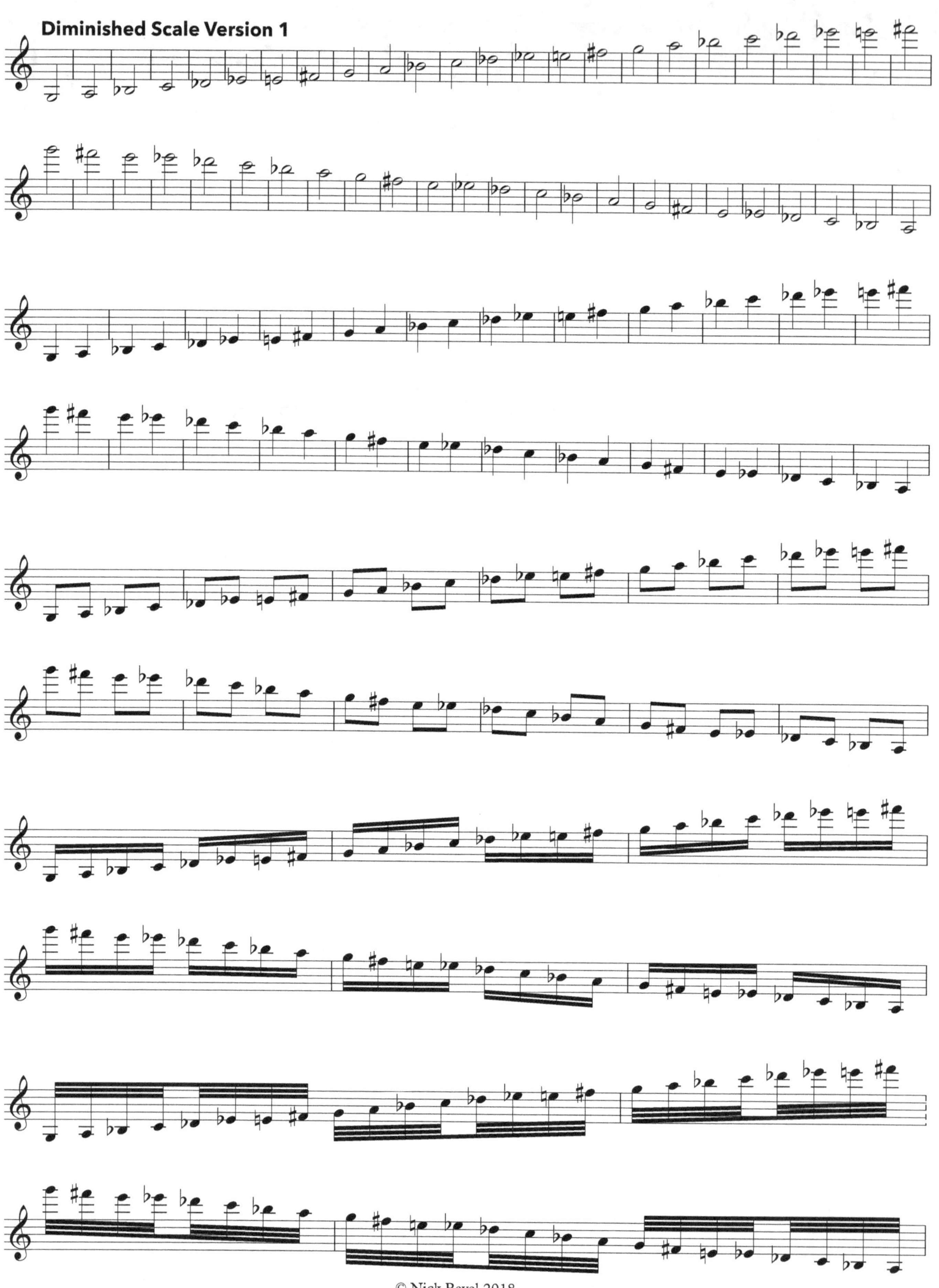

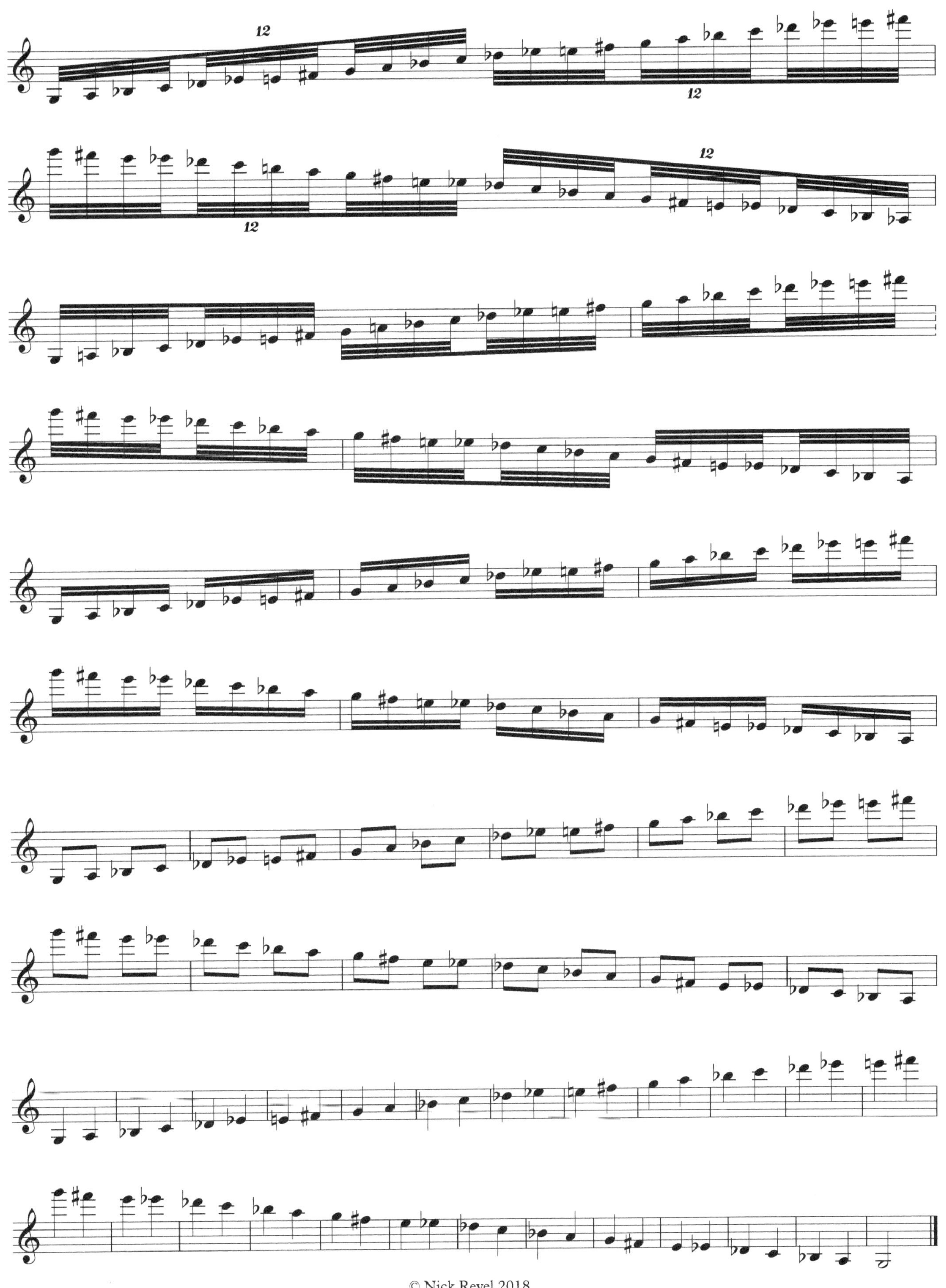



© Nick Revel 2018

## Diminished Scale Version 2

© Nick Revel 2018

12
12
12
12
© Nick Revel 2018

Chromatic
© Nick Revel 2018

## Arpeggios Version 1

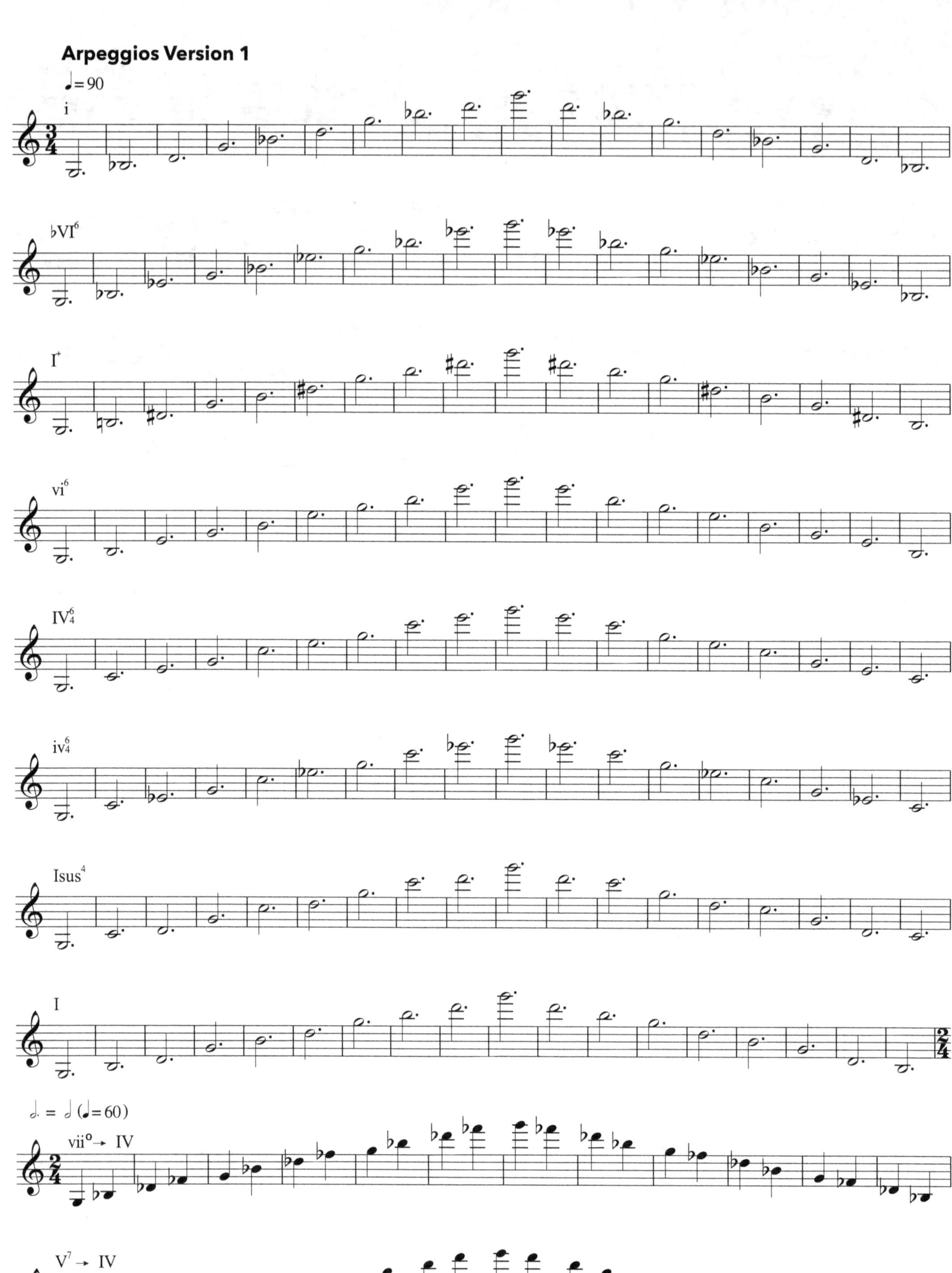


© Nick Revel 2018

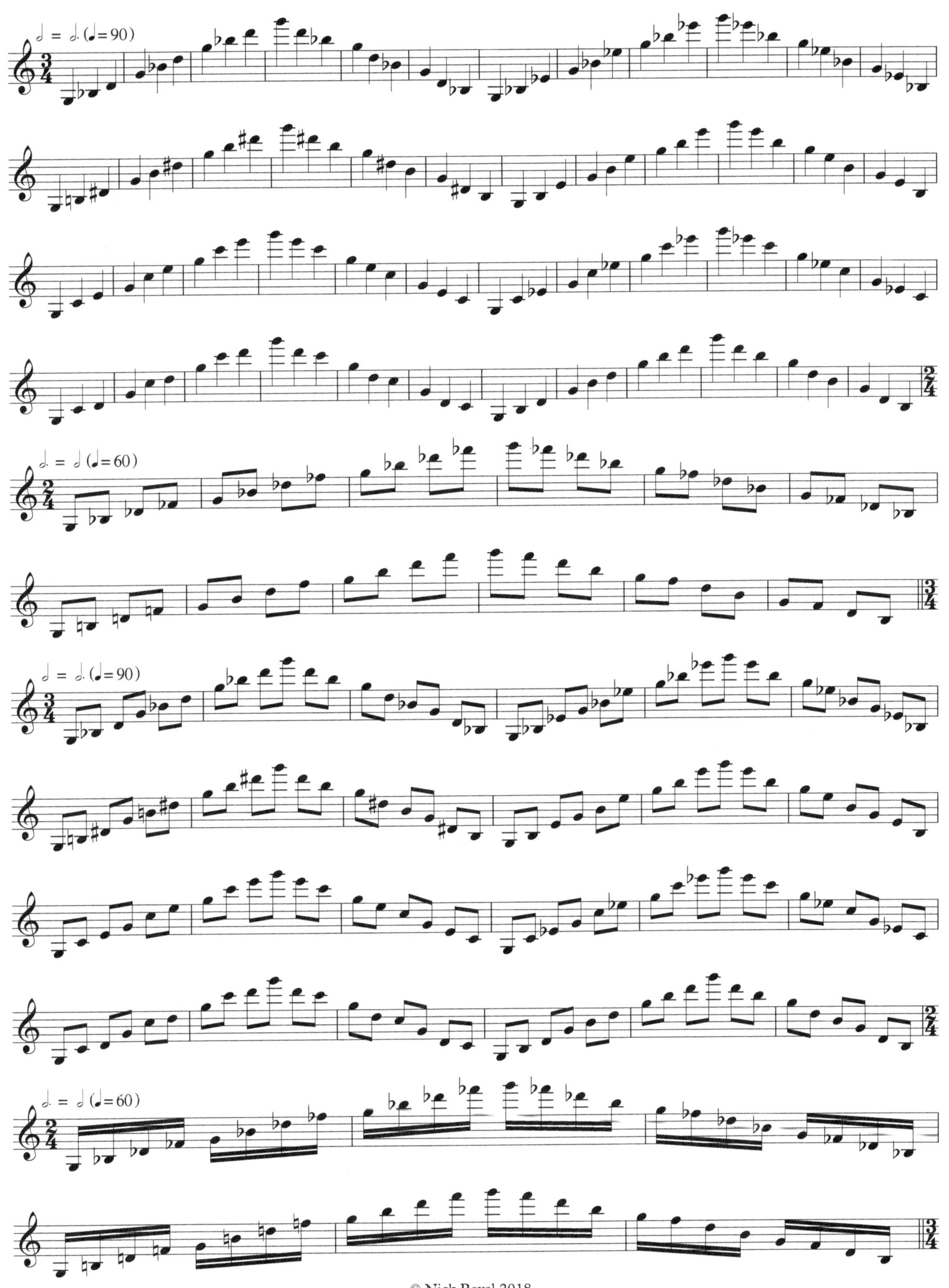

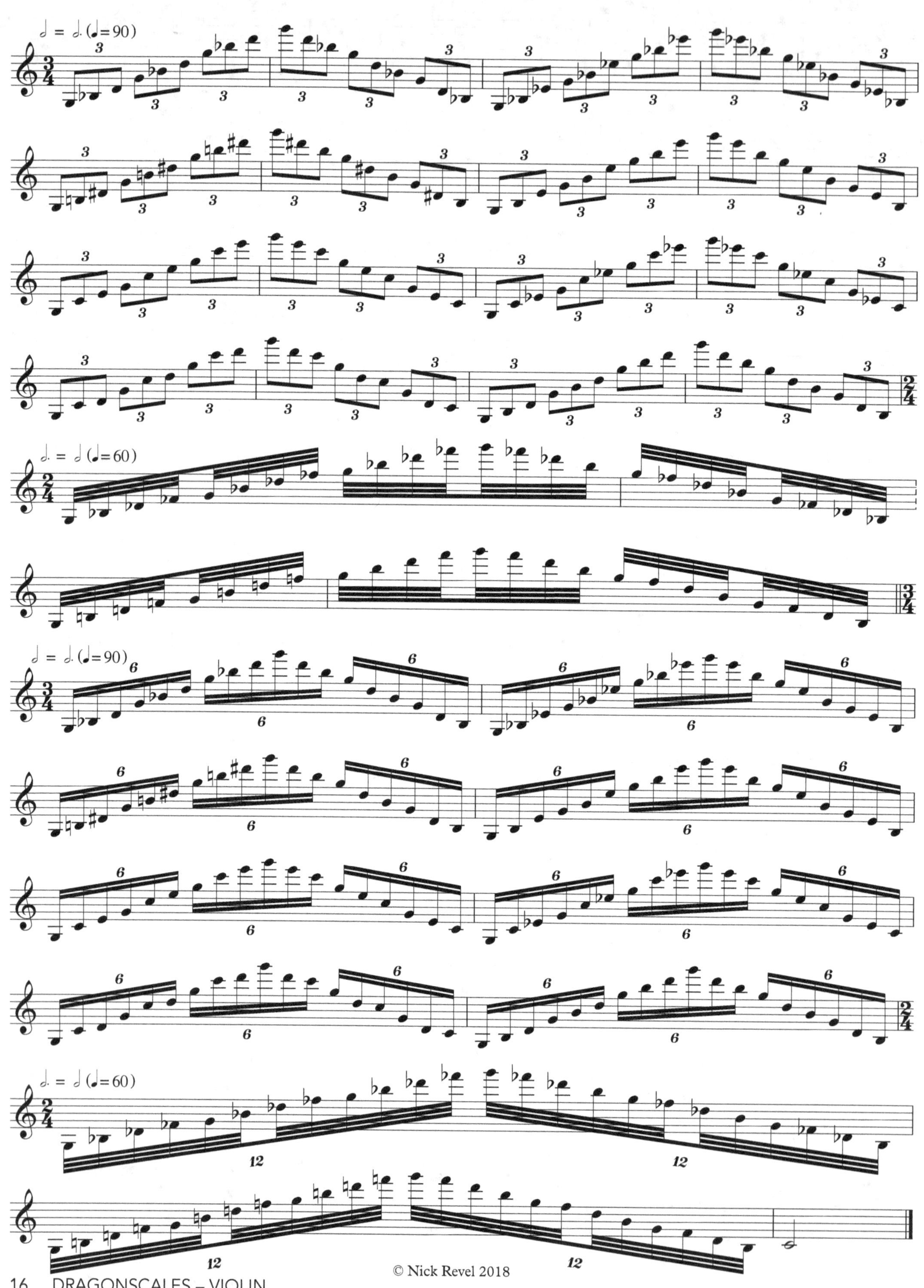

16  DRAGONSCALES – VIOLIN
© Nick Revel 2018

*This page left intentionally blank.*

Arpeggios Version 2
♩ = 90


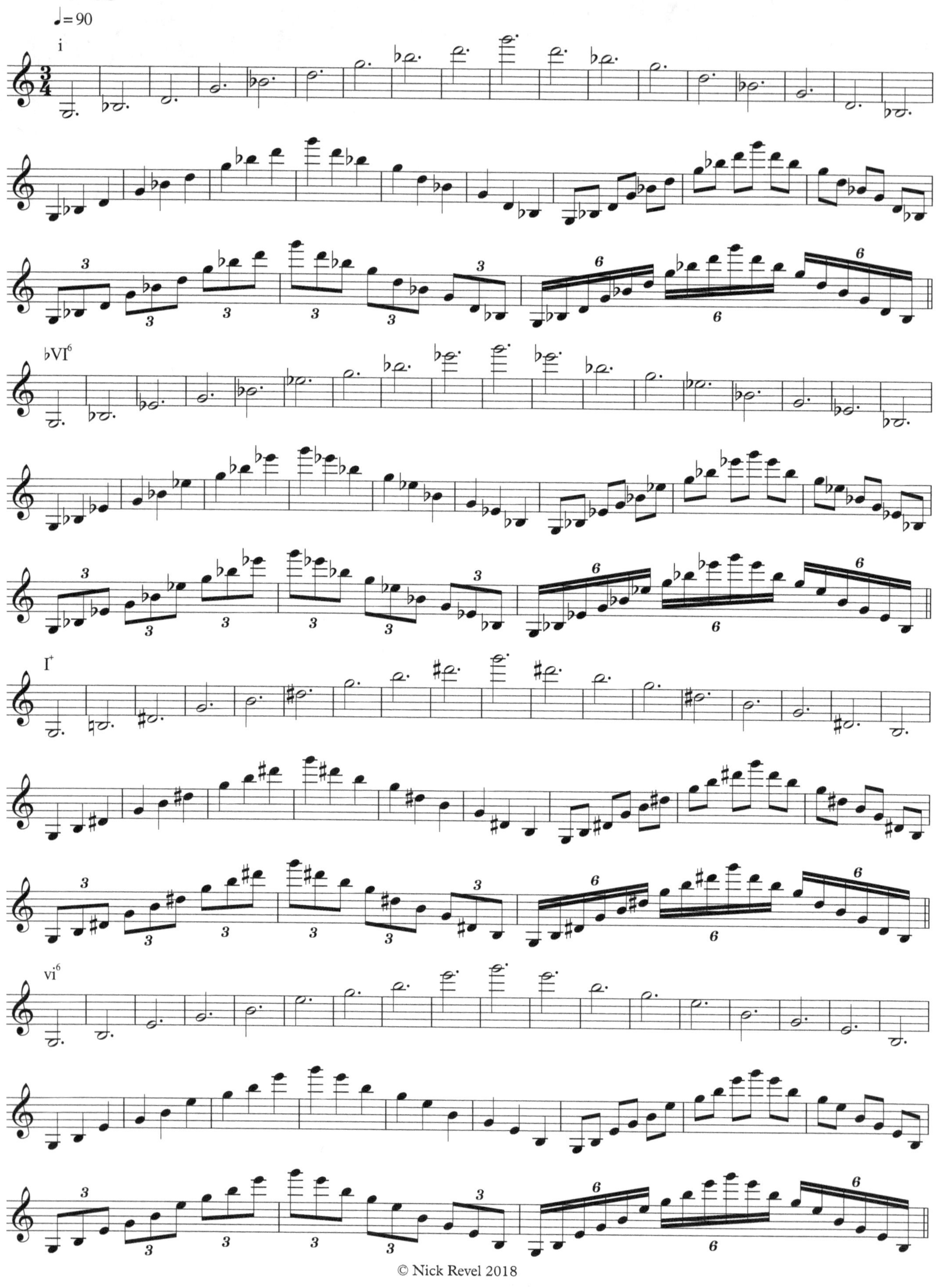


© Nick Revel 2018

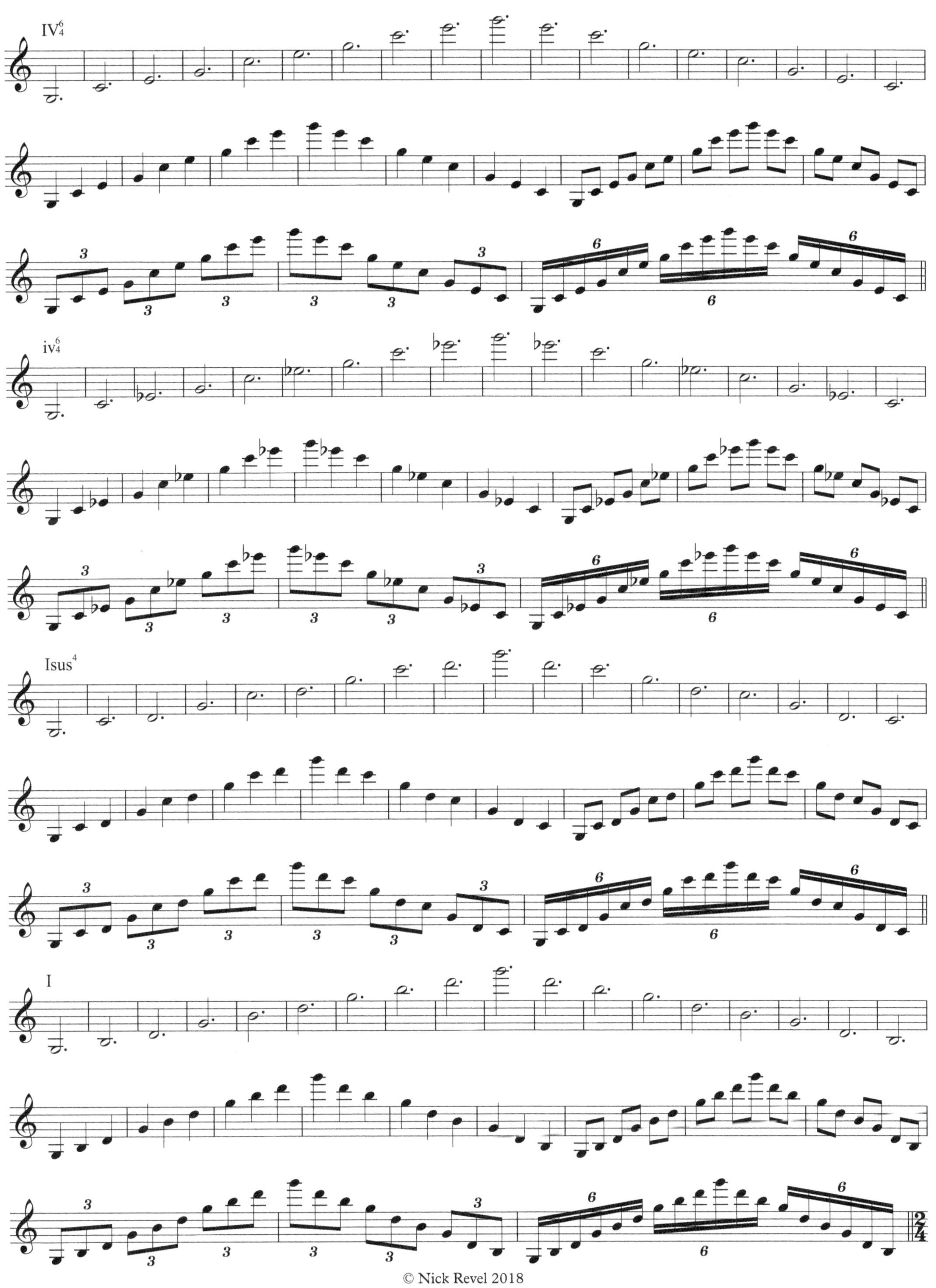

IV⁶₄
iv⁶₄
Isus⁴
I
3
3
3
3
3
3
3
3
3
3
6
6
6
6
6
6
6
6
6
6
6
6
6
6
6
6
2/4

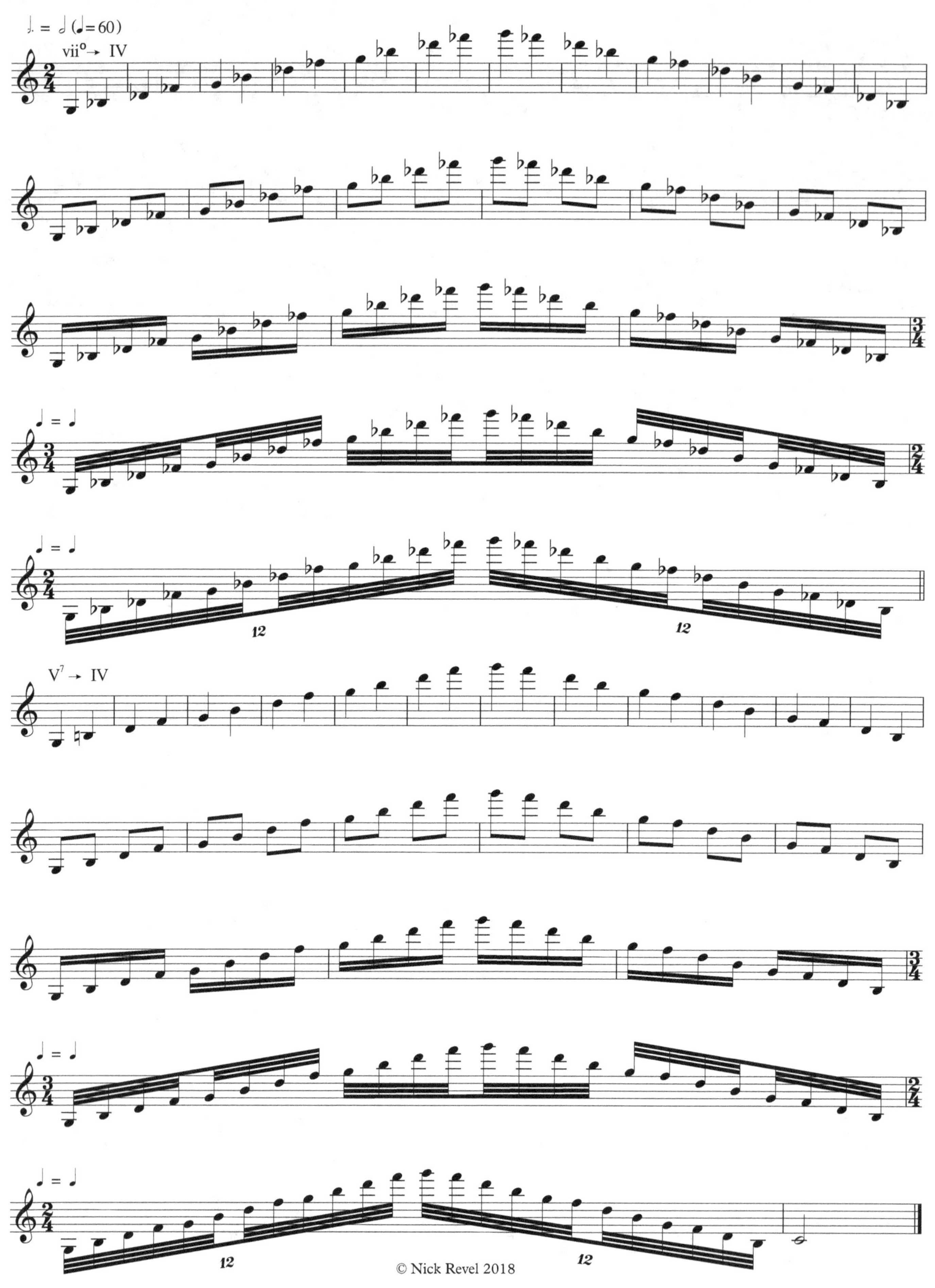

♩. = ♪ (♩=60)
viiº→ IV
V⁷ → IV
12
12
© Nick Revel 2018

# DRAGONSCALES

3-Octave Scales and Arpeggios
In Slow to Fast Rhythms
In All Keys

Nick Revel

# G#/Ab

# DragonScales
## The Complete Set in G#Ab

Nick Revel

**Major**

© Nick Revel 2018

© Nick Revel 2018

© Nick Revel 2018

Whole Tone

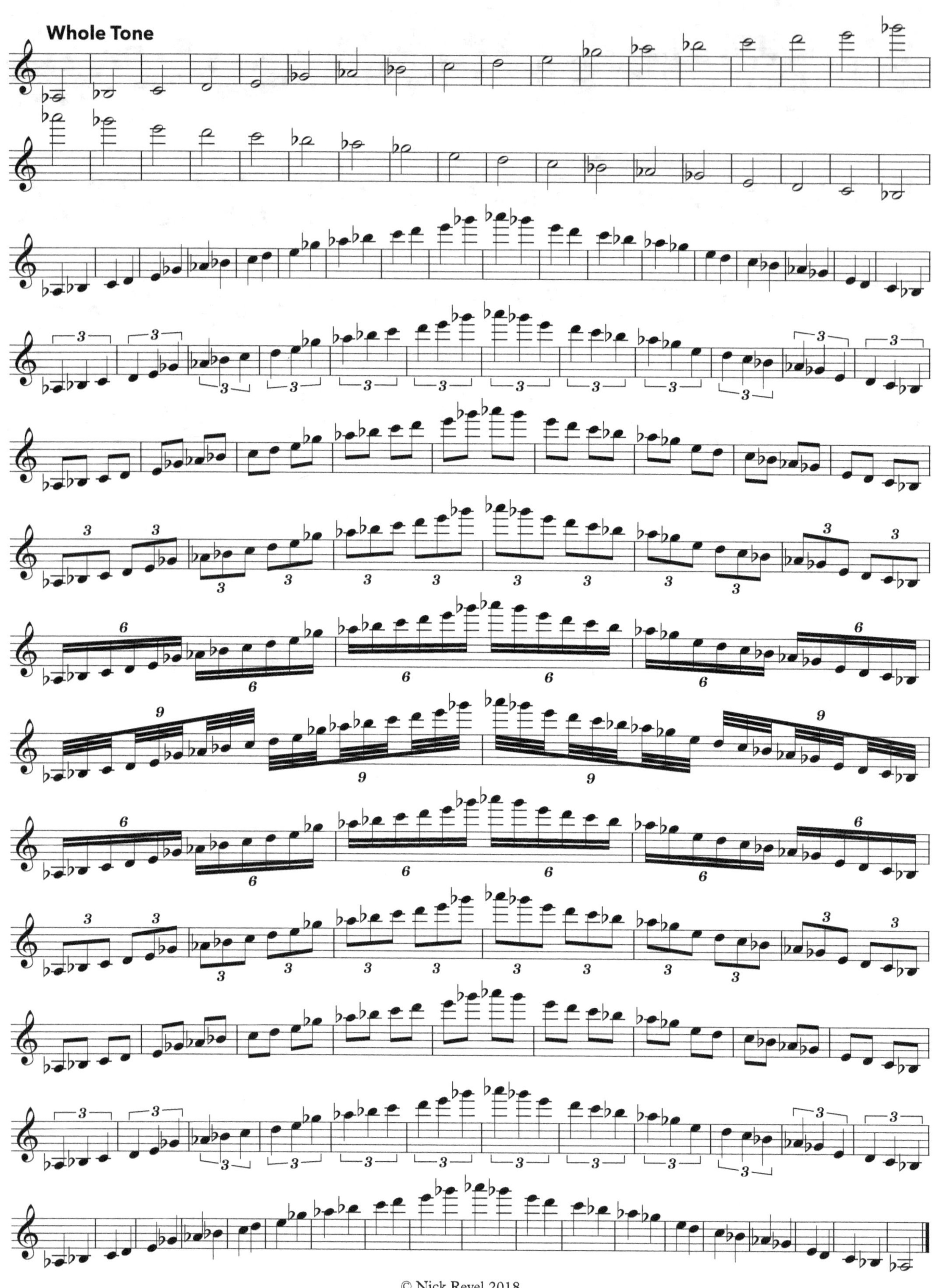

© Nick Revel 2018

*This page left intentionally blank.*

**Diminished Scale Version 1**

© Nick Revel 2018

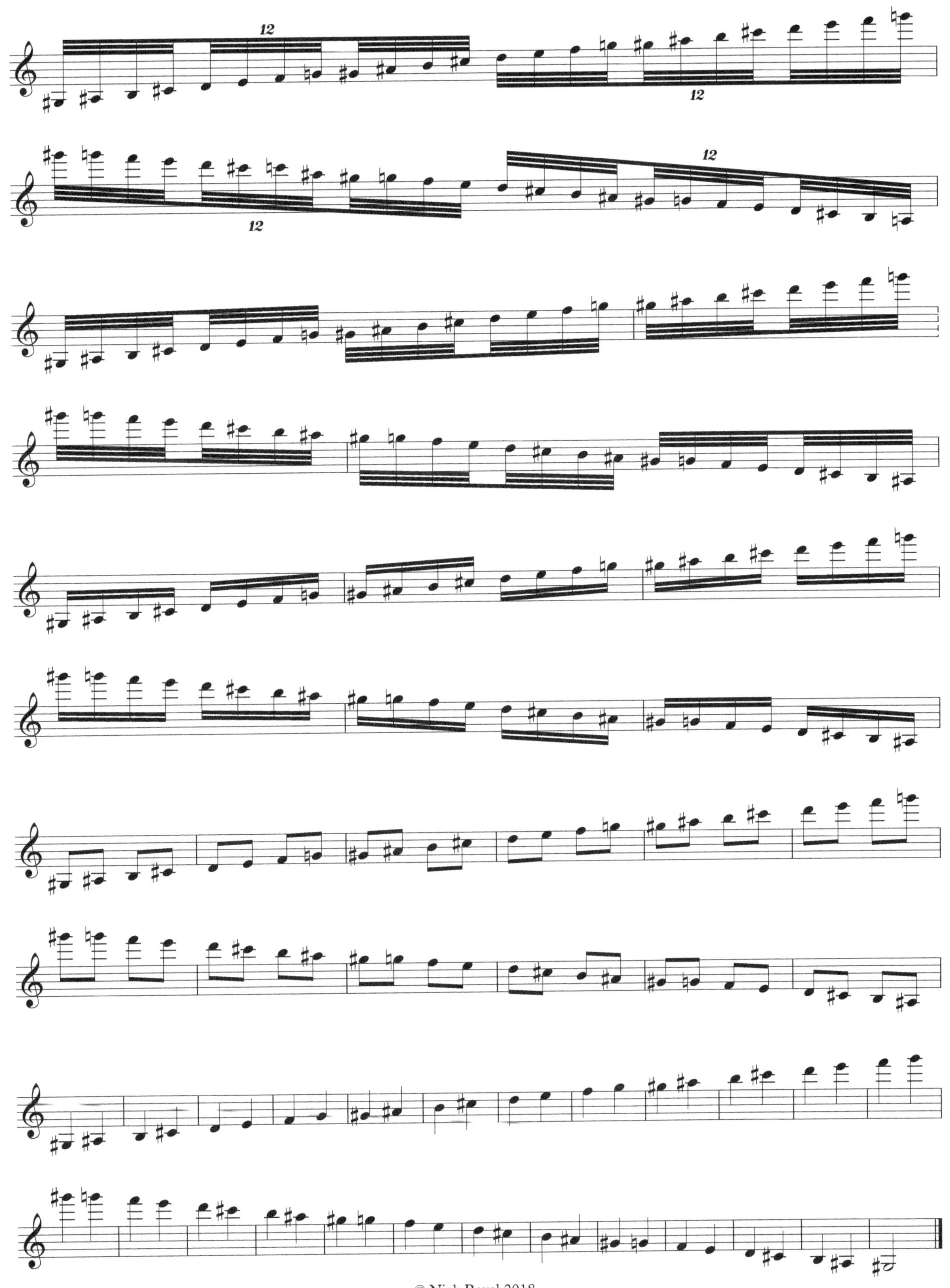

# Diminished Scale Version 2

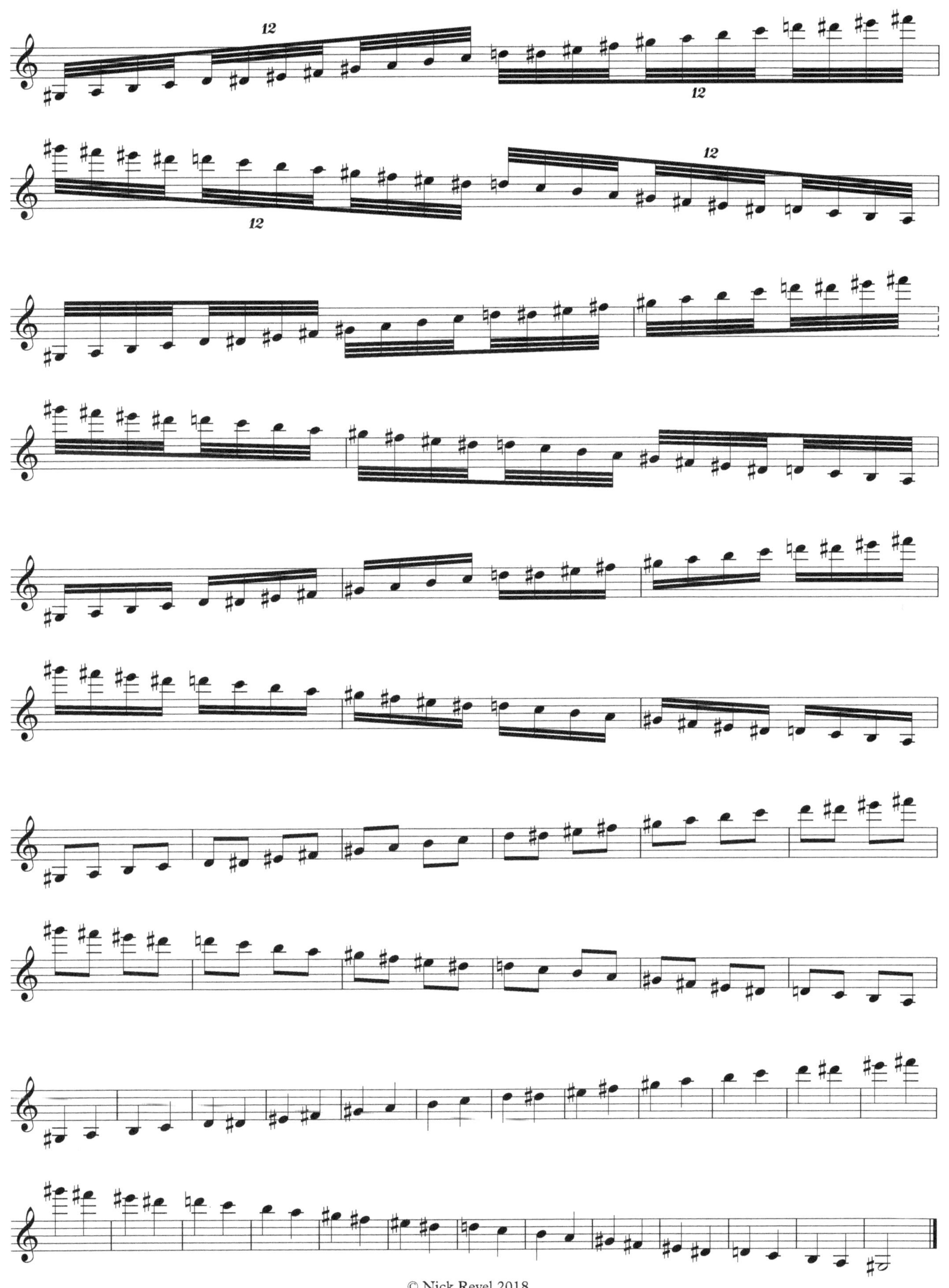


12
12
12
12
© Nick Revel 2018

Chromatic

© Nick Revel 2018

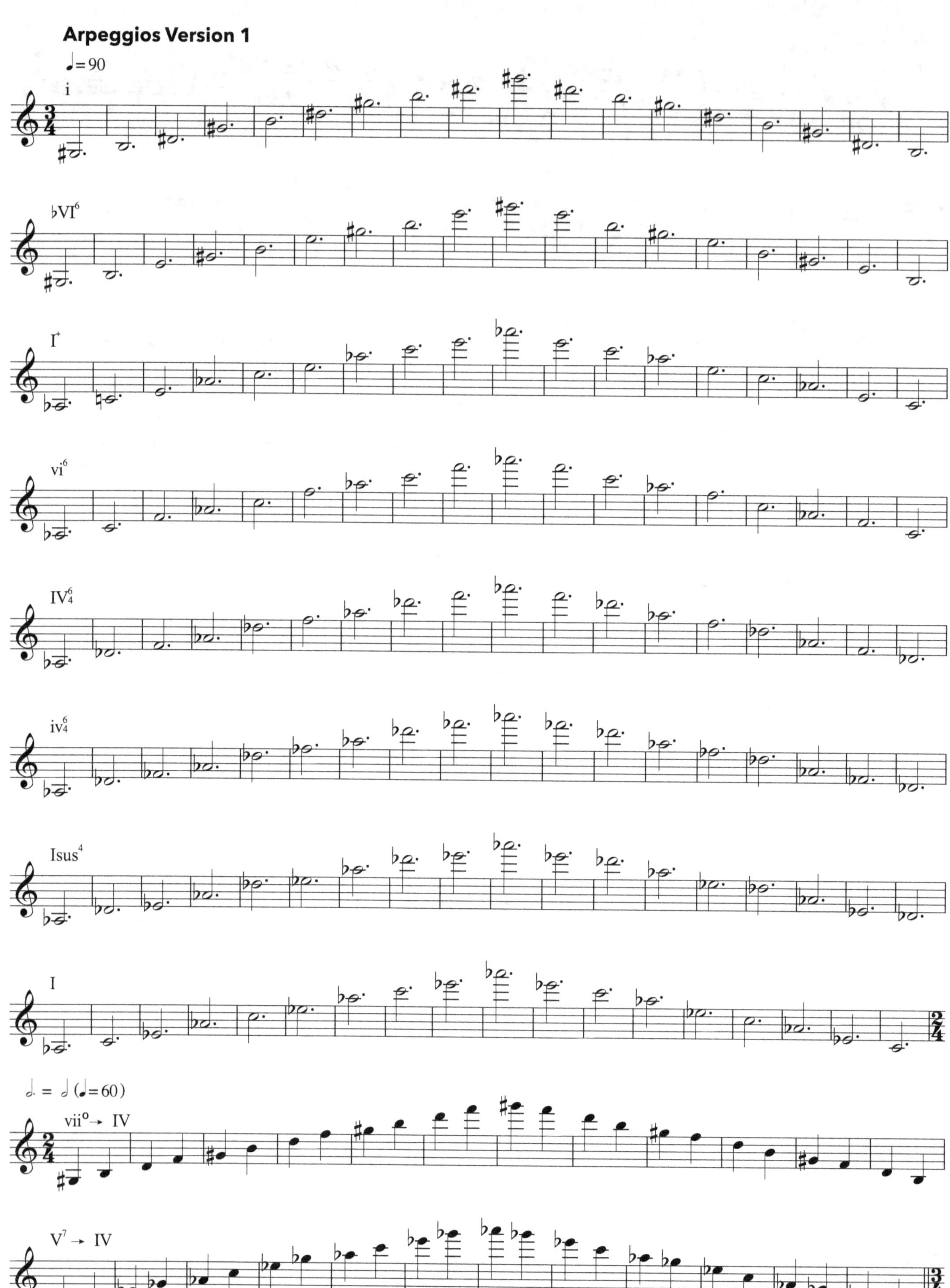


© Nick Revel 2018

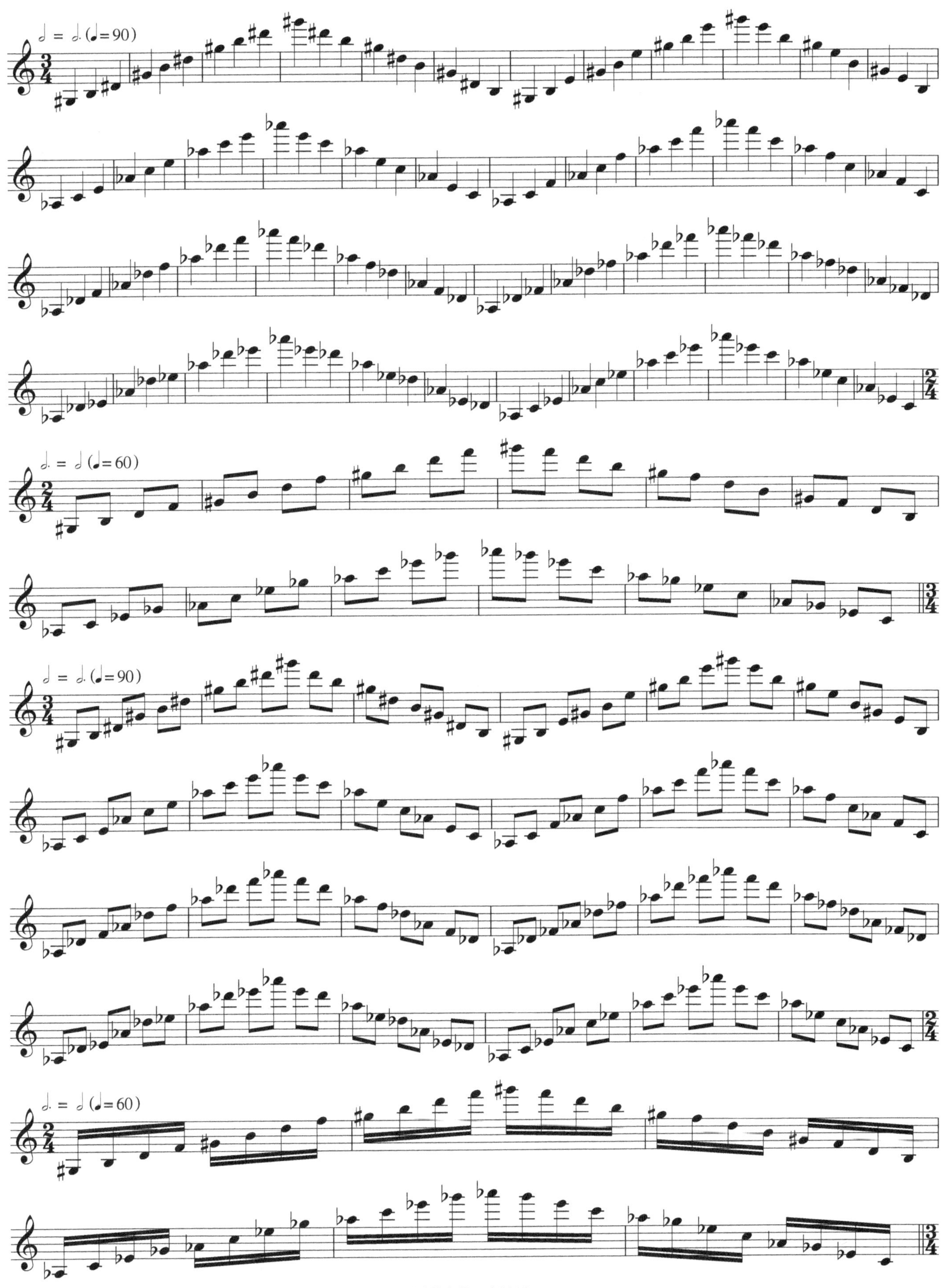


© Nick Revel 2018

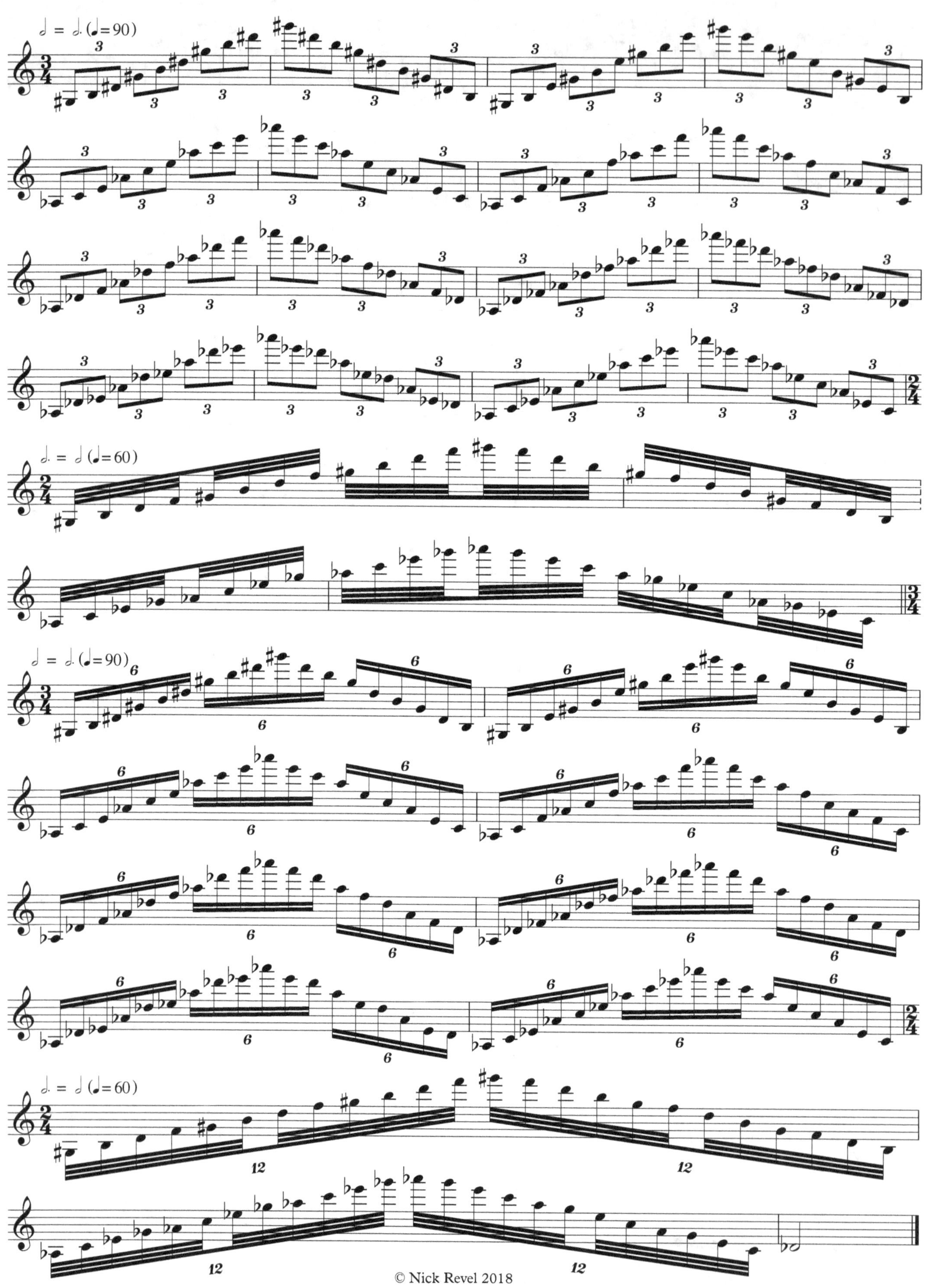

DRAGONSCALES – VIOLIN

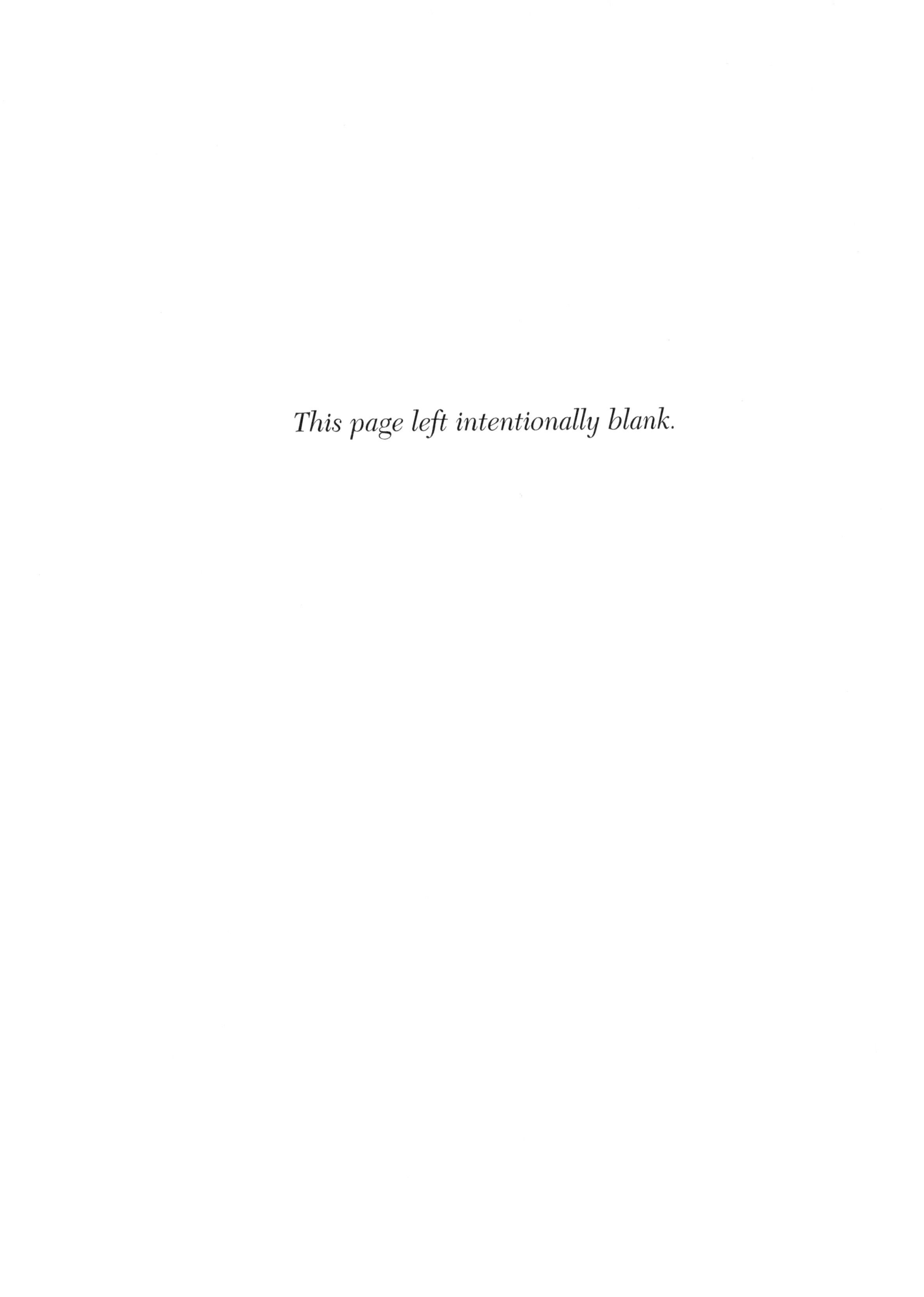

*This page left intentionally blank.*

## Arpeggios Version 2

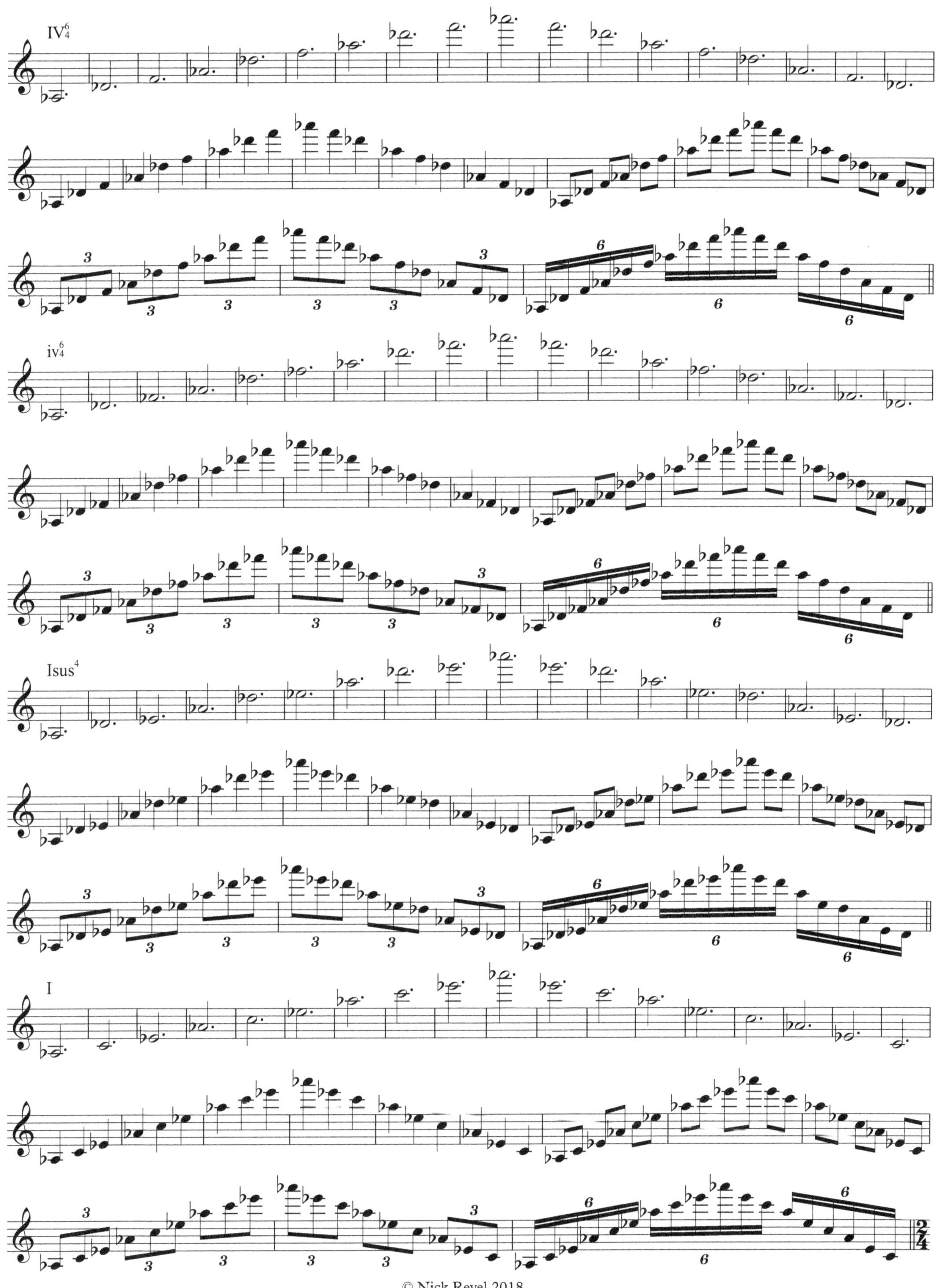

IV6/4
iv6/4
Isus4
I
3   3   3   3   3   6   6
© Nick Revel 2018

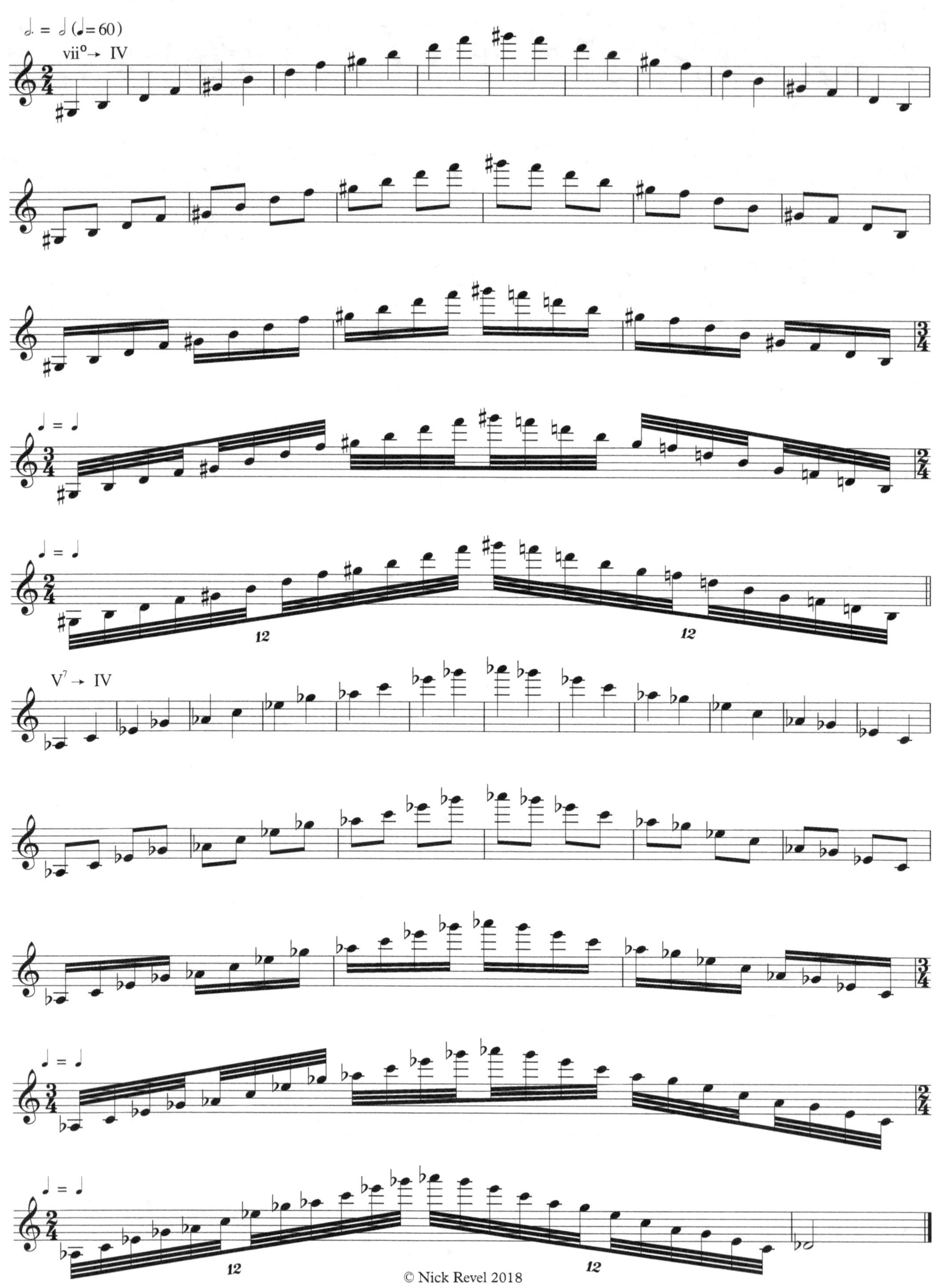

♩. = ♩ (♩=60)
viiº → IV
V⁷ → IV
12
12
12
12
© Nick Revel 2018

# DRAGONSCALES

3-Octave Scales and Arpeggios
In Slow to Fast Rhythms
In All Keys

Nick Revel

A

# DragonScales
## The Complete Set in A

Nick Revel

**Major**

© Nick Revel 2018

© Nick Revel 2018

Minor

© Nick Revel 2018

## Whole Tone

© Nick Revel 2018

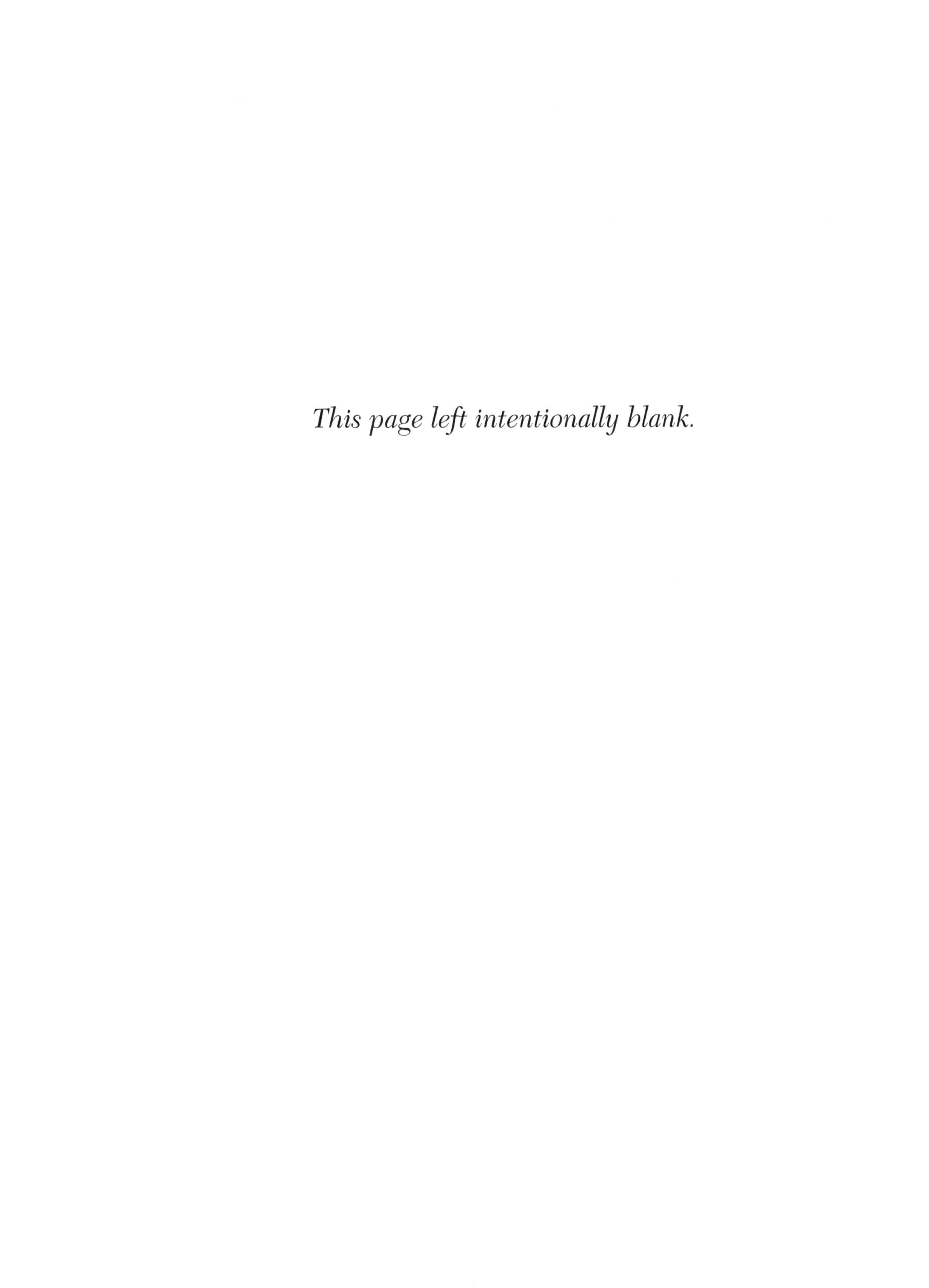

*This page left intentionally blank.*

Diminished Scale Version 1

© Nick Revel 2018

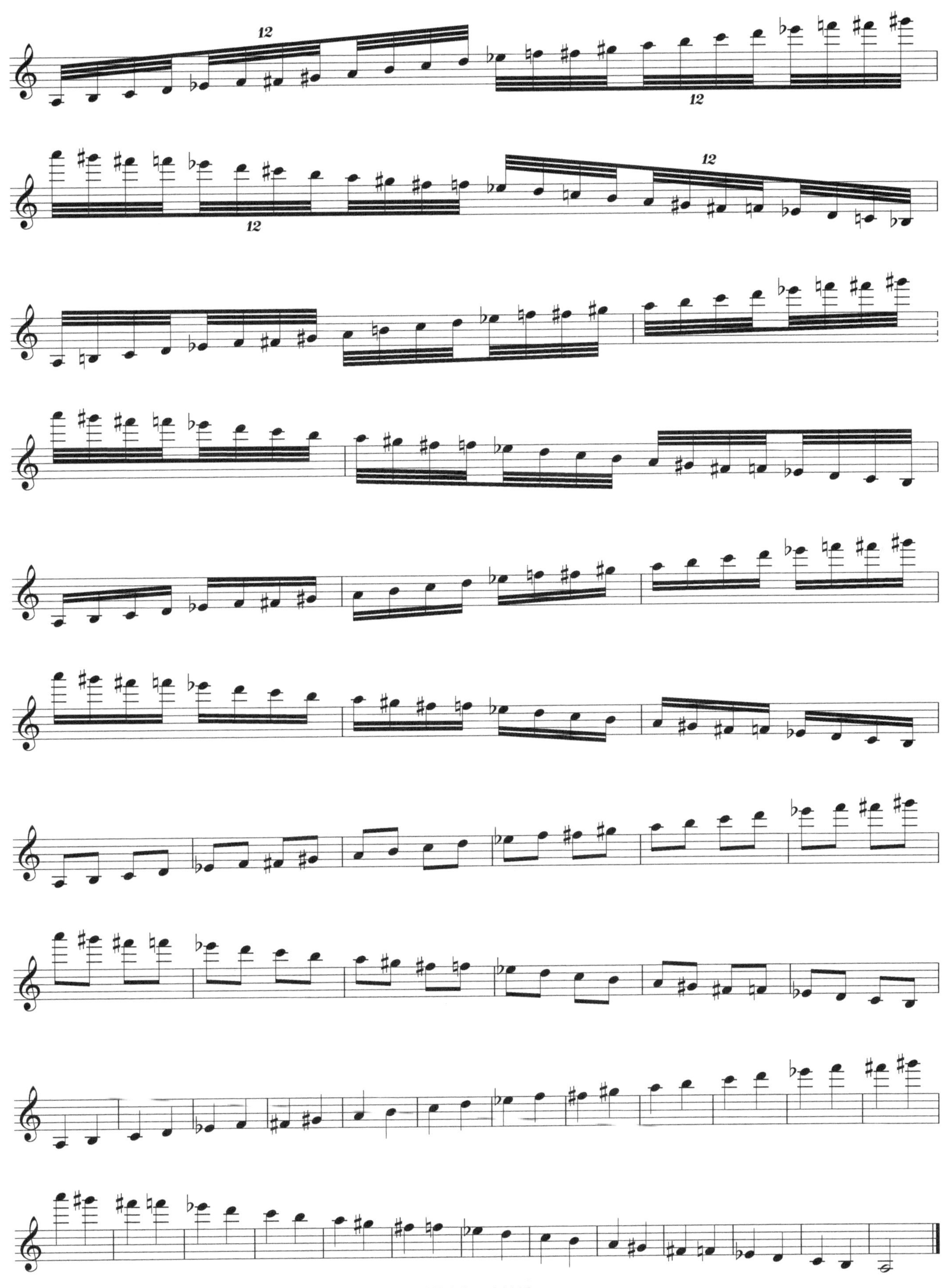



© Nick Revel 2018

**Diminished Scale Version 2**

12
12
12
12

# Chromatic

## Arpeggios Version 1

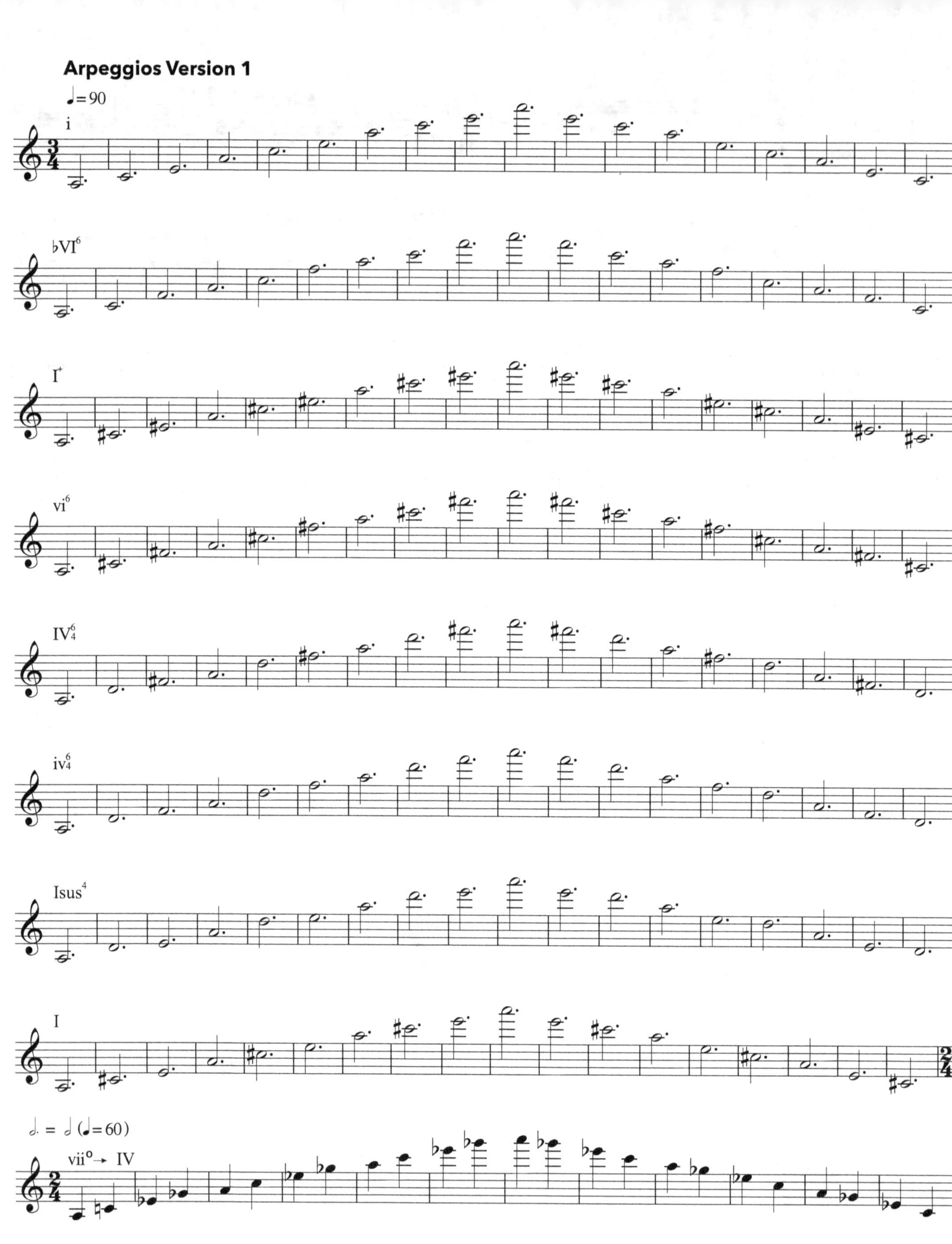

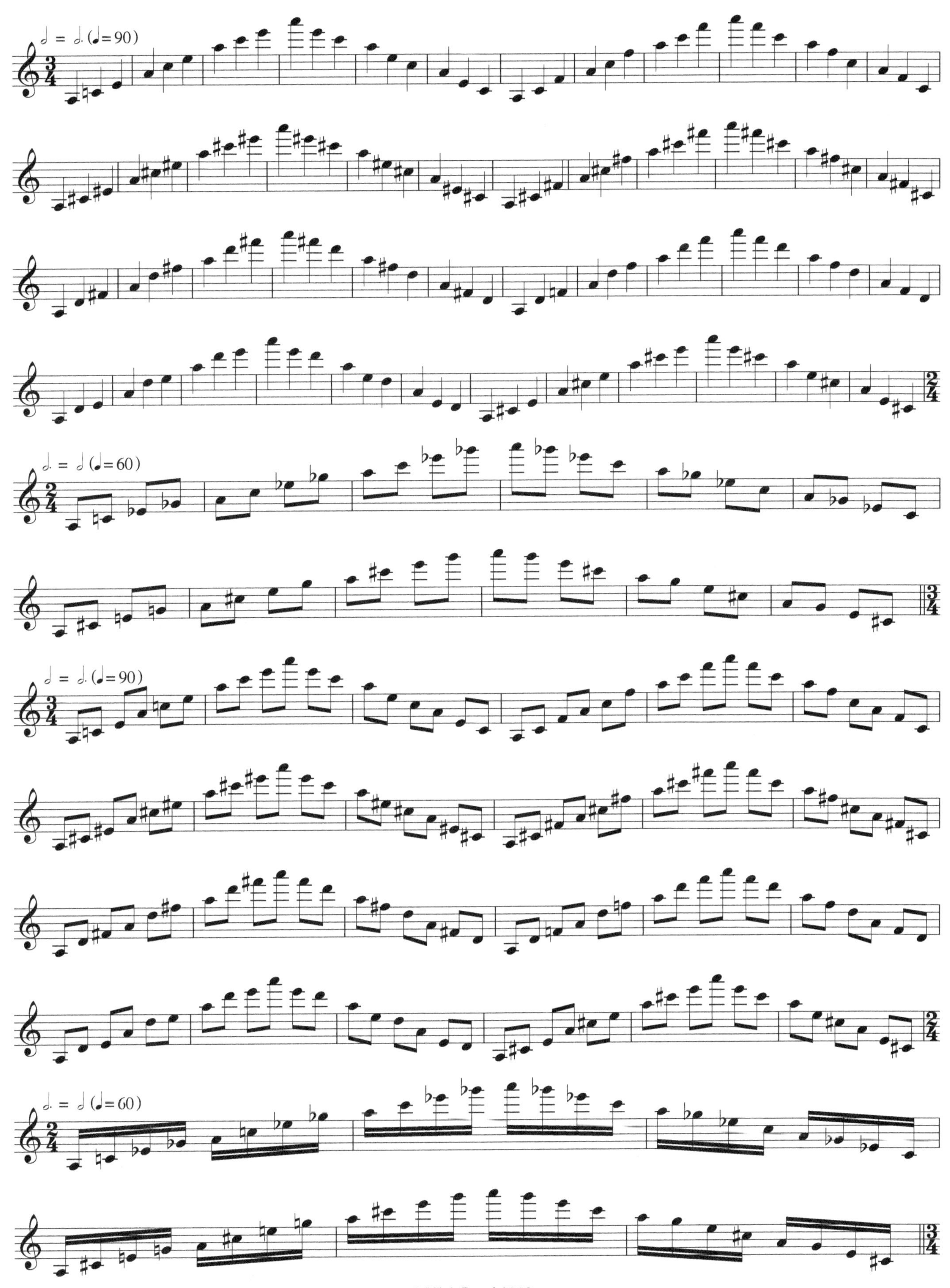
DRAGONSCALES – VIOLIN    55

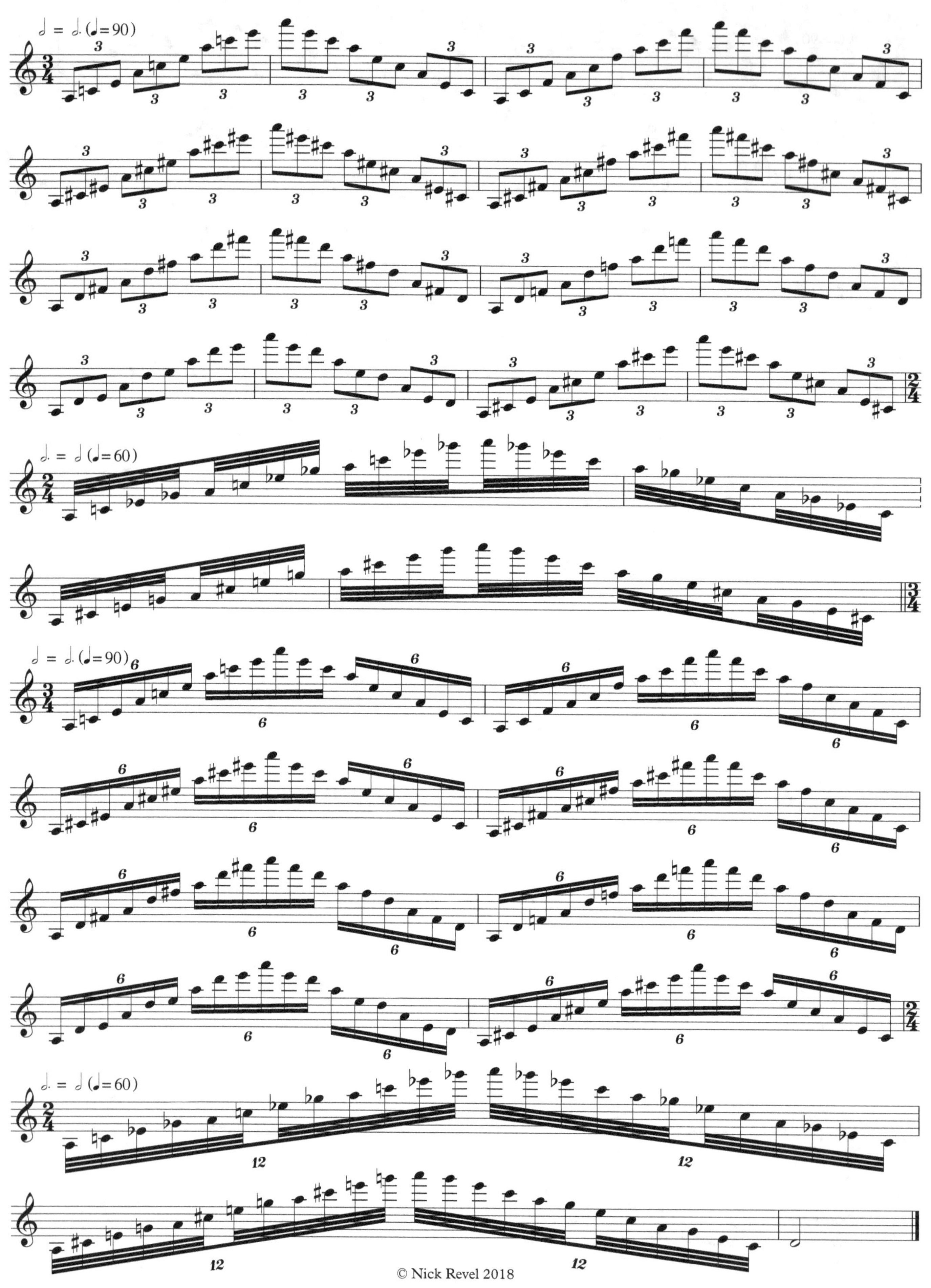

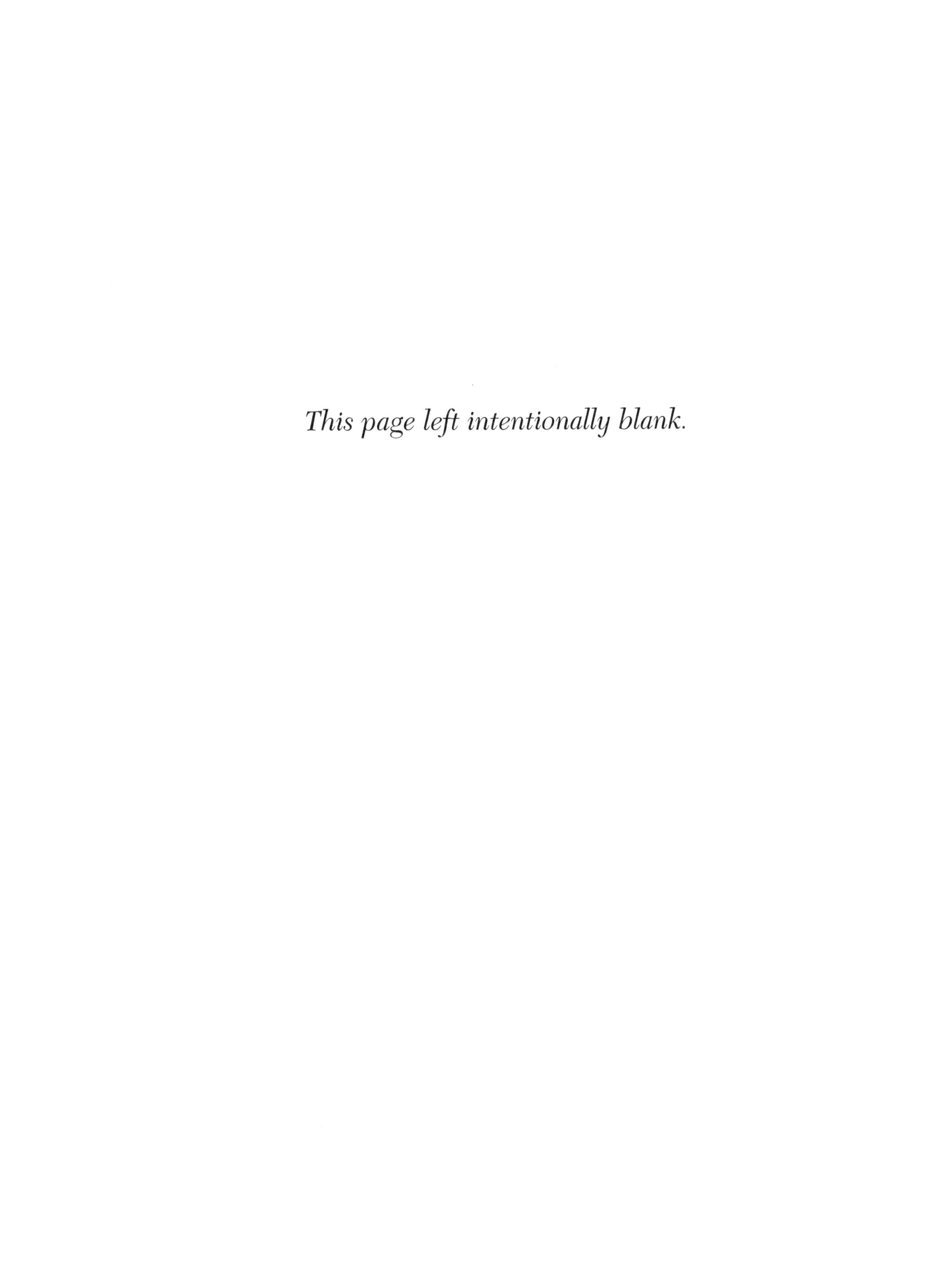

*This page left intentionally blank.*

# Arpeggios Version 2

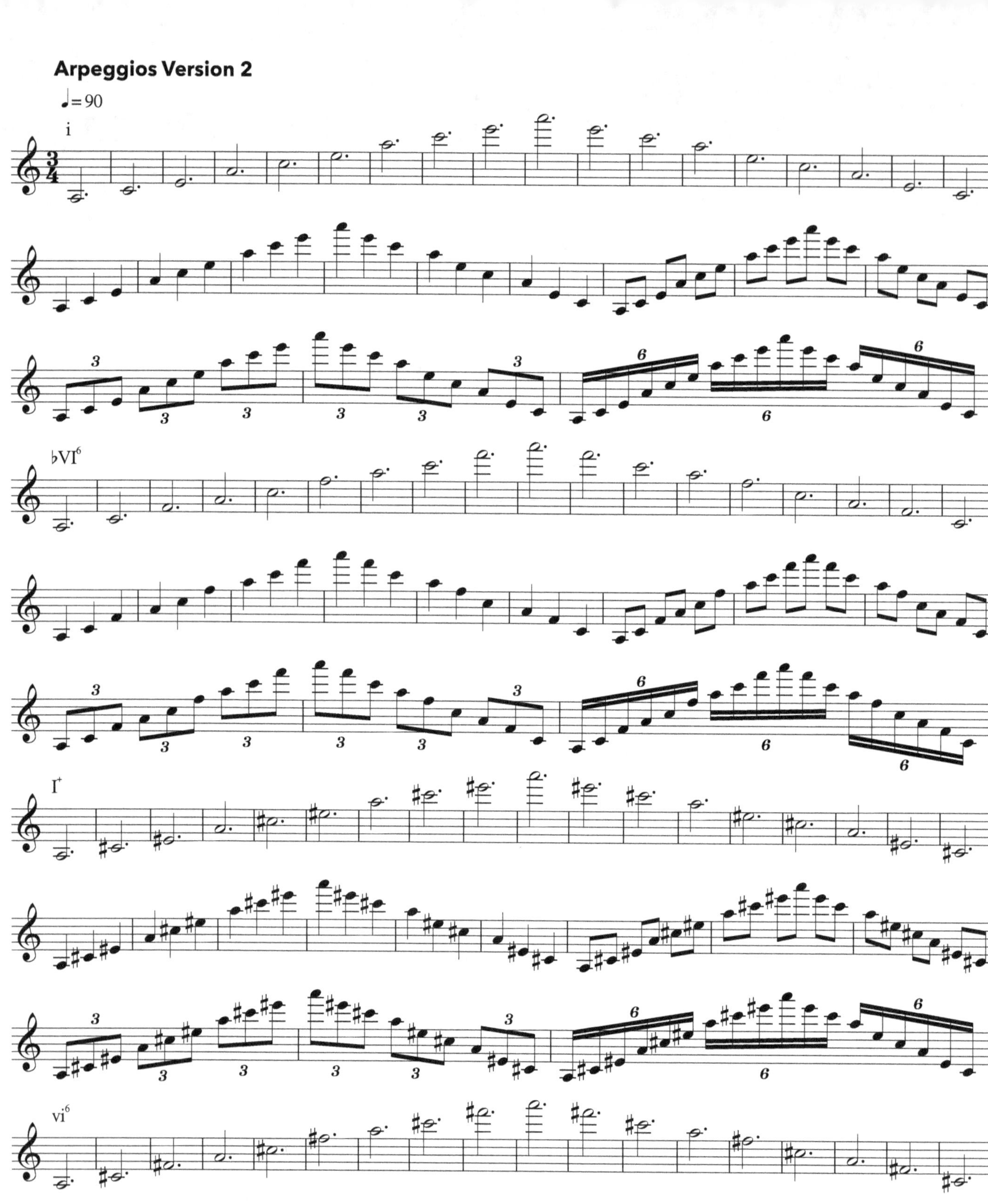


© Nick Revel 2018

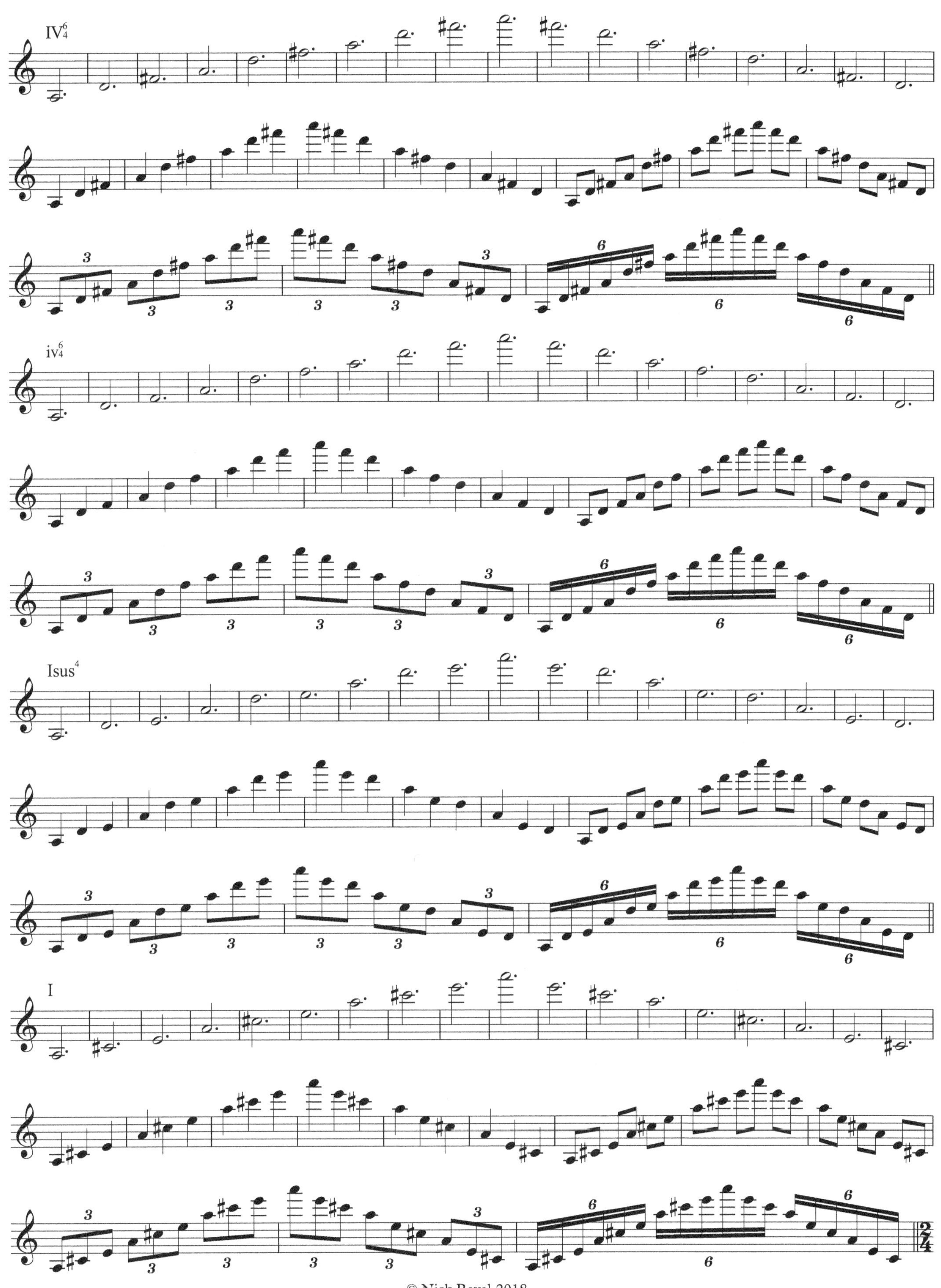

IV6/4
iv6/4
Isus4
I

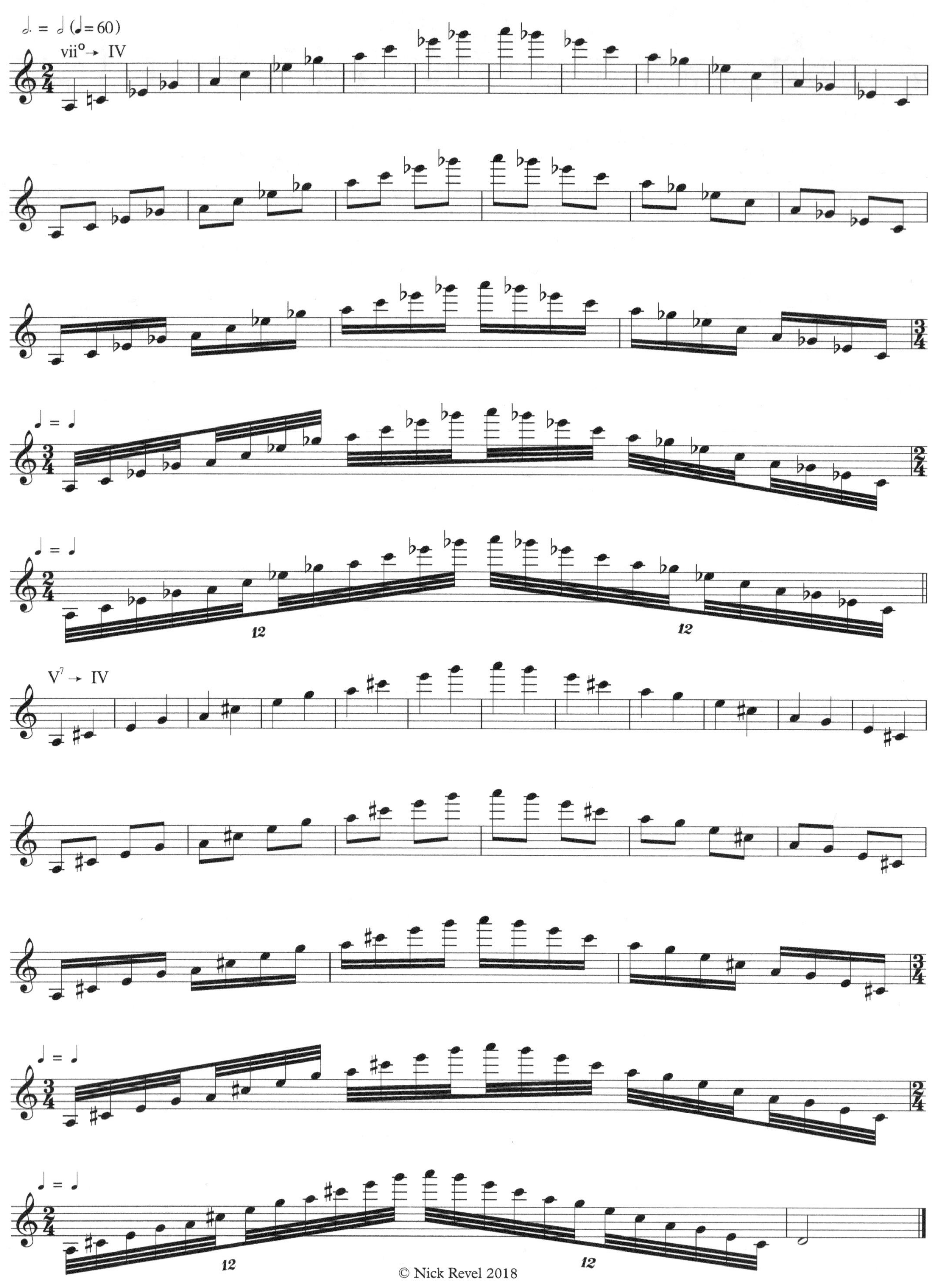
♩. = ♩ (♩ = 60)
vii° → IV
© Nick Revel 2018

# DRAGONSCALES

3-Octave Scales and Arpeggios
In Slow to Fast Rhythms
In All Keys

Nick Revel

# Bb

# DragonScales
## The Complete Set in Bb

Nick Revel

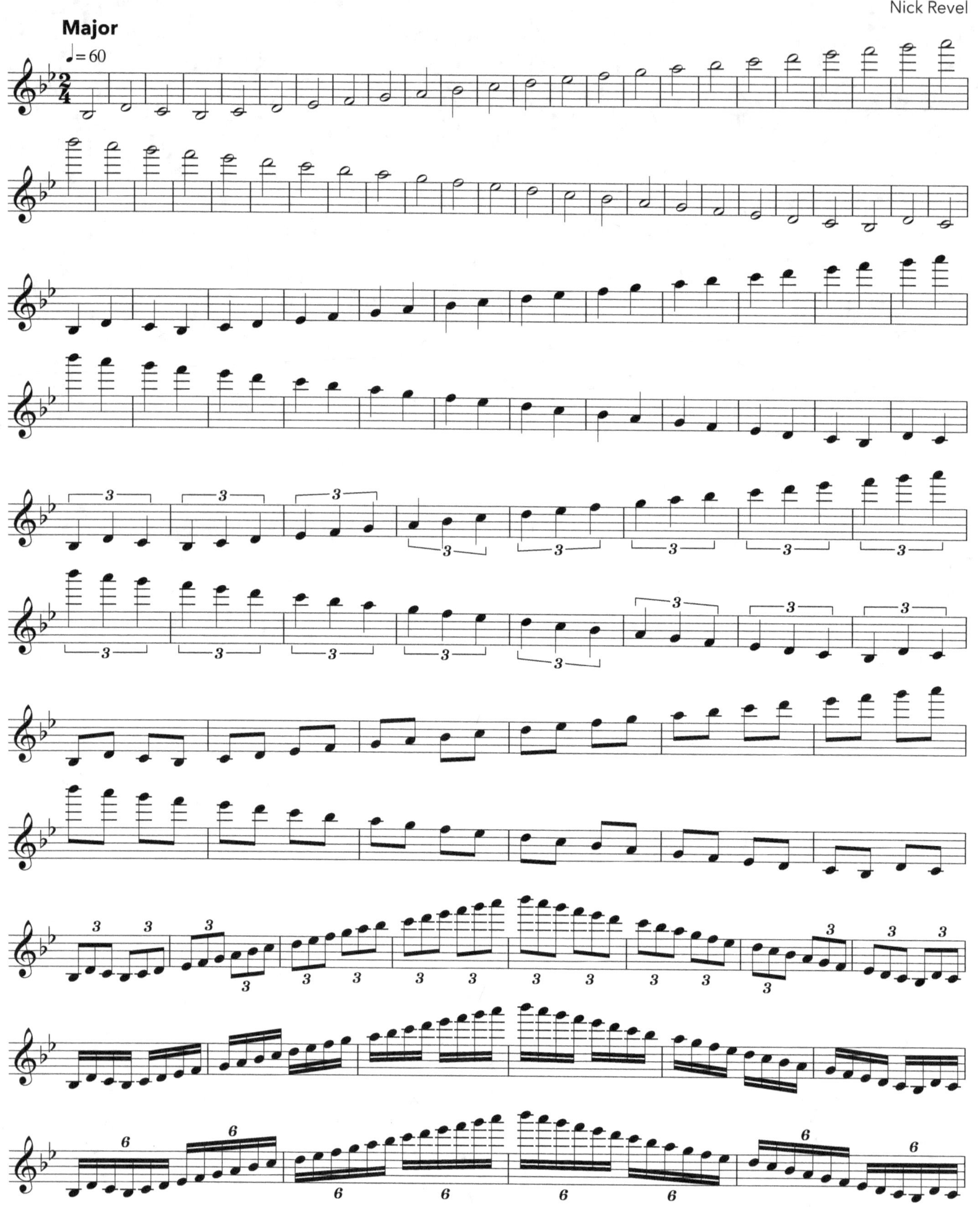

© Nick Revel 2018

# Whole Tone

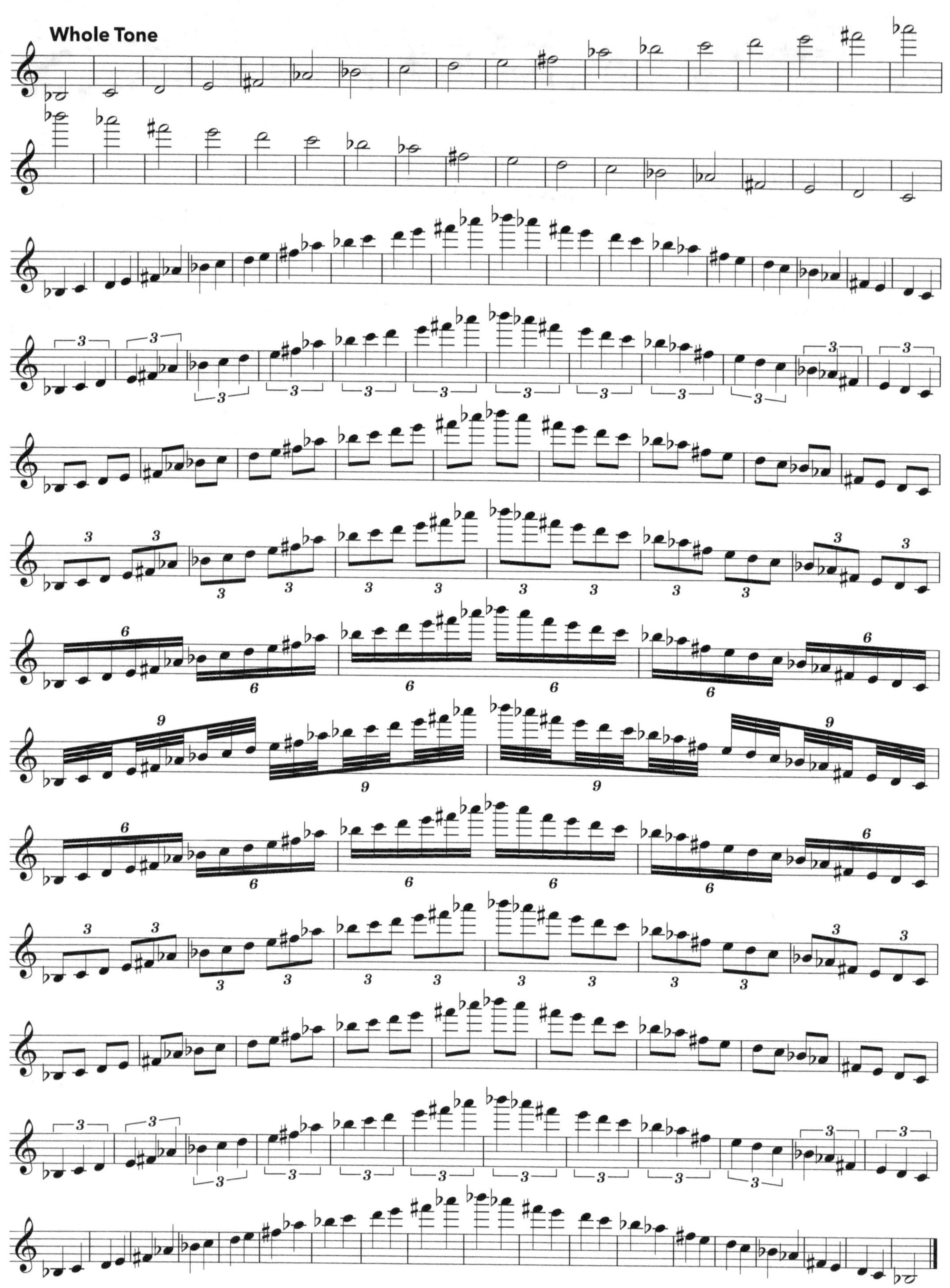

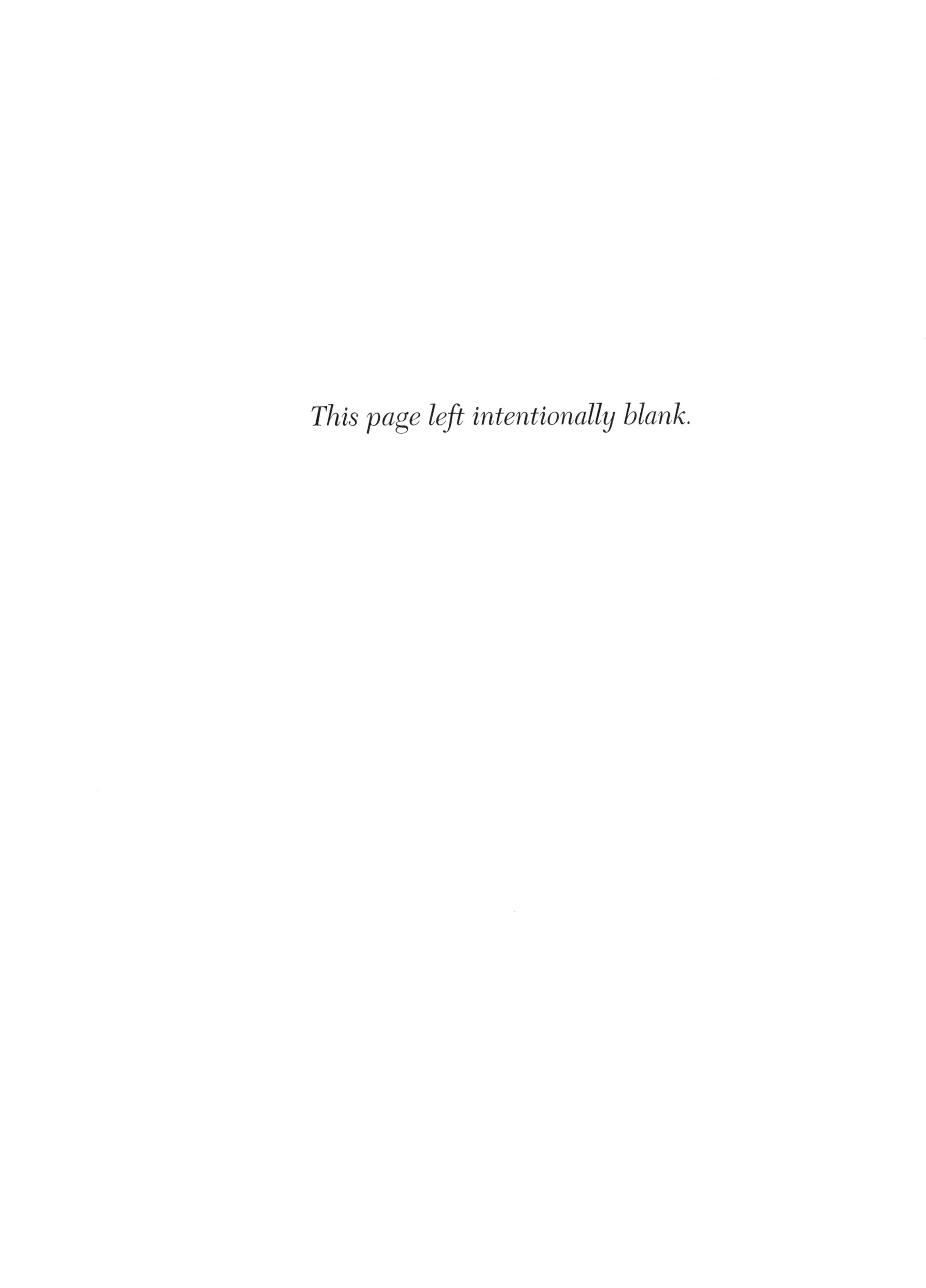

*This page left intentionally blank.*

**Diminished Scale Version 1**

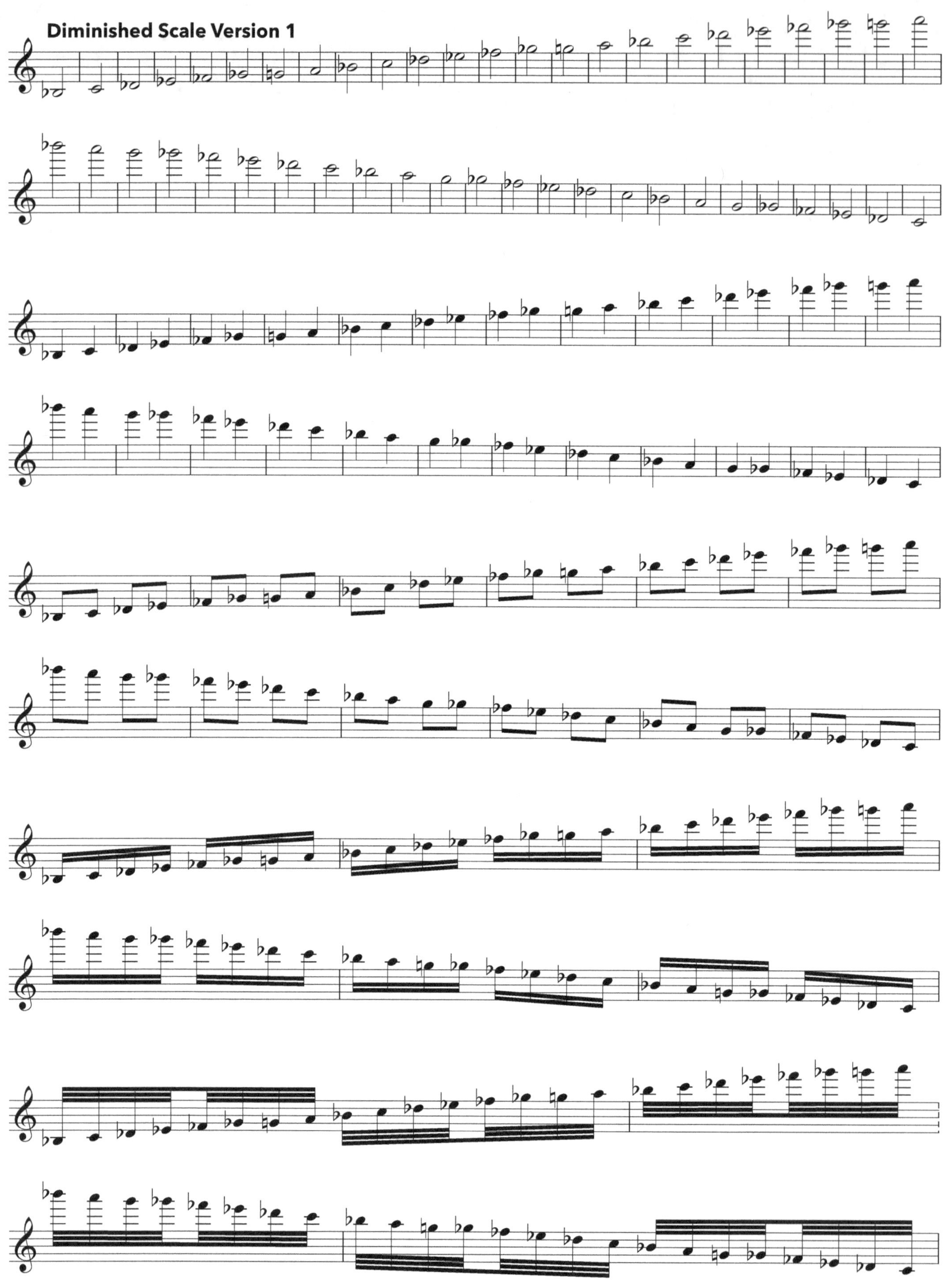

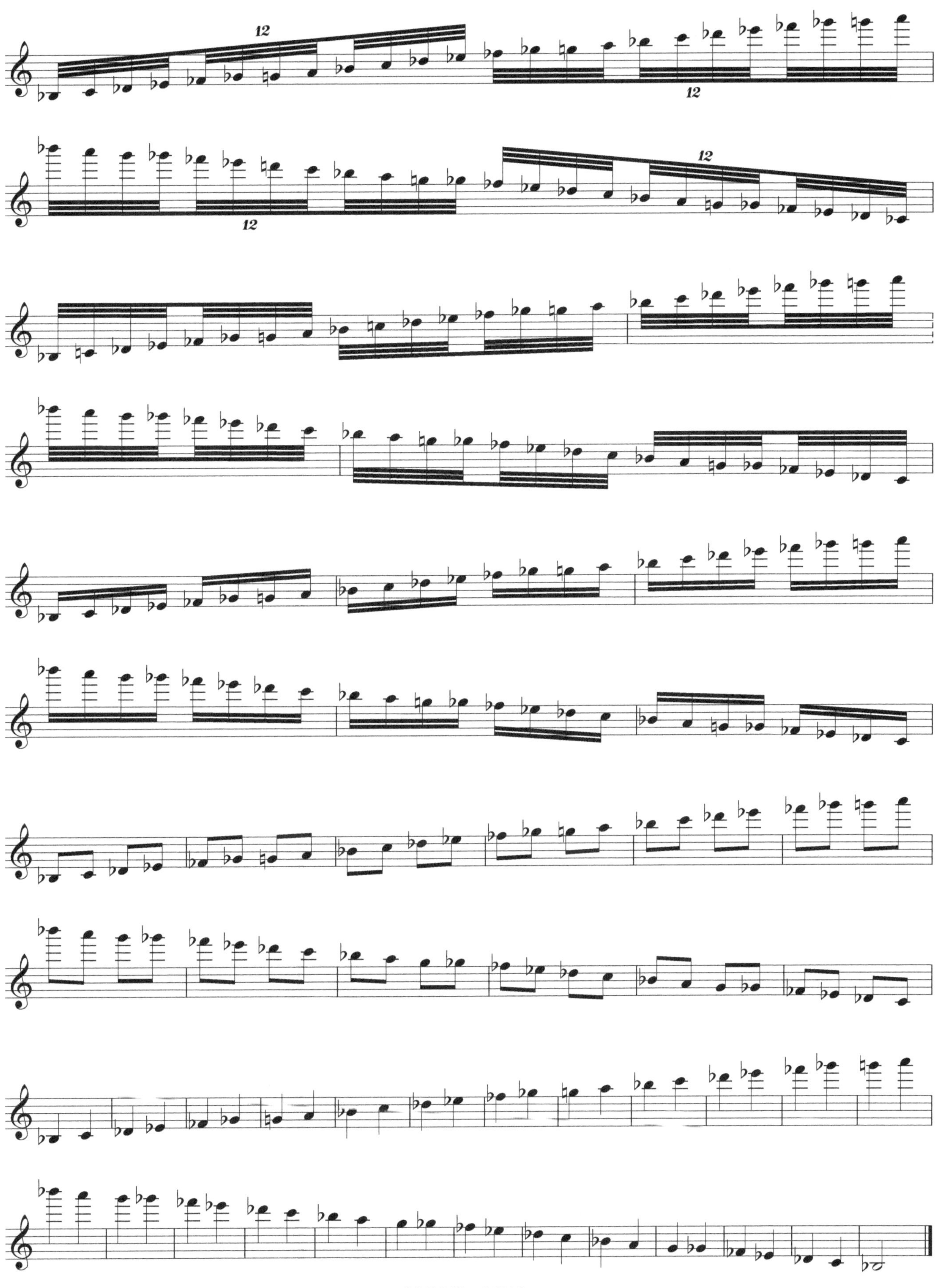

Diminished Scale Version 2

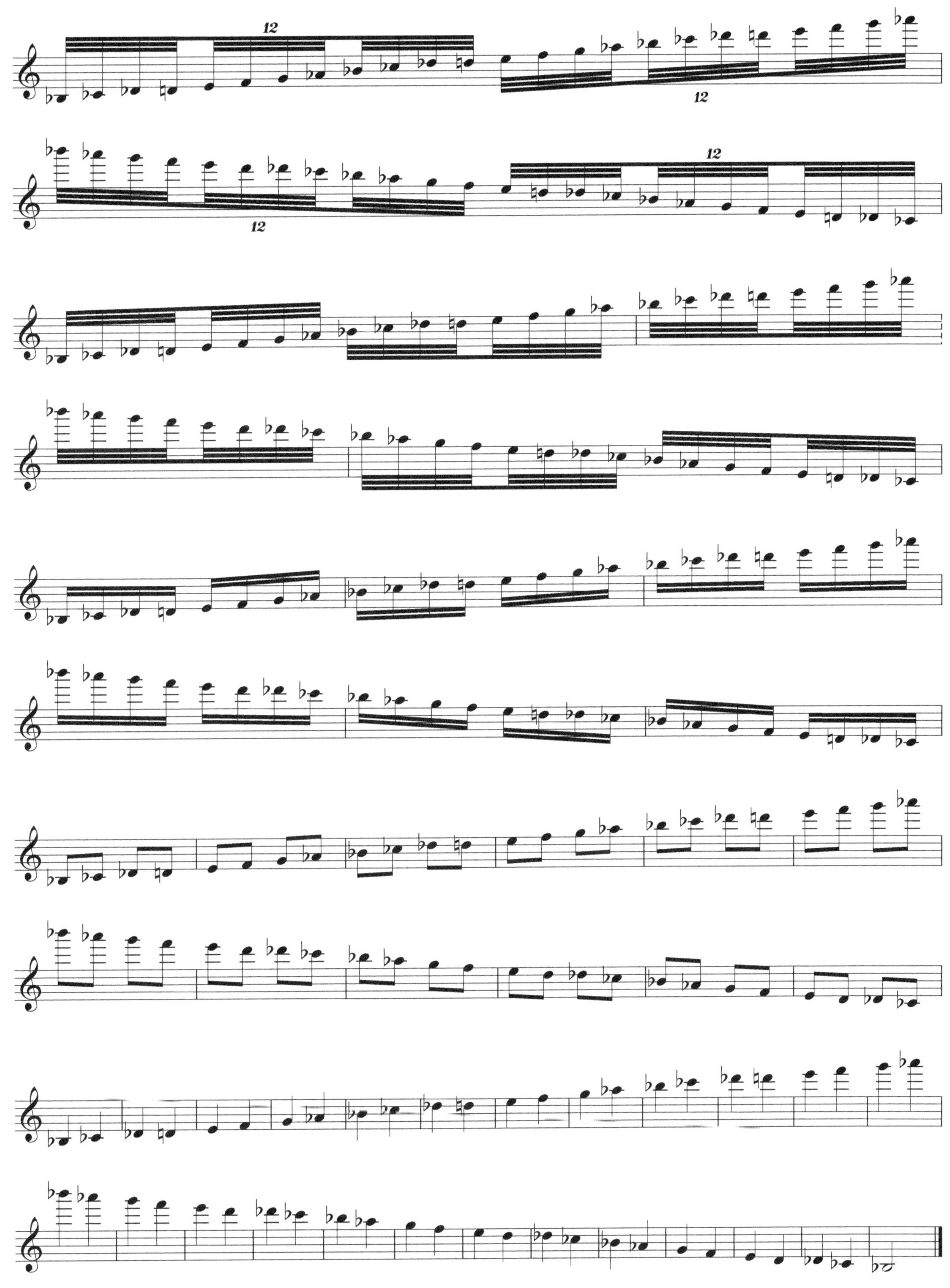



© Nick Revel 2018

# Chromatic

© Nick Revel 2018

**Arpeggios Version 1**

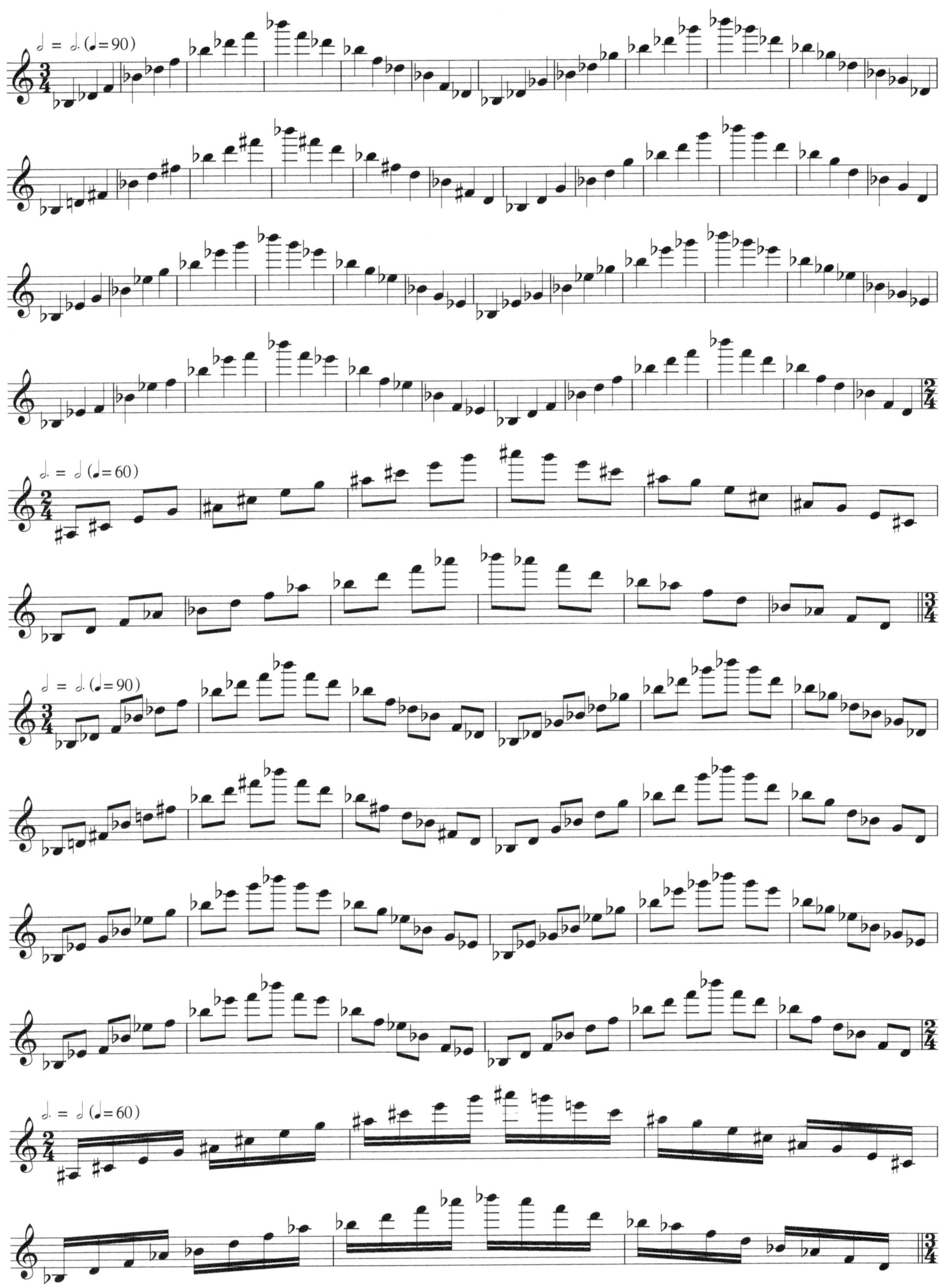

© Nick Revel 2018

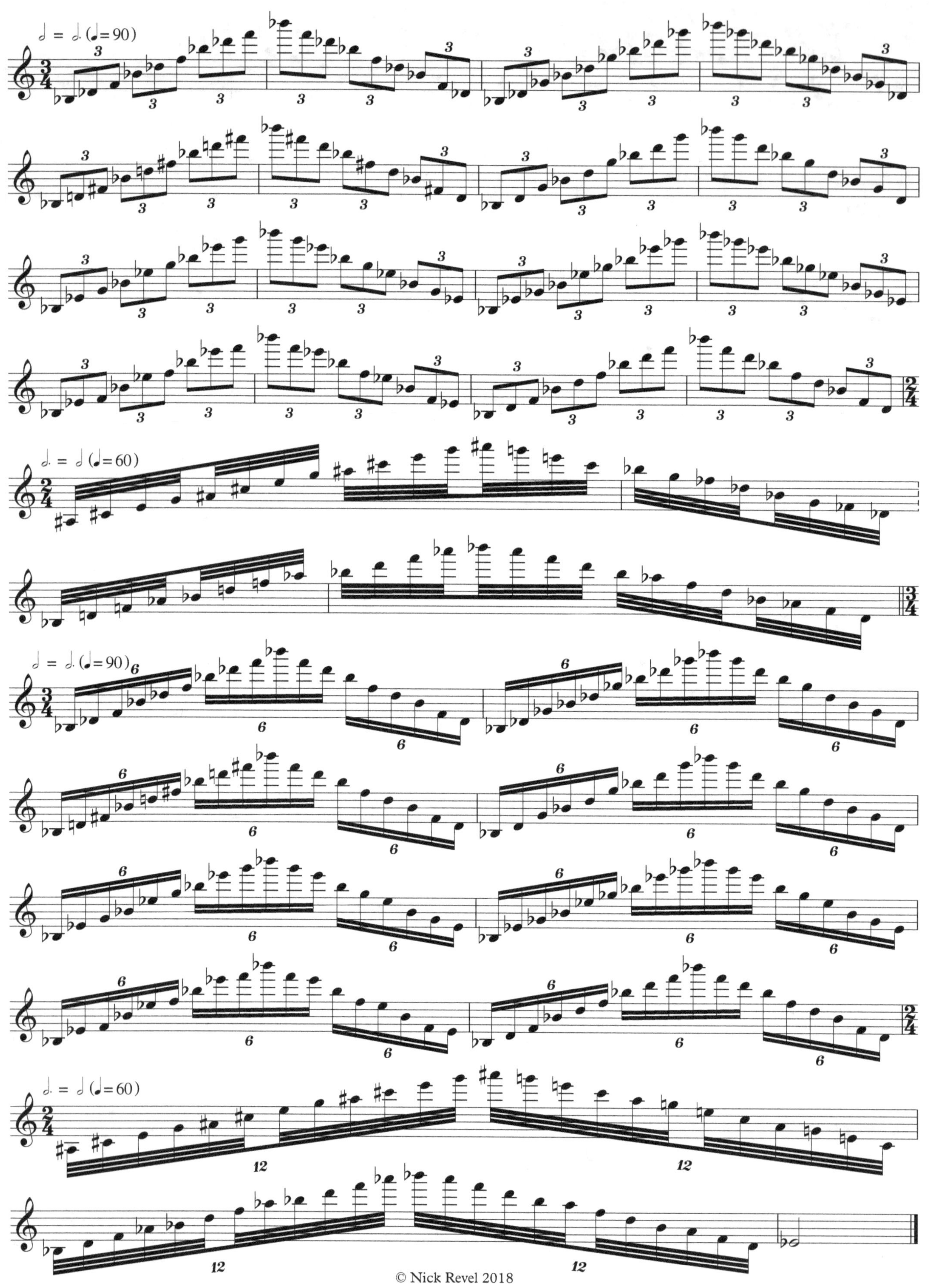

© Nick Revel 2018

This page left intentionally blank.

# Arpeggios Version 2

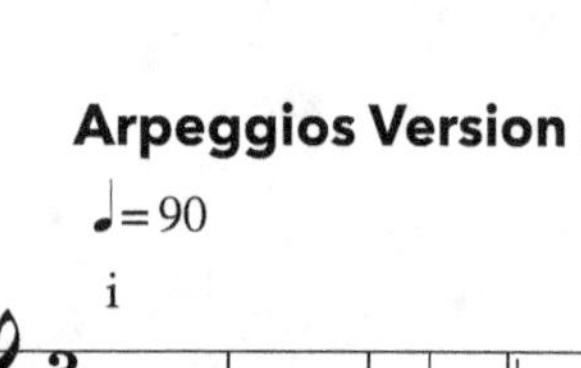

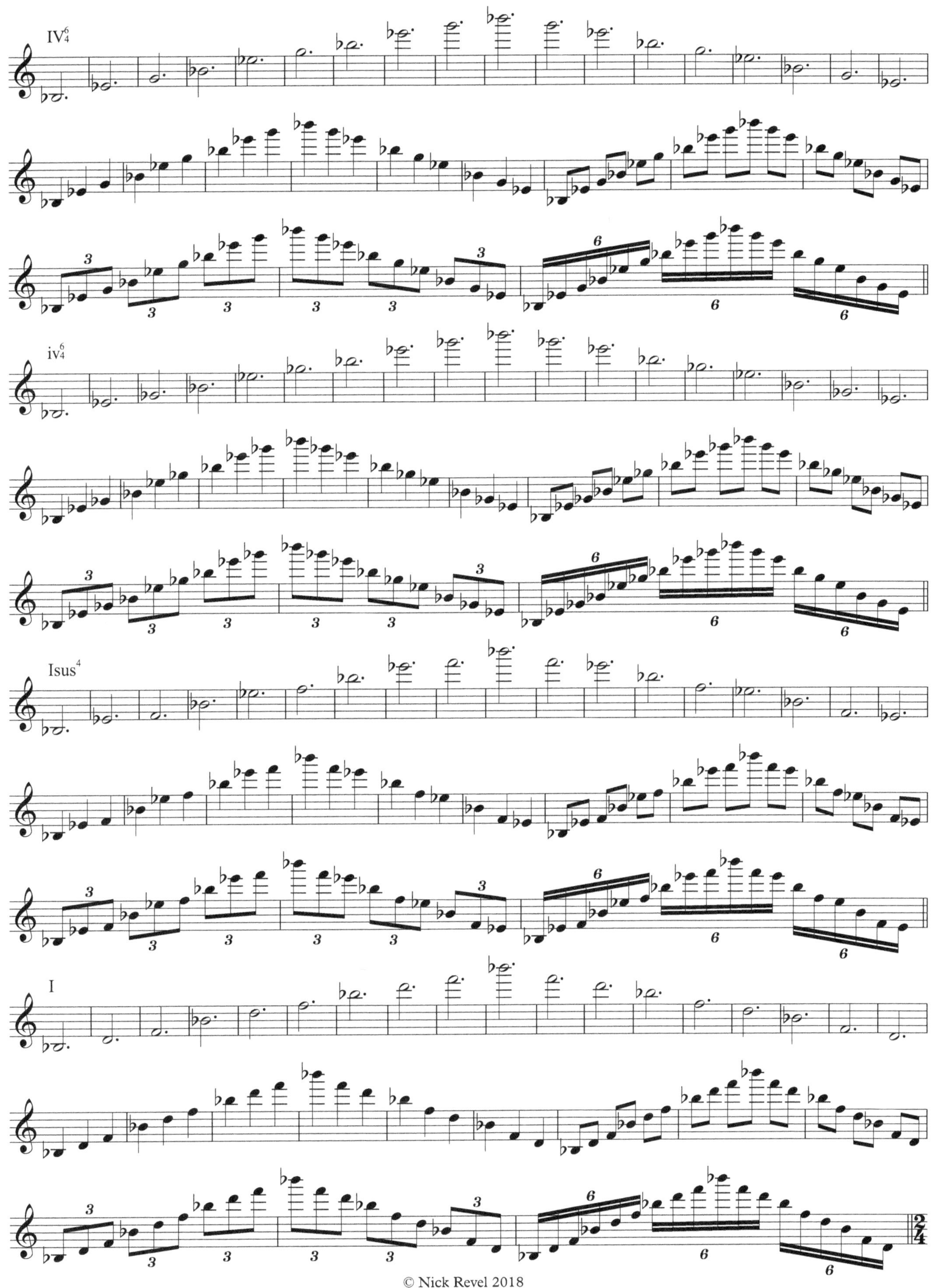

IV⁶₄
iv⁶₄
Isus⁴
I

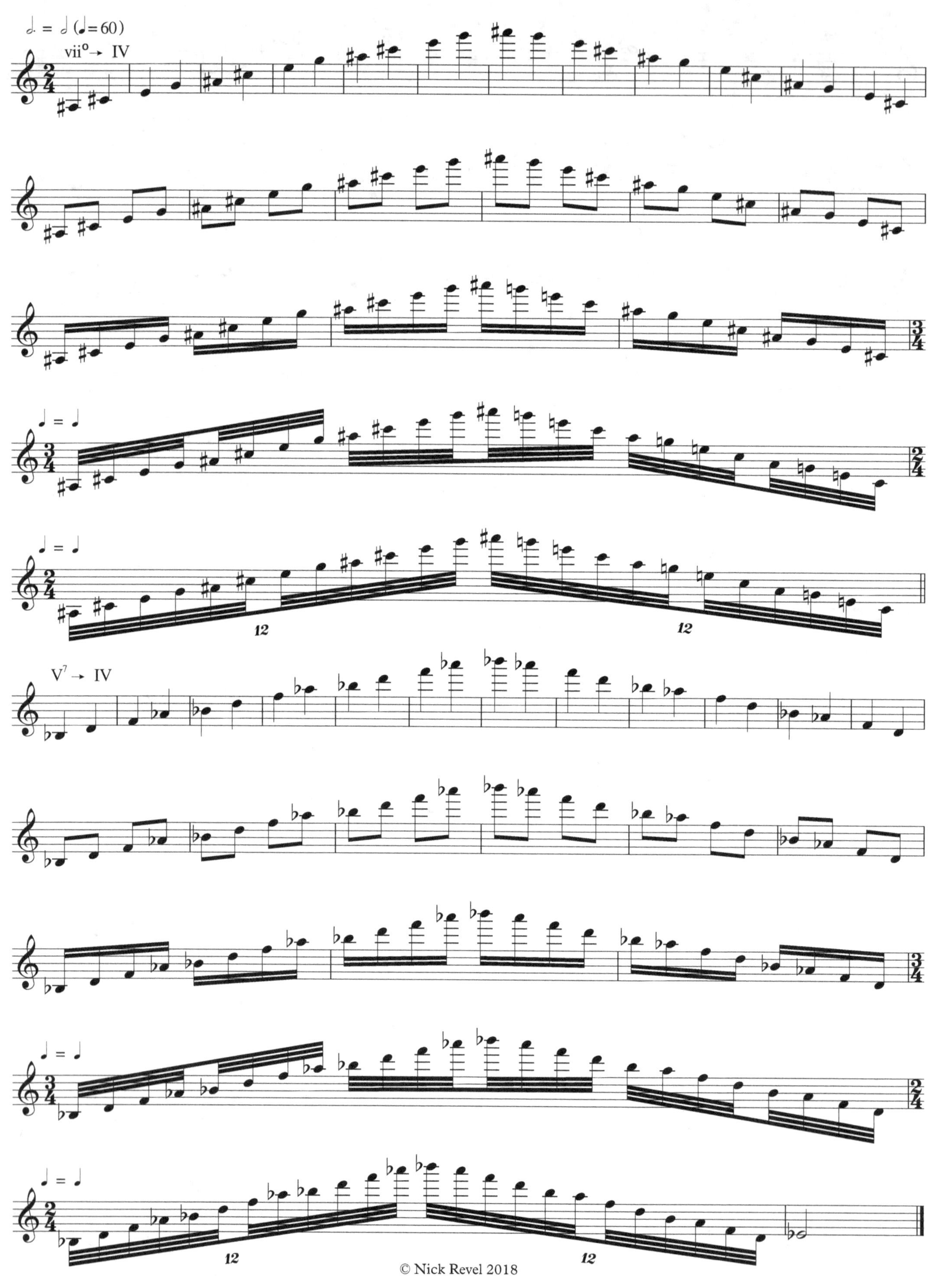

♩. = ♩ (♩ = 60)
vii° → IV
V⁷ → IV
12
12
12
12
© Nick Revel 2018

# DRAGONSCALES

3-Octave Scales and Arpeggios
In Slow to Fast Rhythms
In All Keys

Nick Revel

# B

# DragonScales
## The Complete Set in B

Nick Revel

© Nick Revel 2018

© Nick Revel 2018

Whole Tone

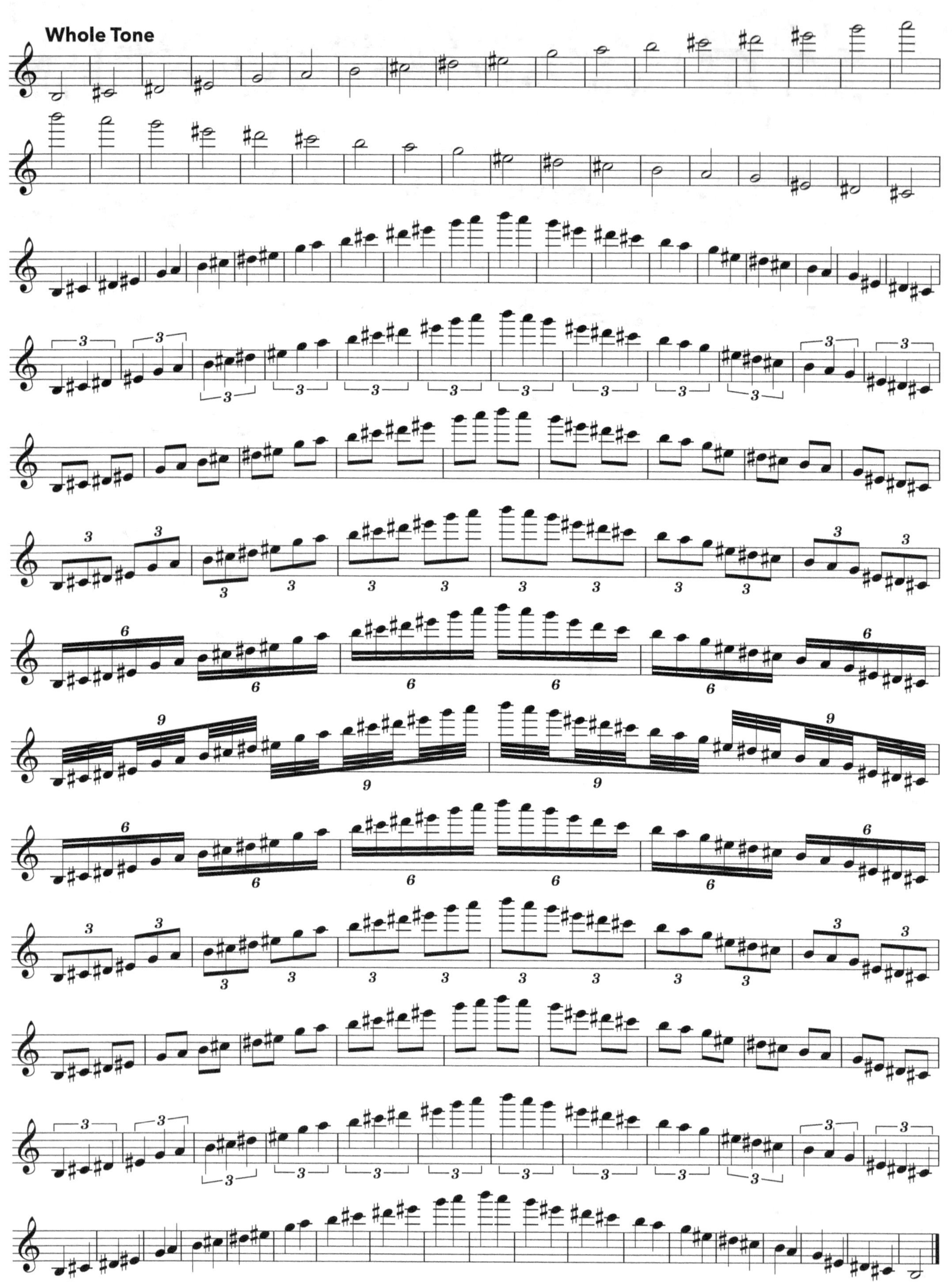

© Nick Revel 2018

*This page left intentionally blank.*

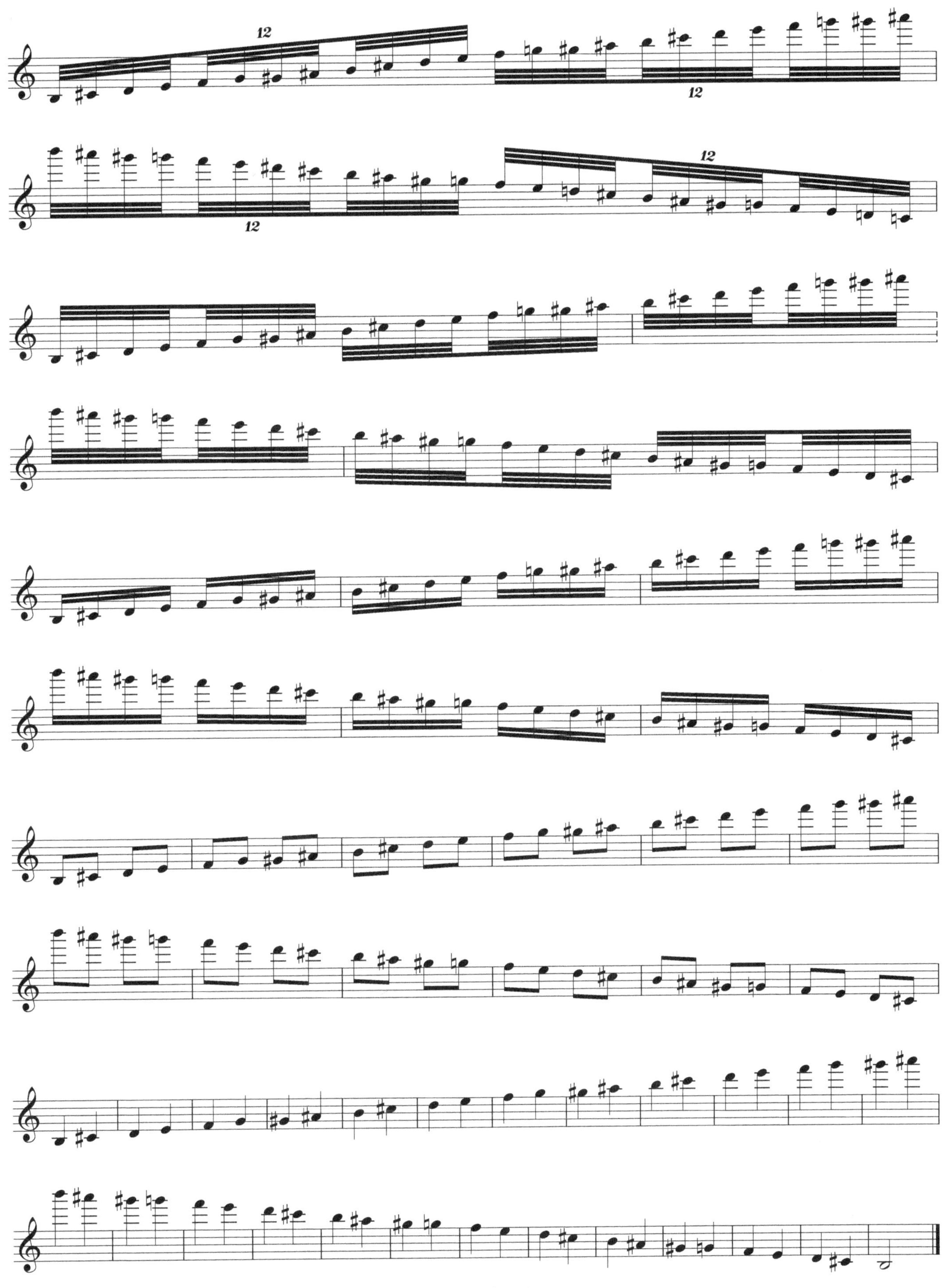

Diminished Scale Version 2
© Nick Revel 2018

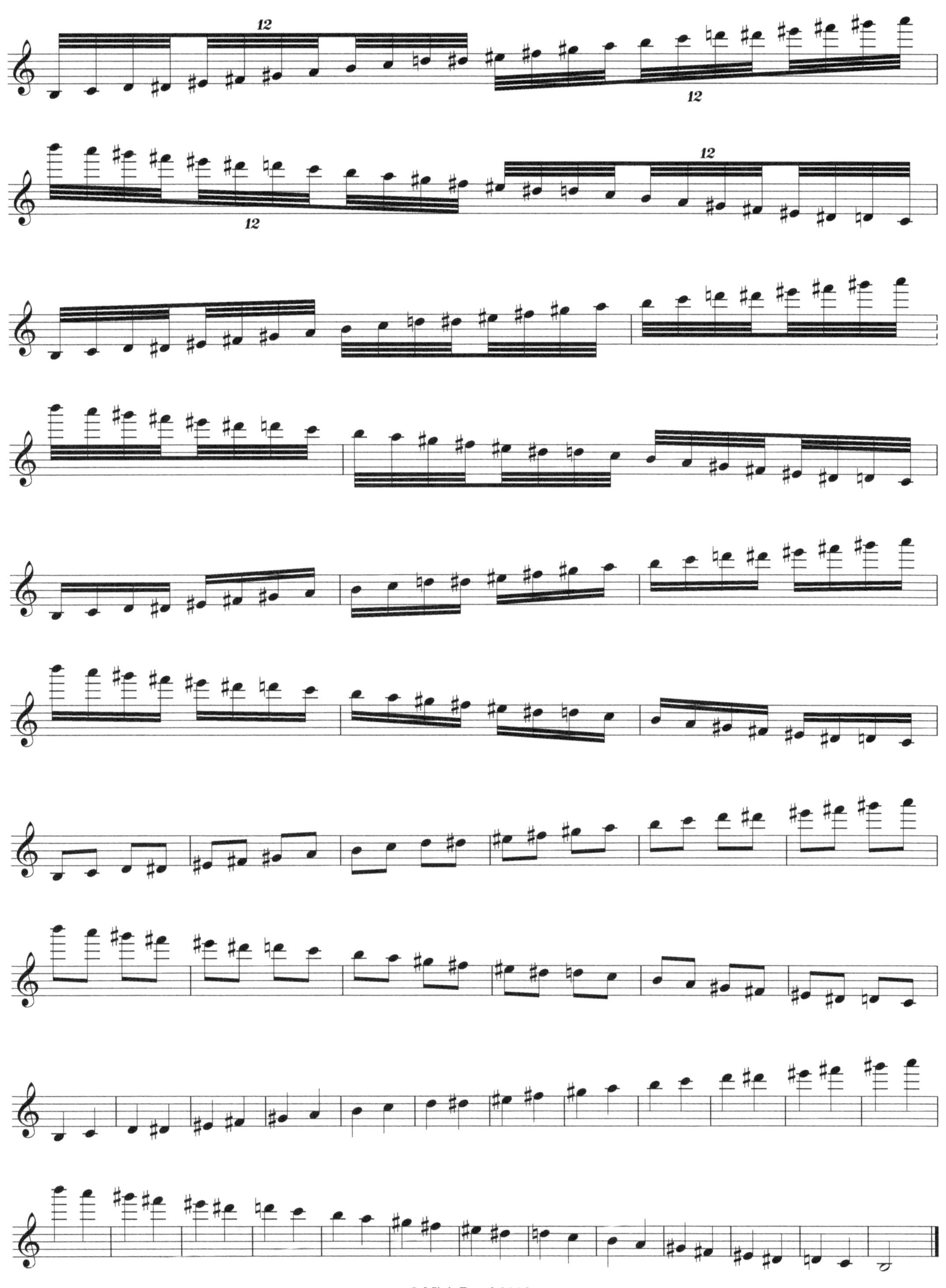

Chromatic

DRAGONSCALES – VIOLIN    93

© Nick Revel 2018

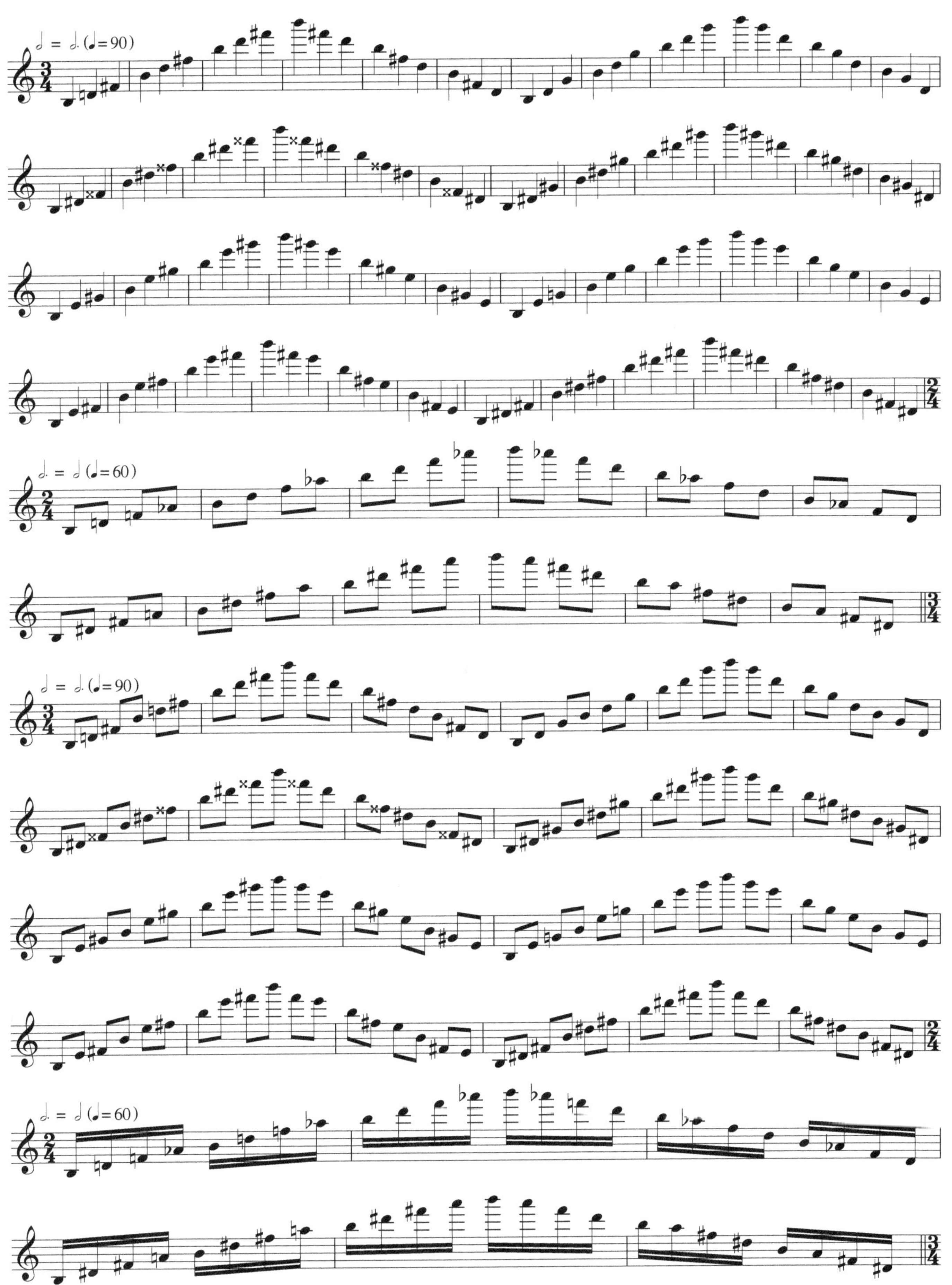
DRAGONSCALES – VIOLIN 95

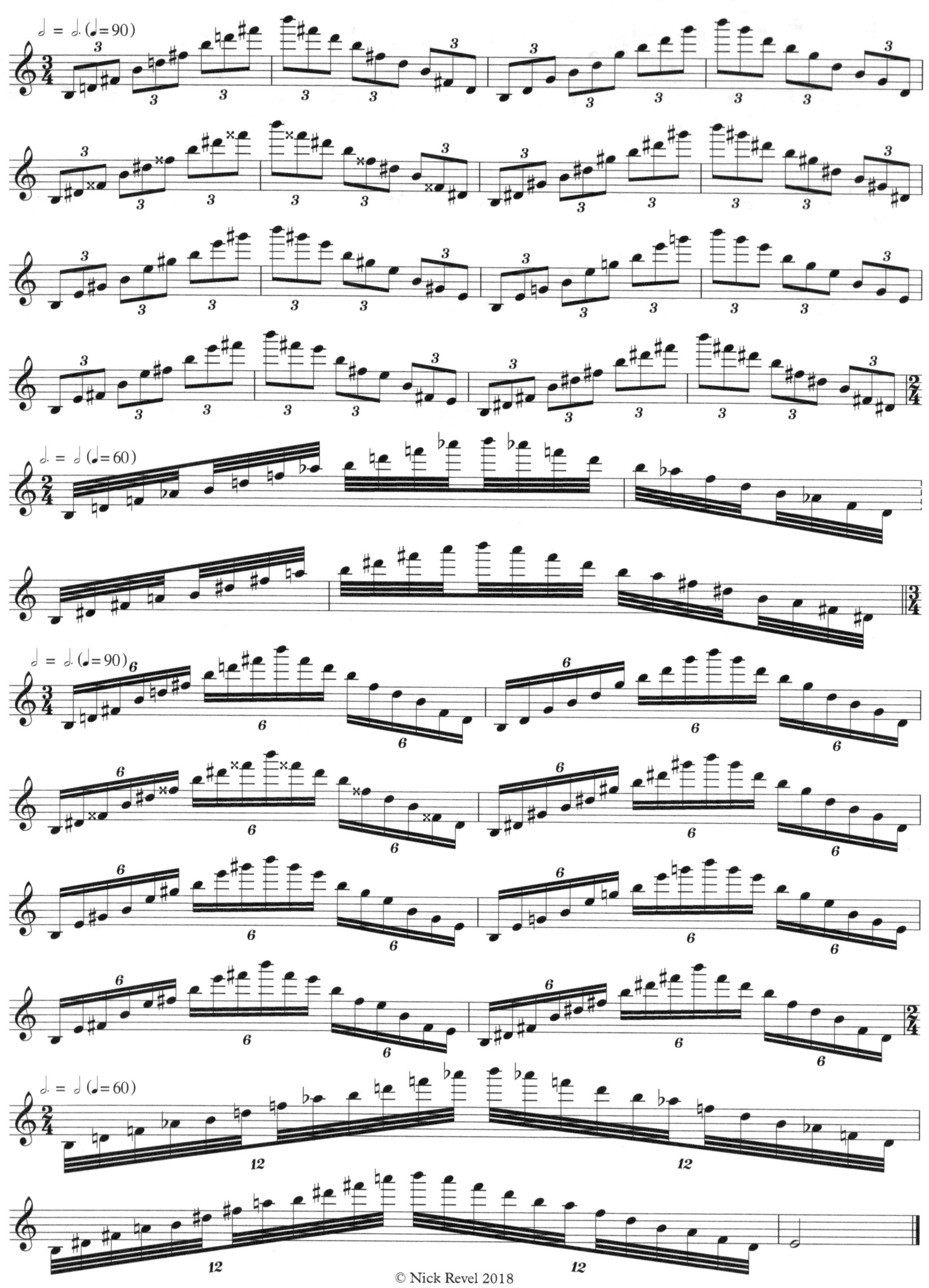

♩ = ♩. (♩=90)
♩. = ♩ (♩=60)
♩ = ♩. (♩=90)
♩. = ♩ (♩=60)
© Nick Revel 2018

*This page left intentionally blank.*

## Arpeggios Version 2

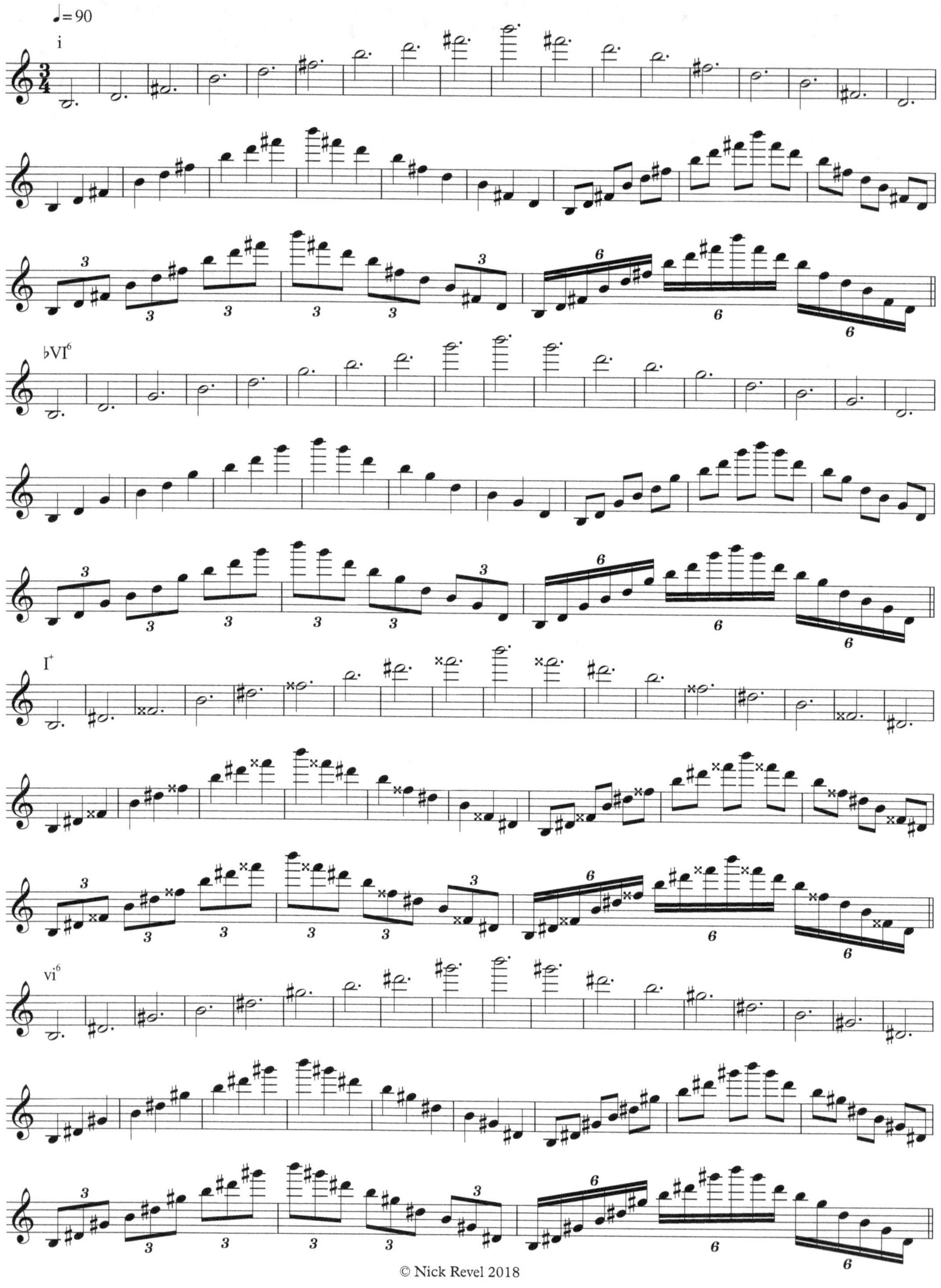

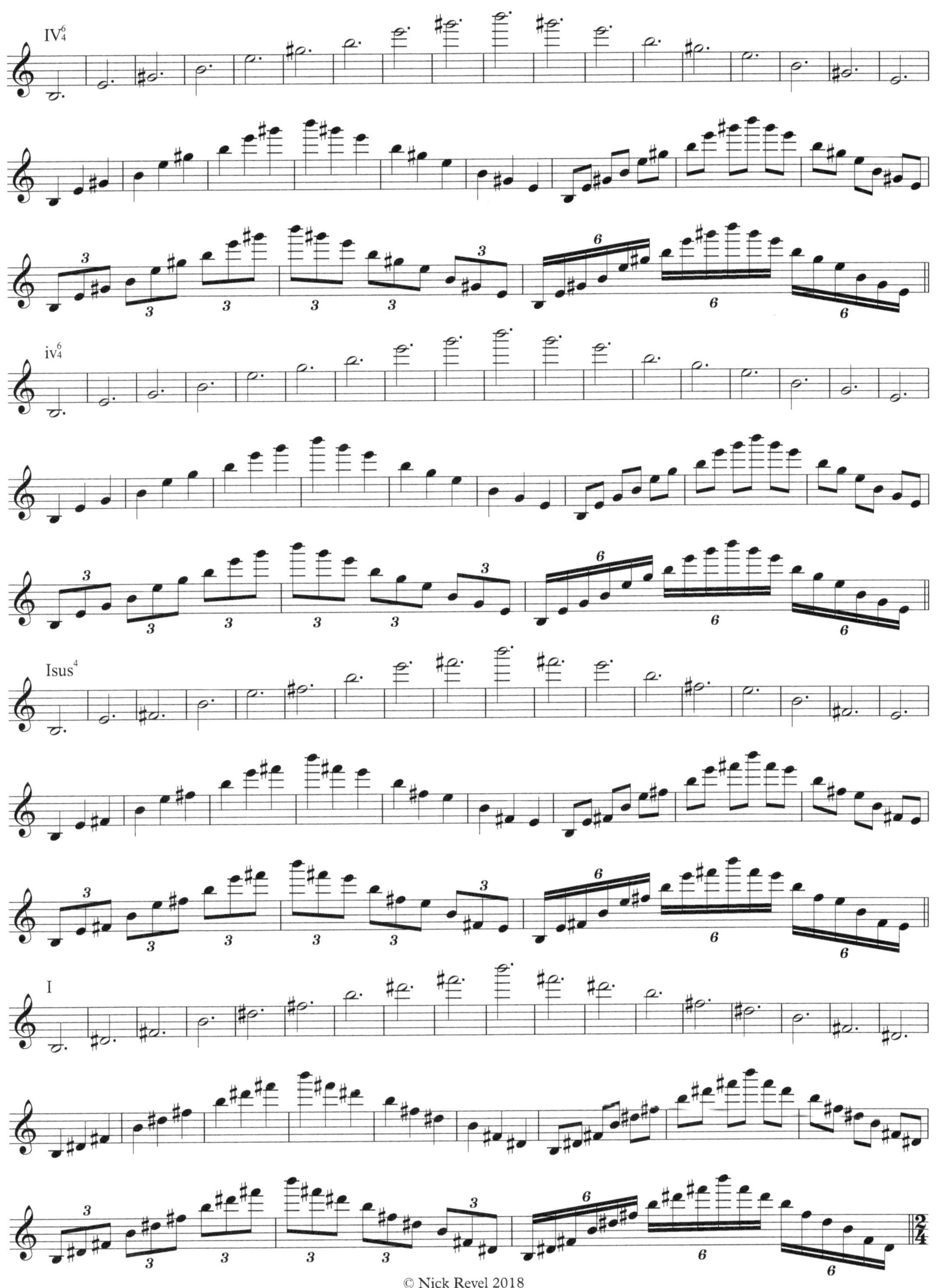

IV6/4
iv6/4
Isus4
I
© Nick Revel 2018

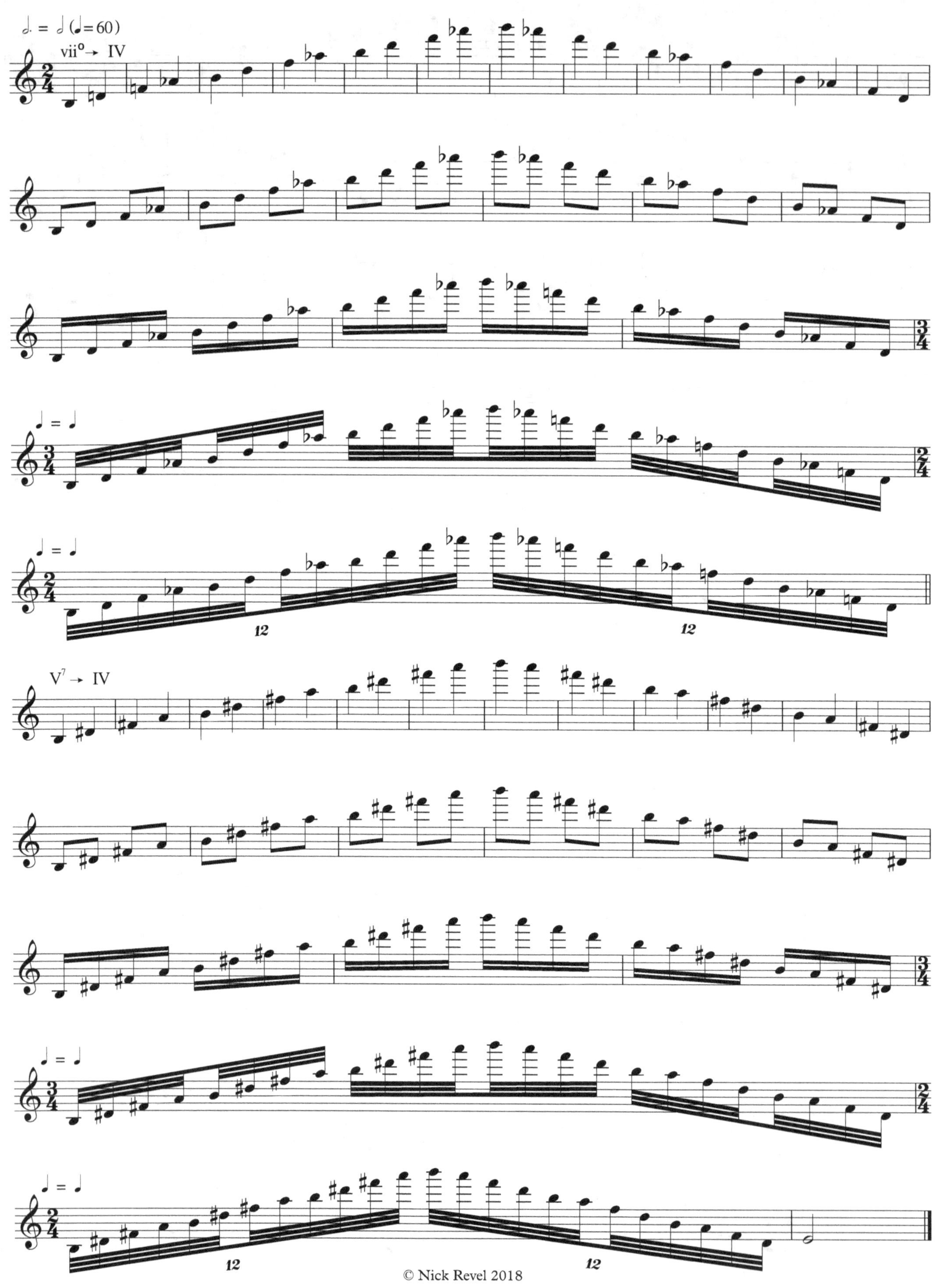

♩. = ♪ (♩ = 60)
vii° → IV
2/4
3/4
♩ = ♩
3/4
2/4
♩ = ♩
2/4
12
12
V⁷ → IV
3/4
♩ = ♩
3/4
2/4
♩ = ♩
2/4
12
12

# DRAGONSCALES

3-Octave Scales and Arpeggios
In Slow to Fast Rhythms
In All Keys

Nick Revel

C

# DragonScales
## The Complete Set in C

Nick Revel

© Nick Revel 2018

**Minor**

© Nick Revel 2018

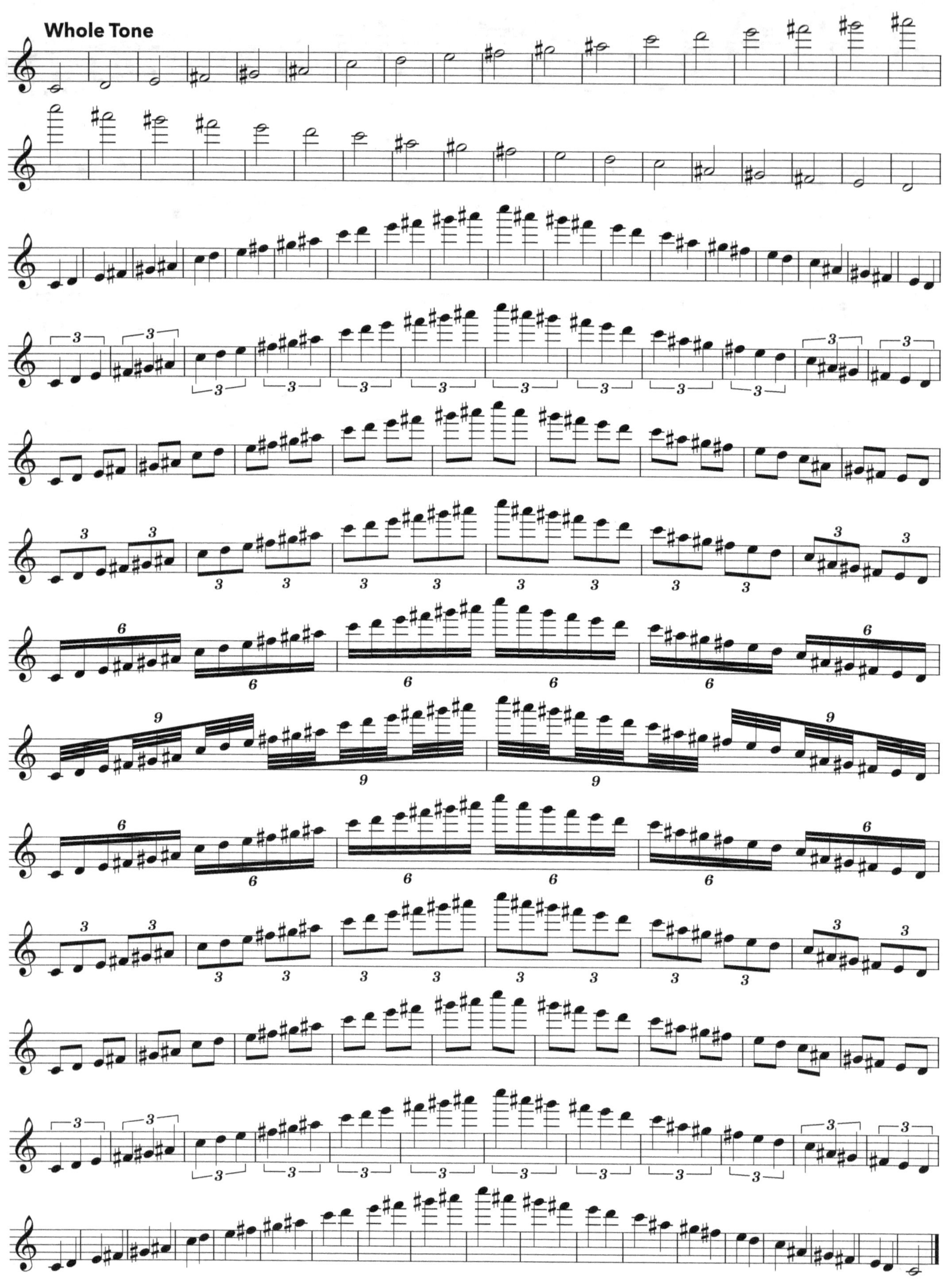


© Nick Revel 2018

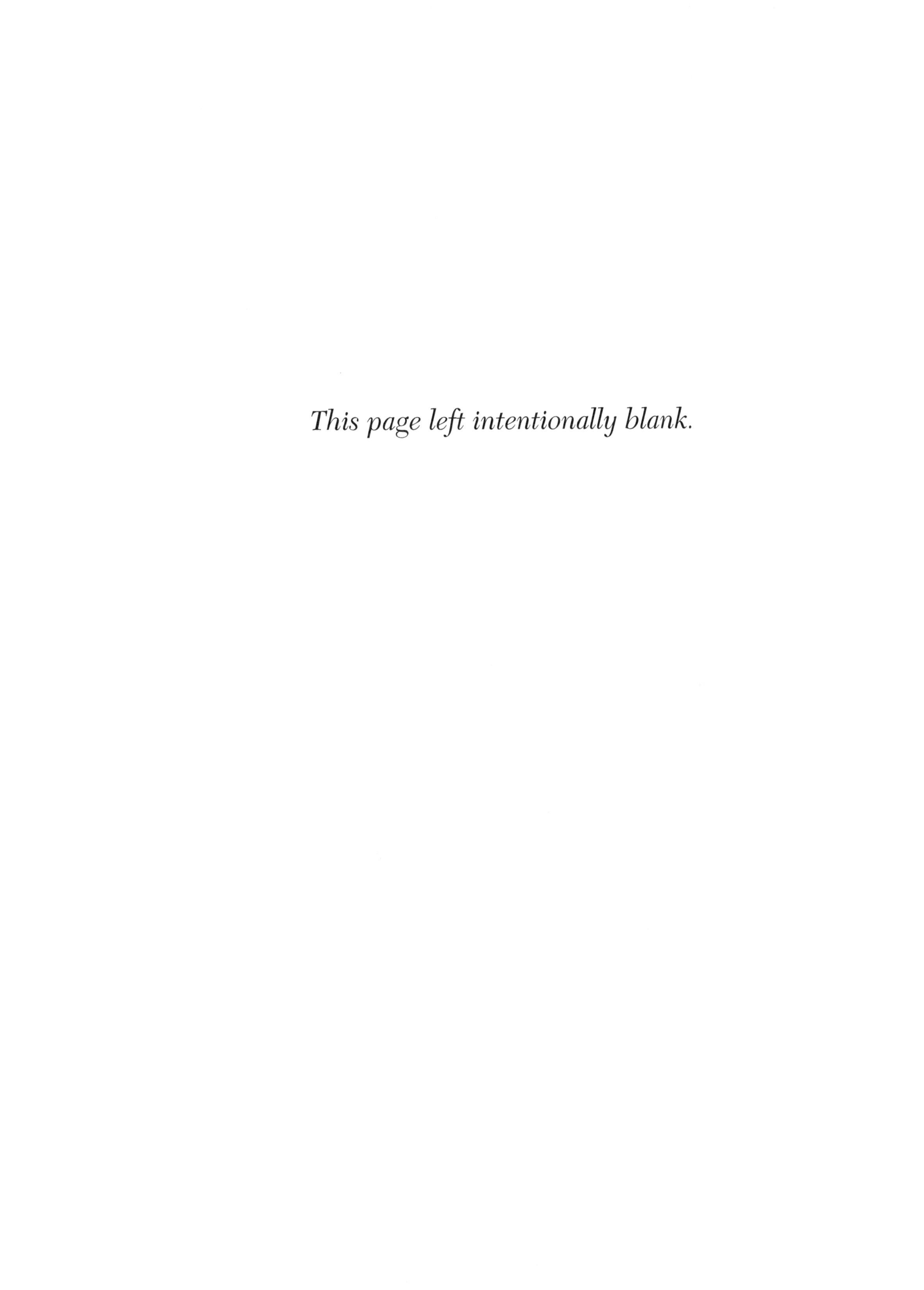

*This page left intentionally blank.*

**Diminished Scale Version 1**

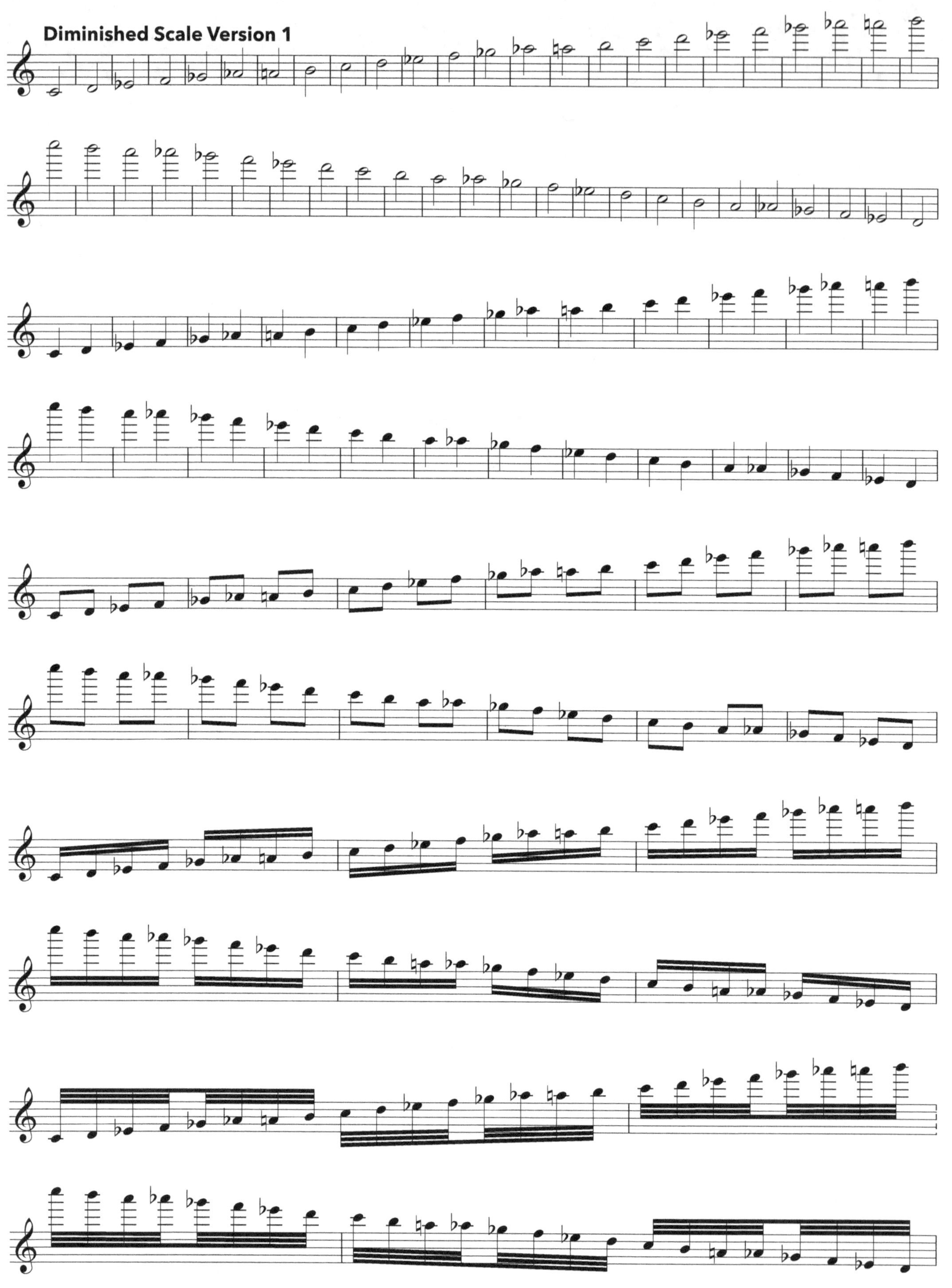

© Nick Revel 2018

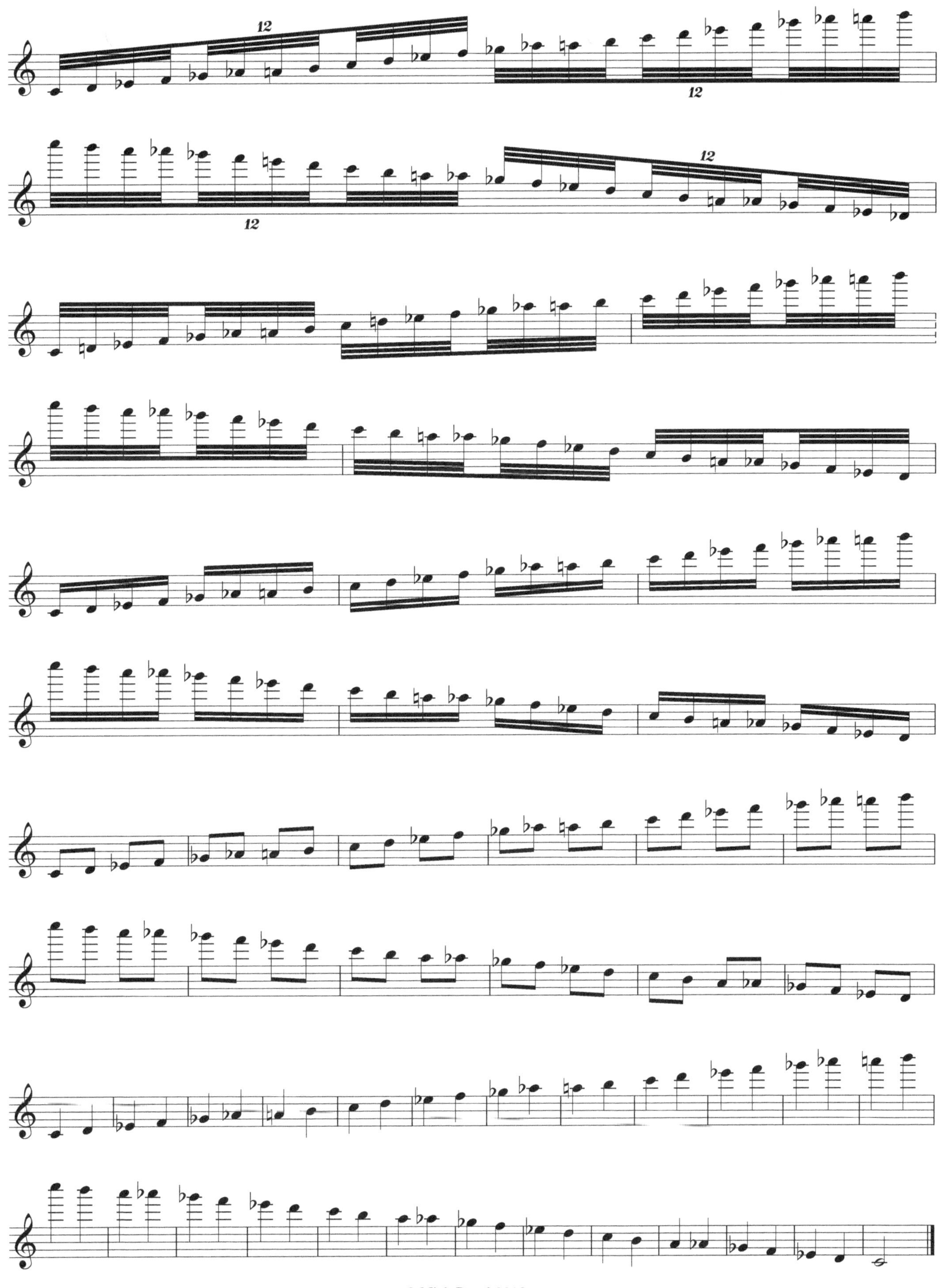

Diminished Scale Version 2

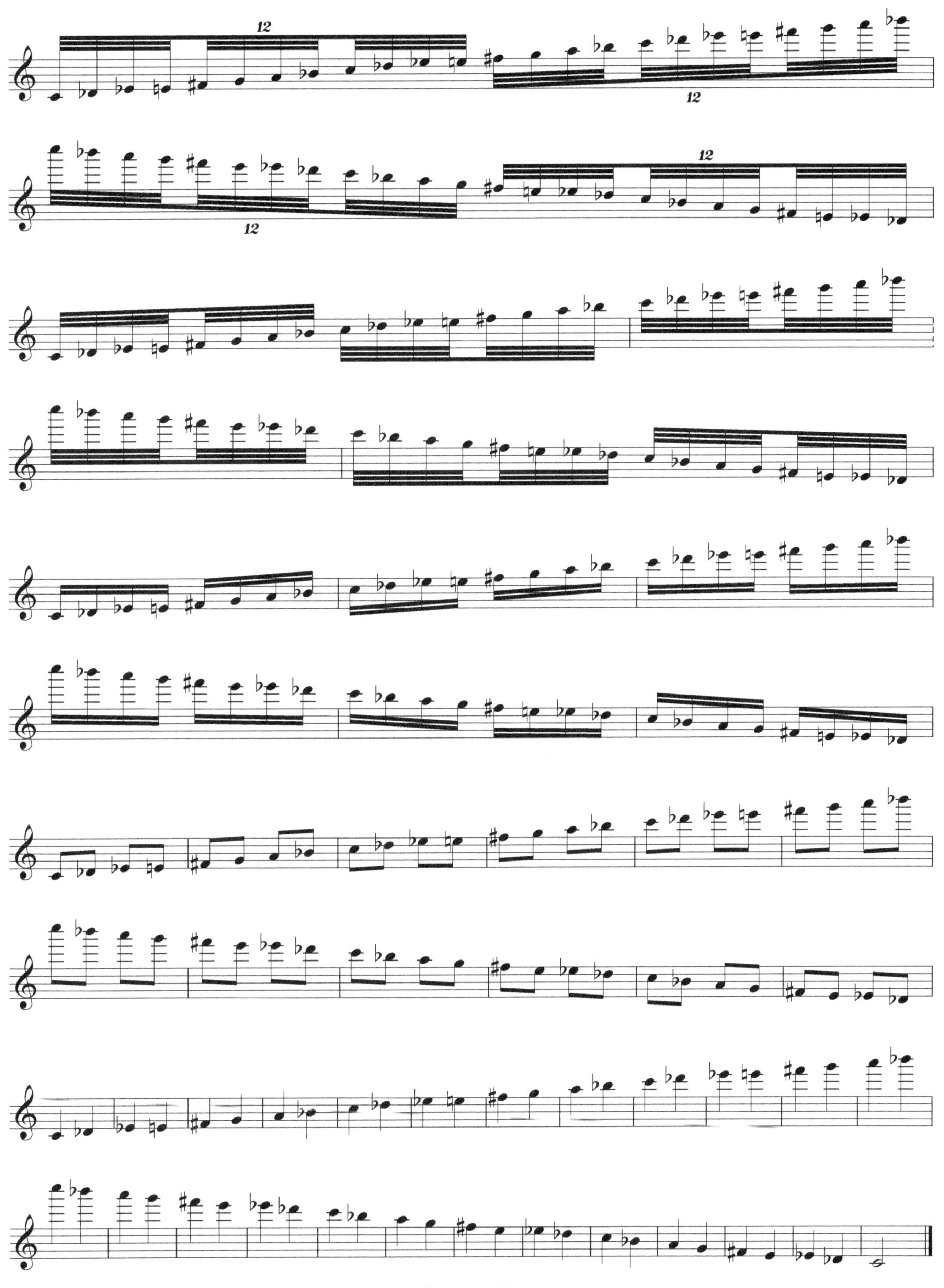

12
12
12

**Chromatic**

© Nick Revel 2018

© Nick Revel 2018

**Arpeggios Version 1**



© Nick Revel 2018

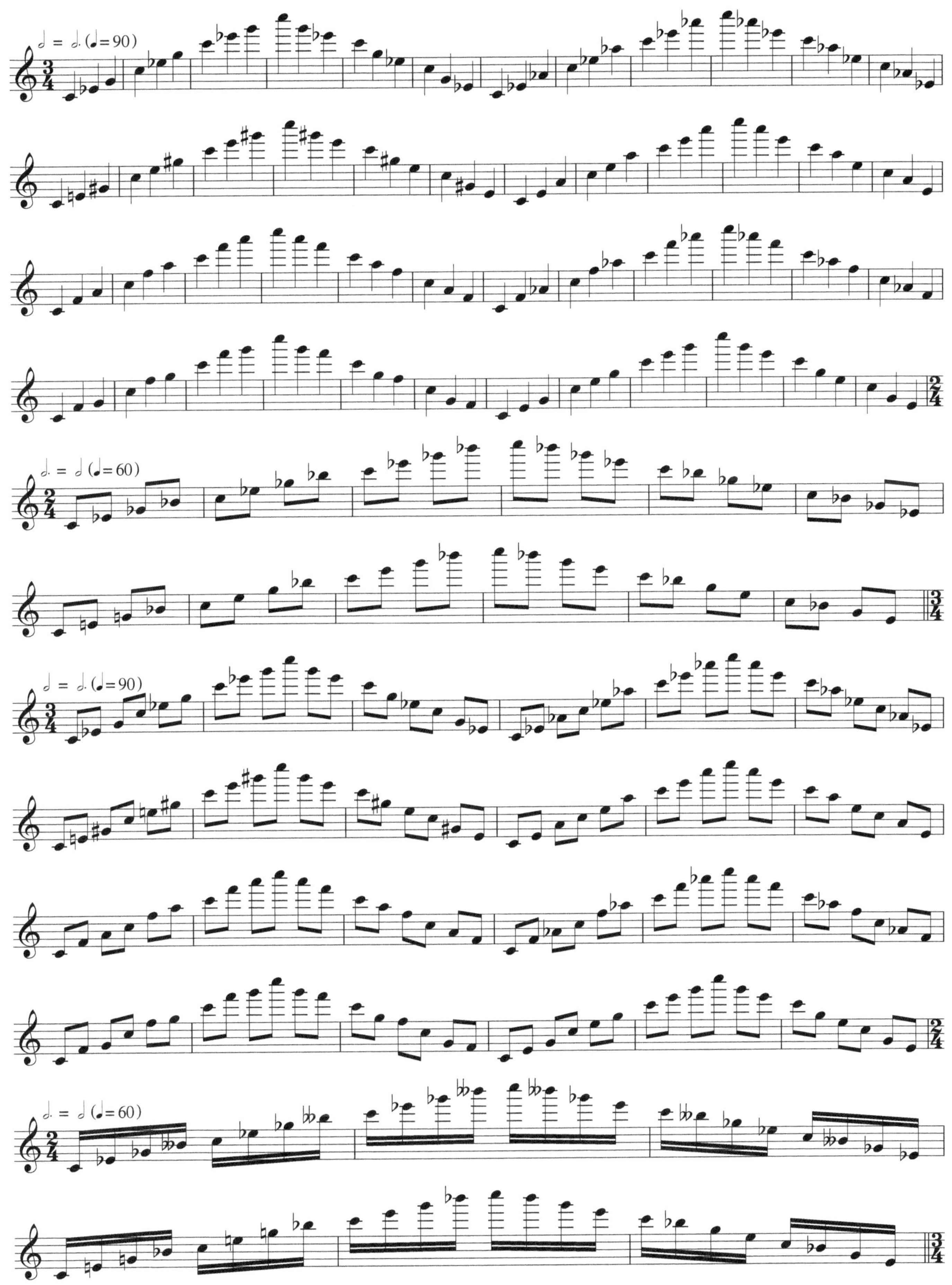

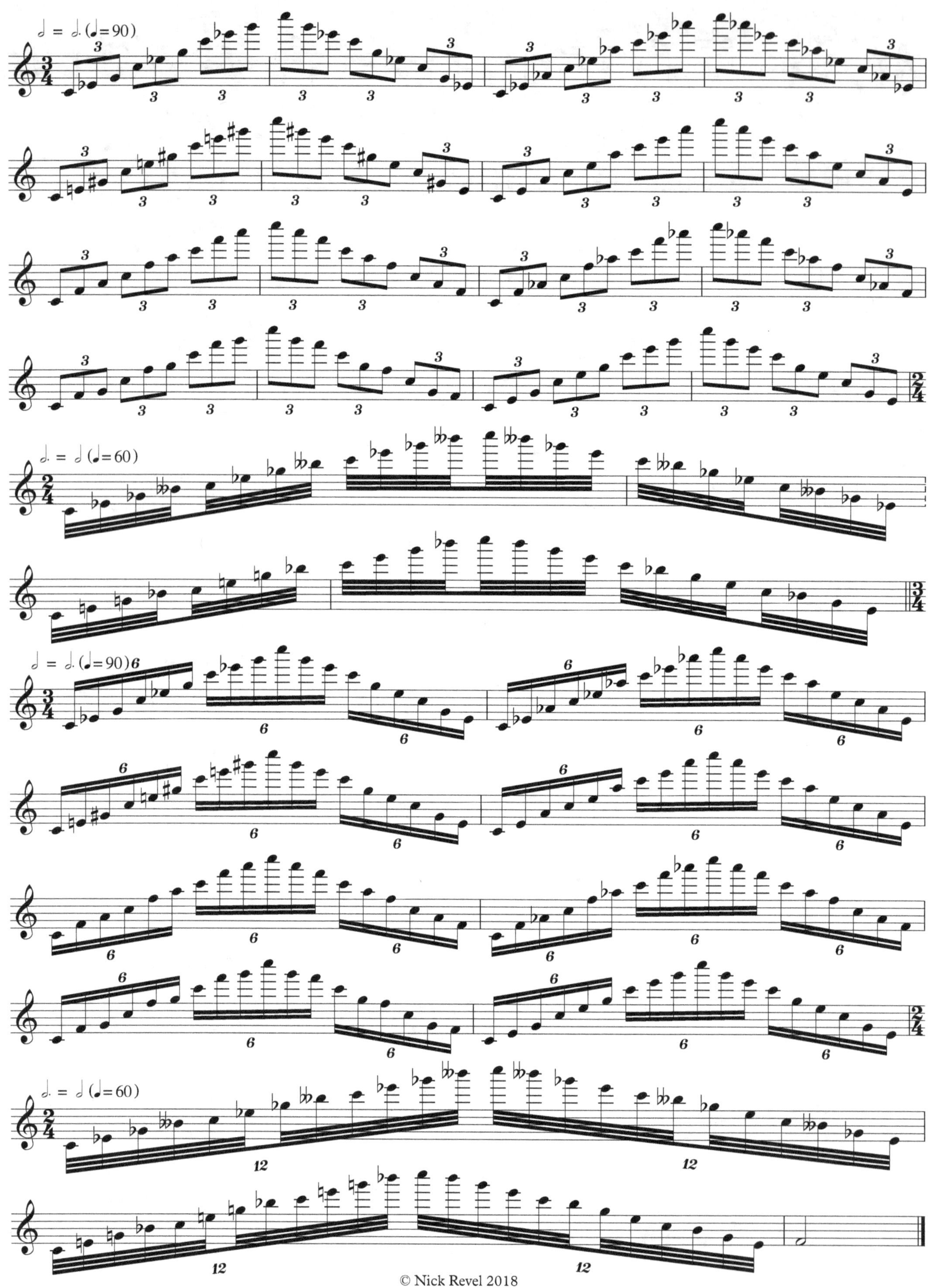
© Nick Revel 2018

*This page left intentionally blank.*

# Arpeggios Version 2

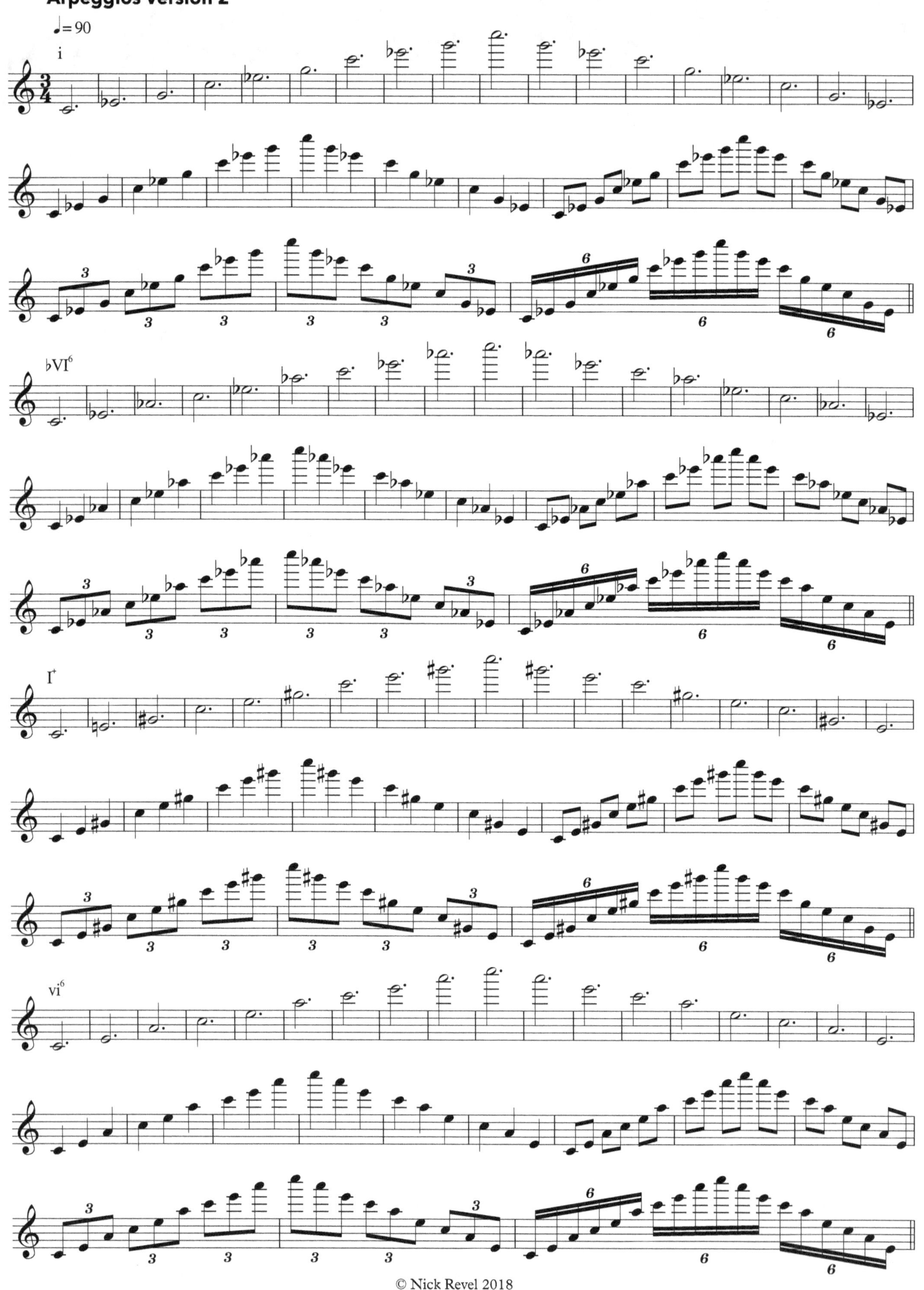

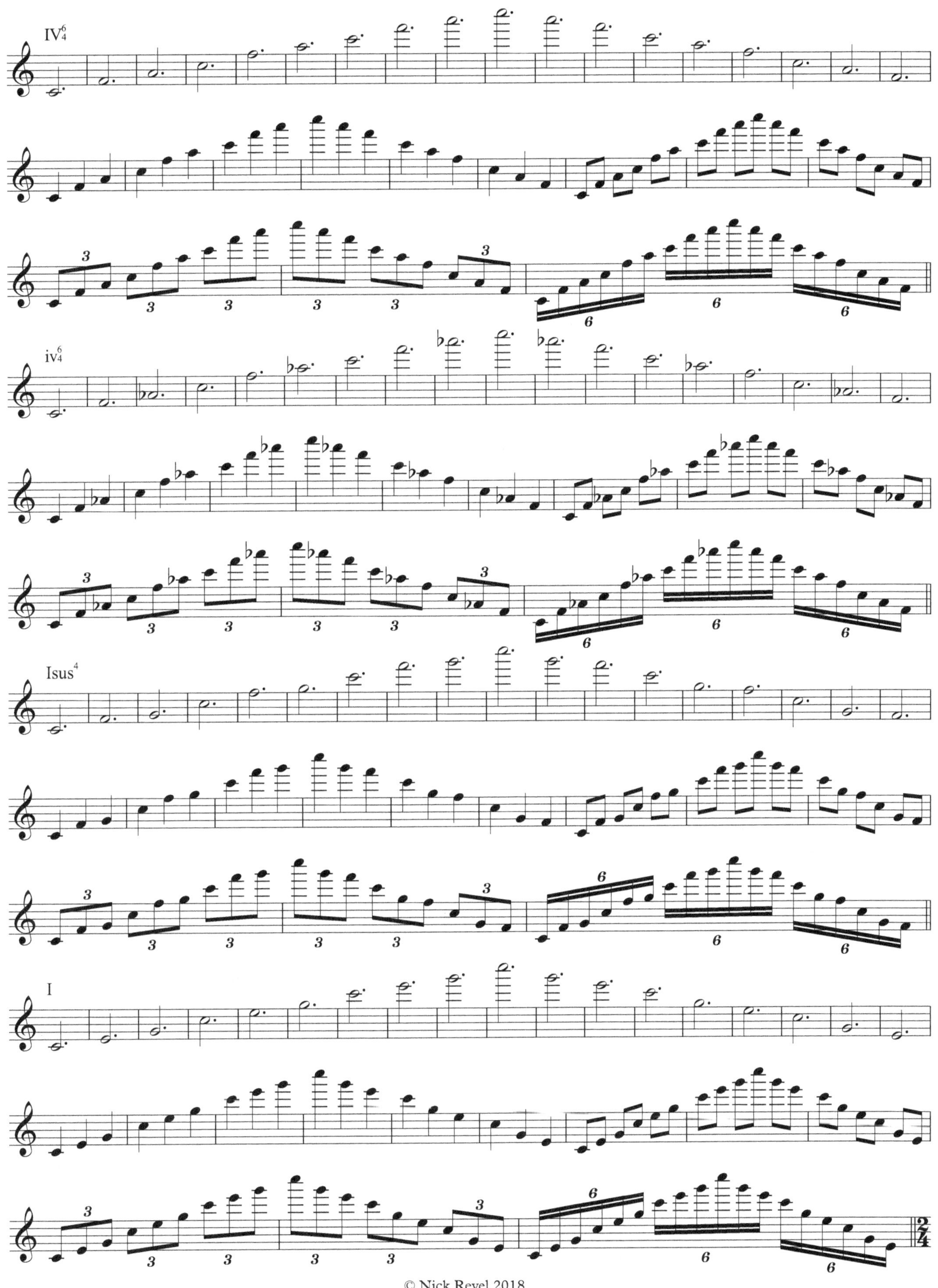

IV⁶₄
iv⁶₄
Isus⁴
I
© Nick Revel 2018

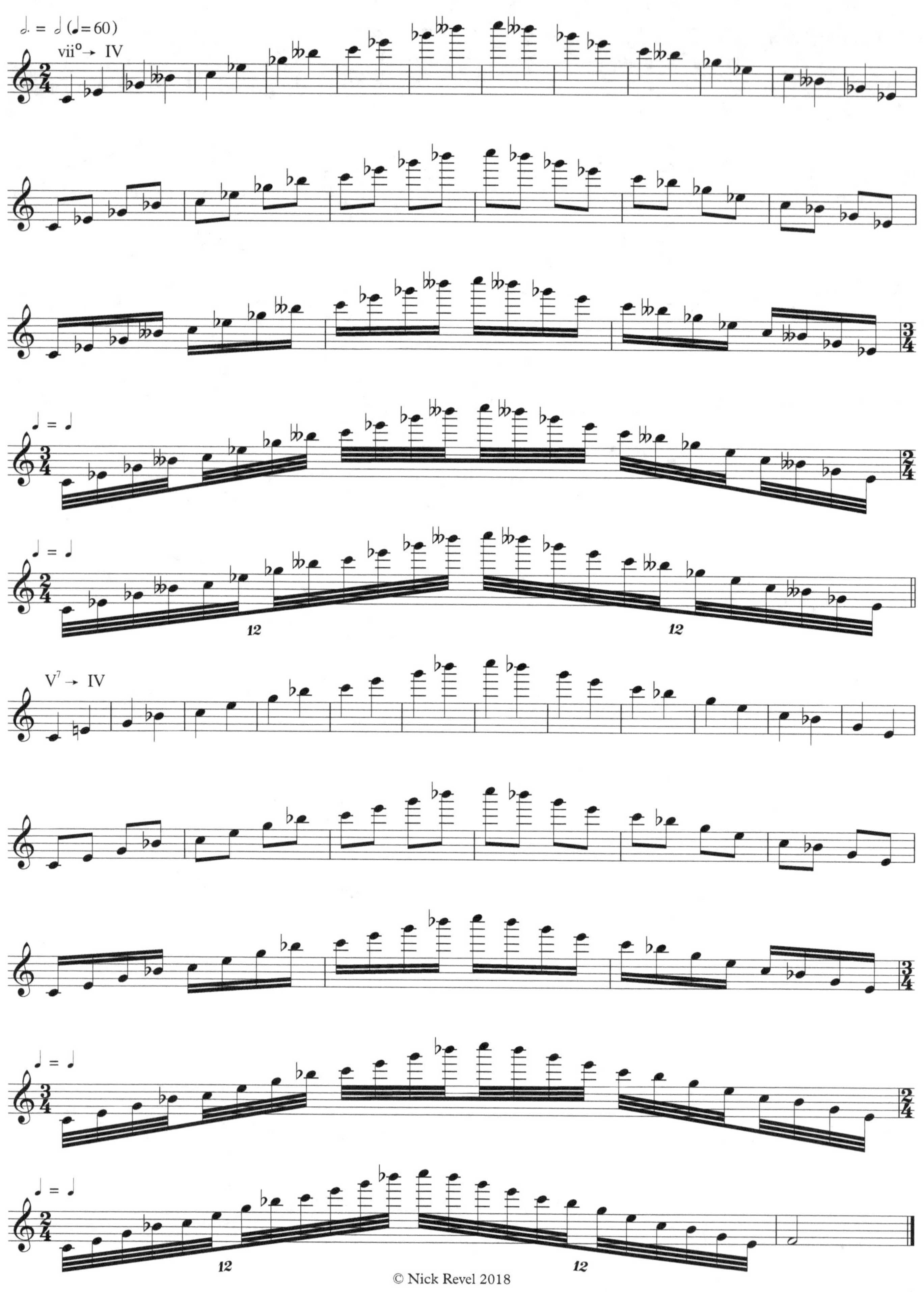

vii° → IV
V⁷ → IV
© Nick Revel 2018
120  DRAGONSCALES – VIOLIN

# DRAGONSCALES

3-Octave Scales and Arpeggios
In Slow to Fast Rhythms
In All Keys

Nick Revel

# C#/Db

DragonScales
The Complete Set in C#Db
Nick Revel
Major
♩ = 60
3
© Nick Revel 2018

12
12
12
12
6
6
6
6
6
6
6
6
3
3
3
3
3
3
3
3
3
3
3
3
3
3
3
3
3
3
3
3
3
3
3
3
3
3
3
3
3
3

Minor

12
12
12
6
6
6
6
6
6
6
6
3 3 3
3 3
3 3 3 3 3
3 3 3 3
3 3 3
3
3 3 3 3 3
3 3 3 3
3 3 3 3
3

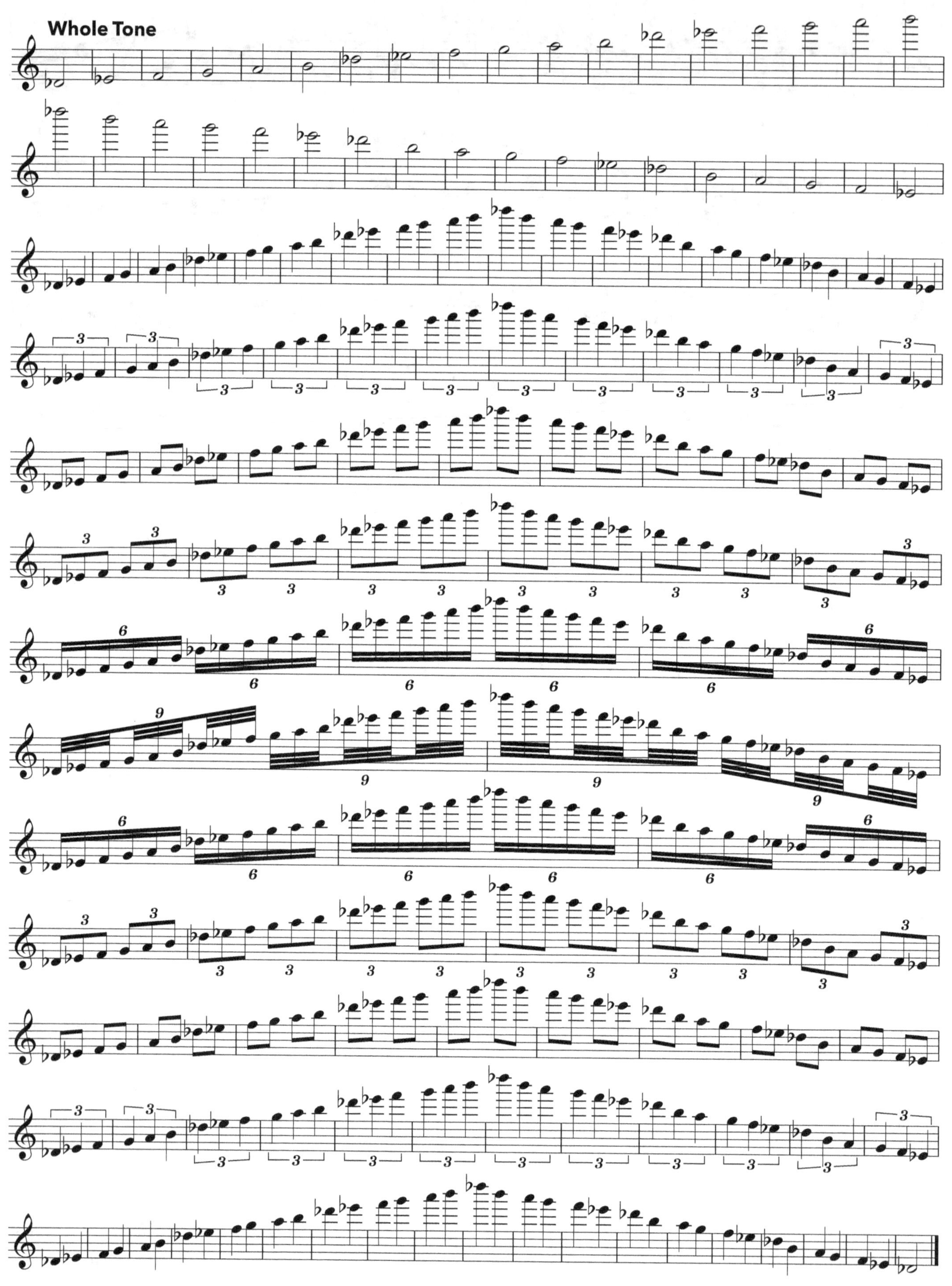


© Nick Revel 2018

© Nick Revel 2018

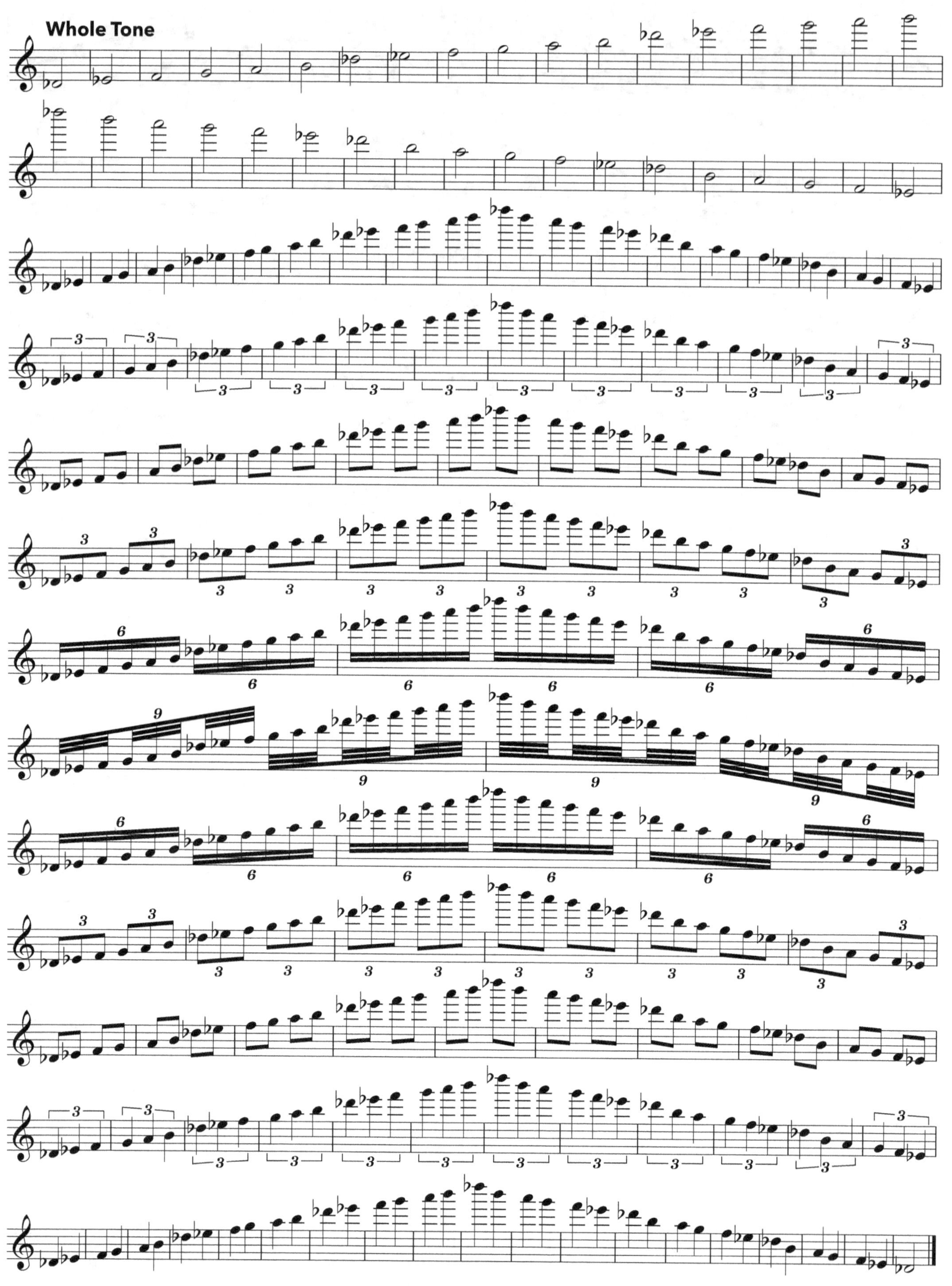


© Nick Revel 2018

*This page left intentionally blank.*

# Diminished Scale Version 1

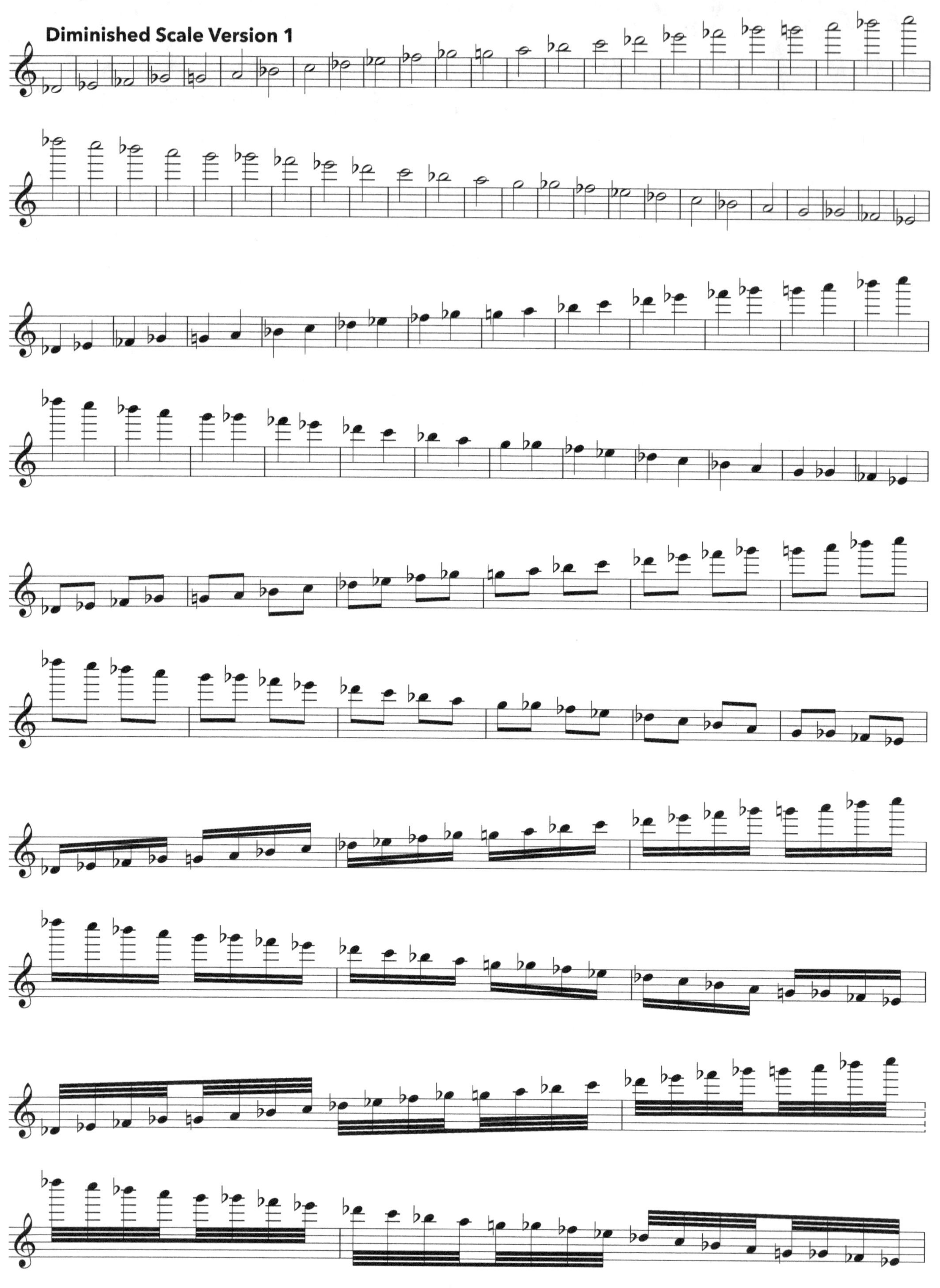

© Nick Revel 2018

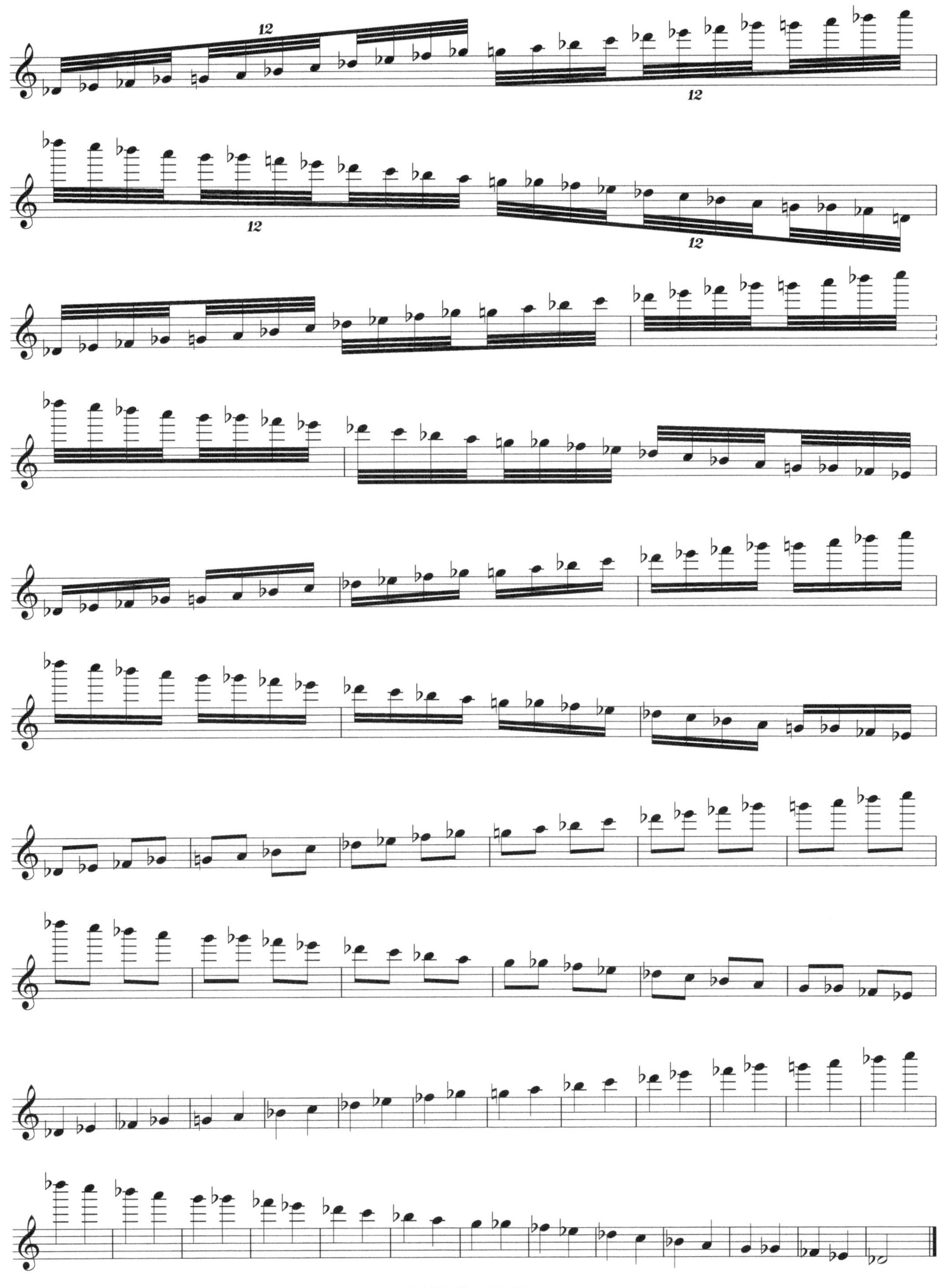


© Nick Revel 2018

# Diminished Scale Version 2

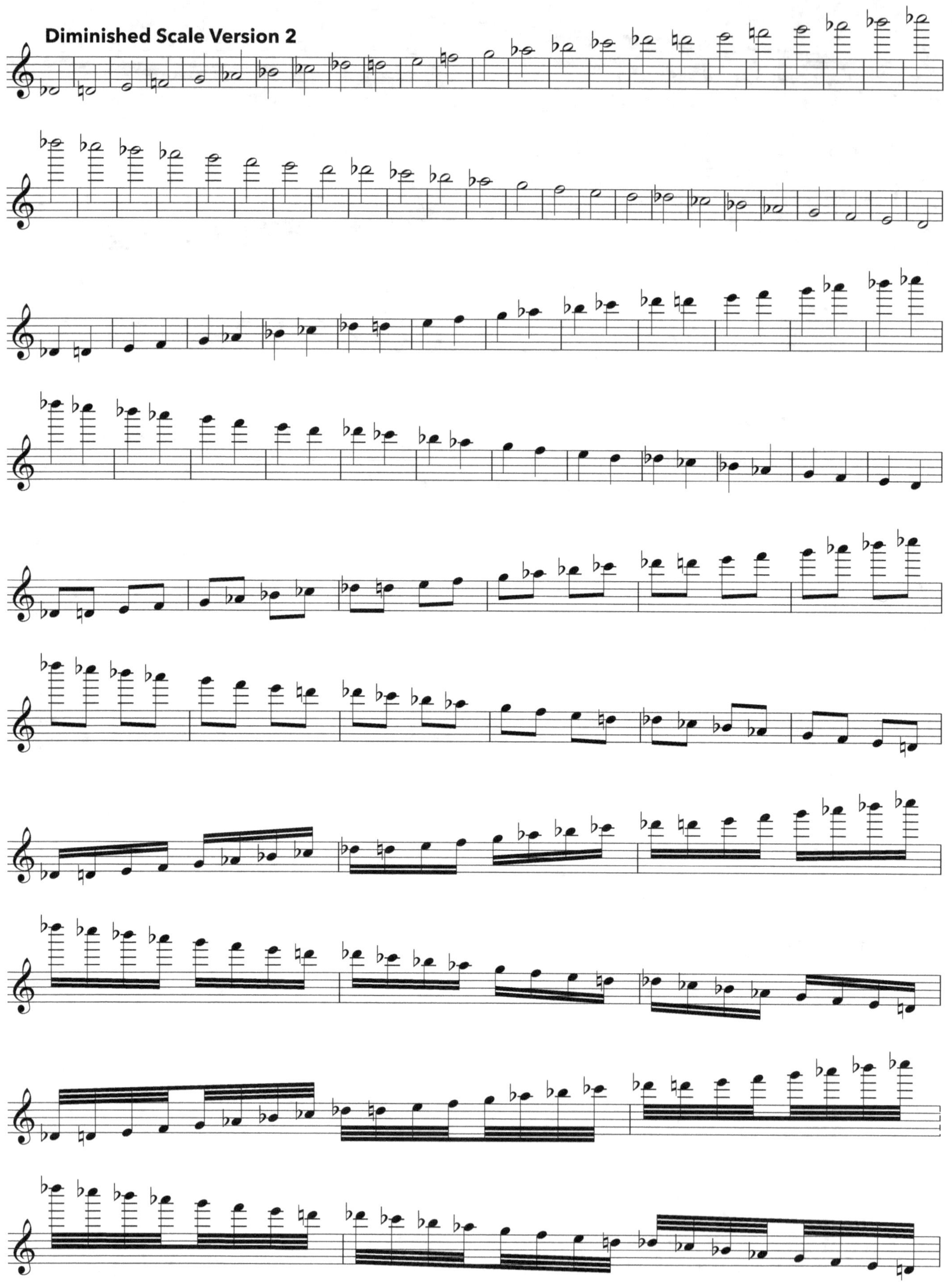

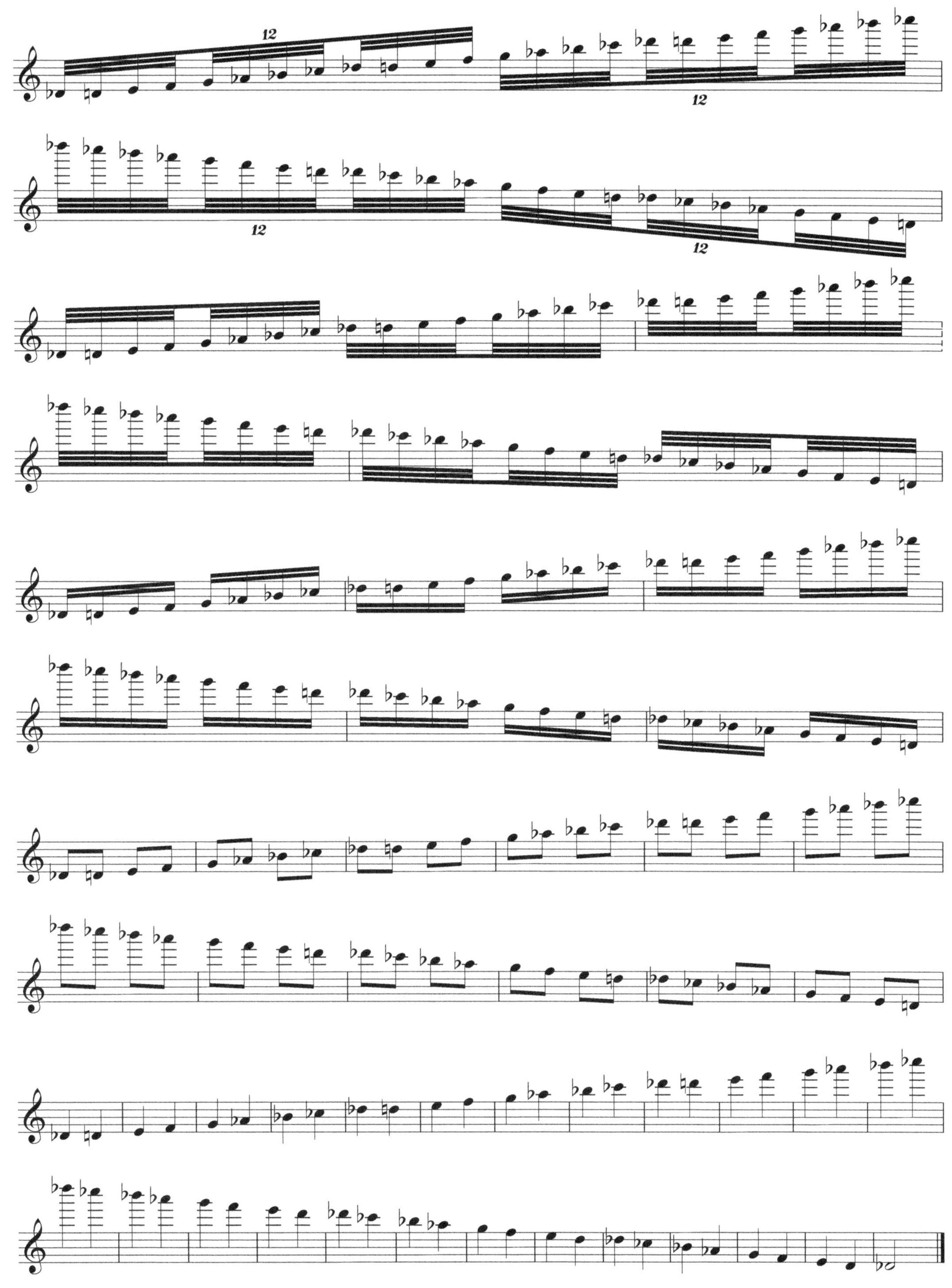

## Chromatic

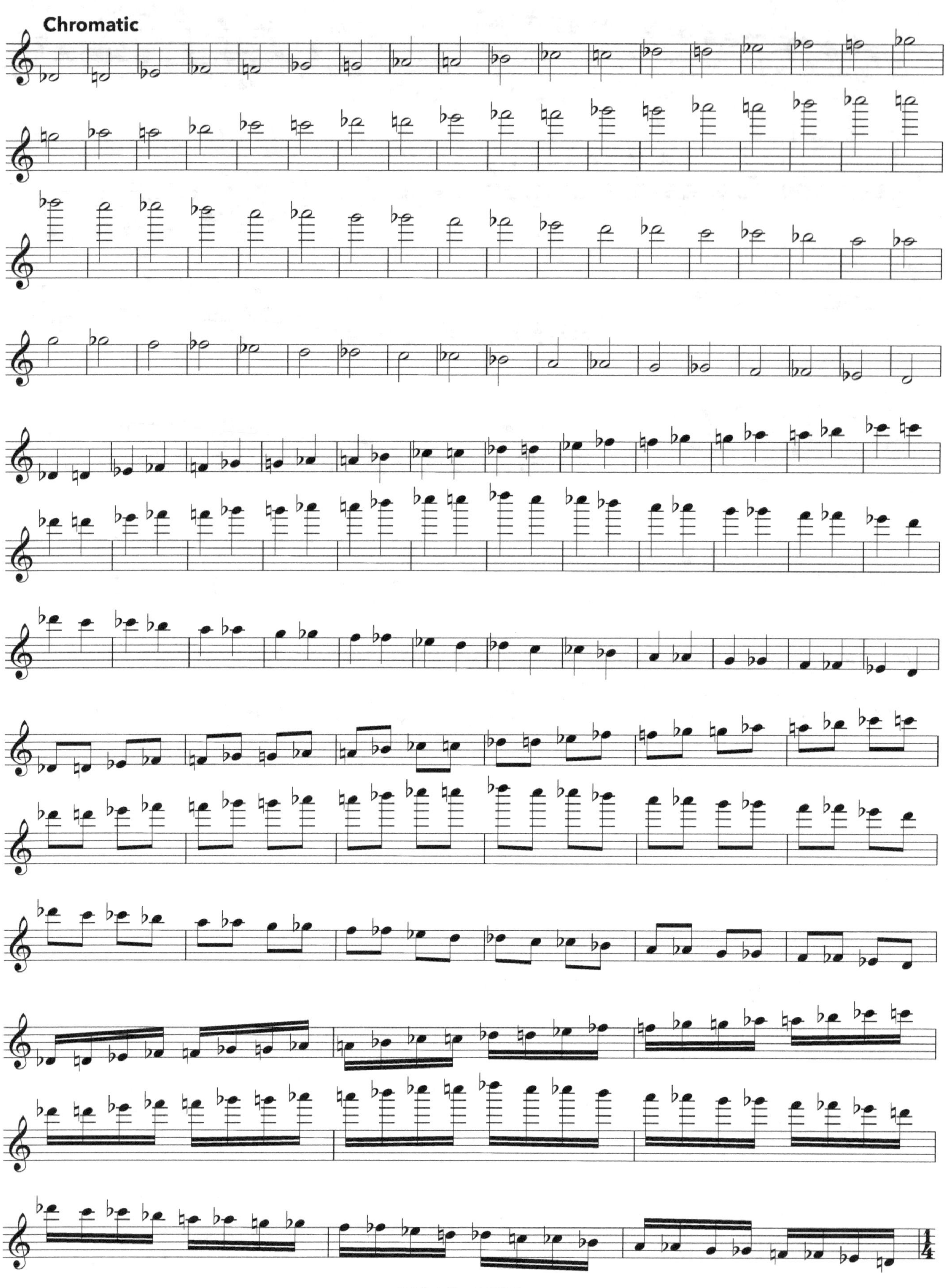


© Nick Revel 2018

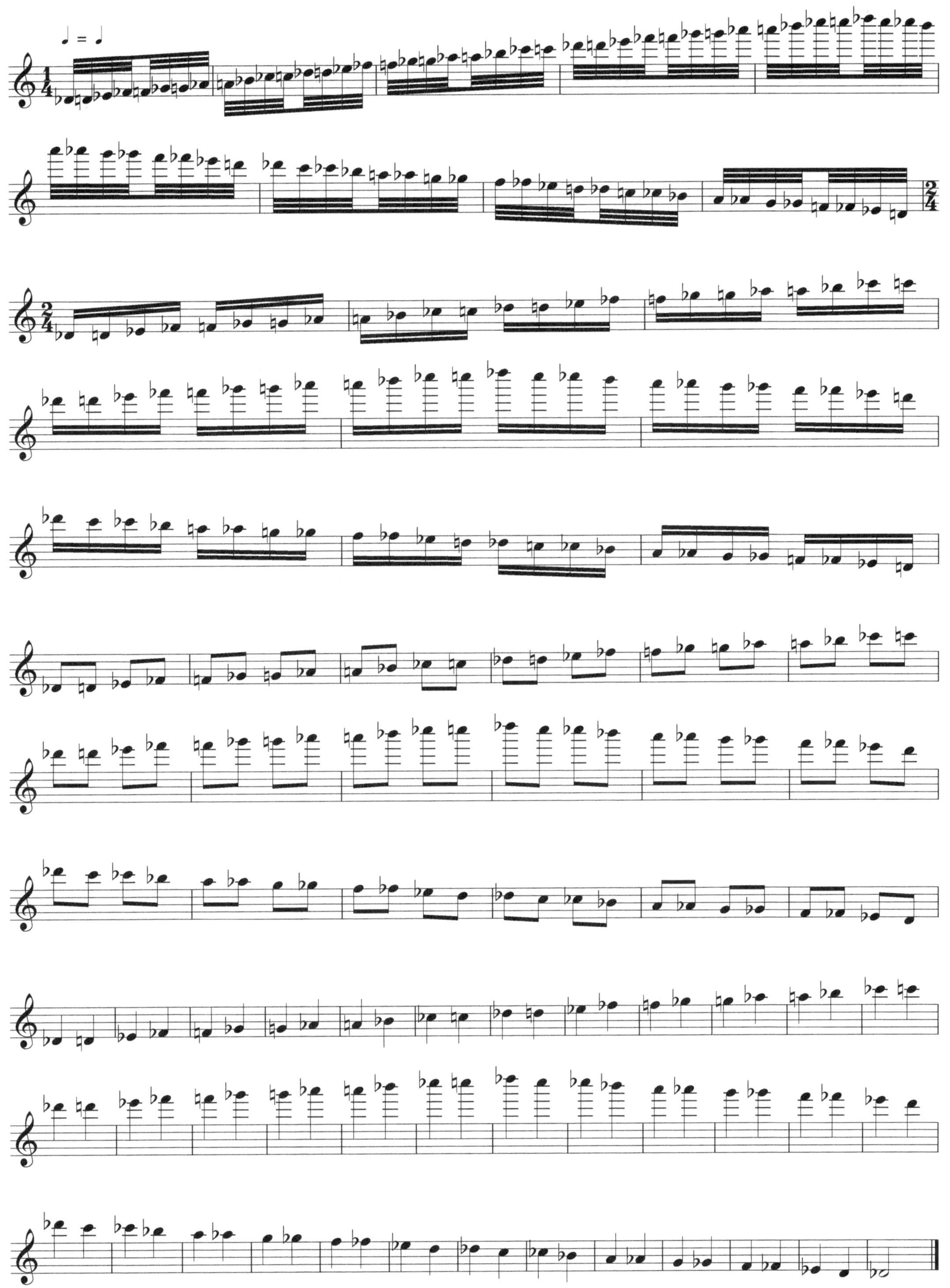

© Nick Revel 2018

## Arpeggios Version 1

© Nick Revel 2018

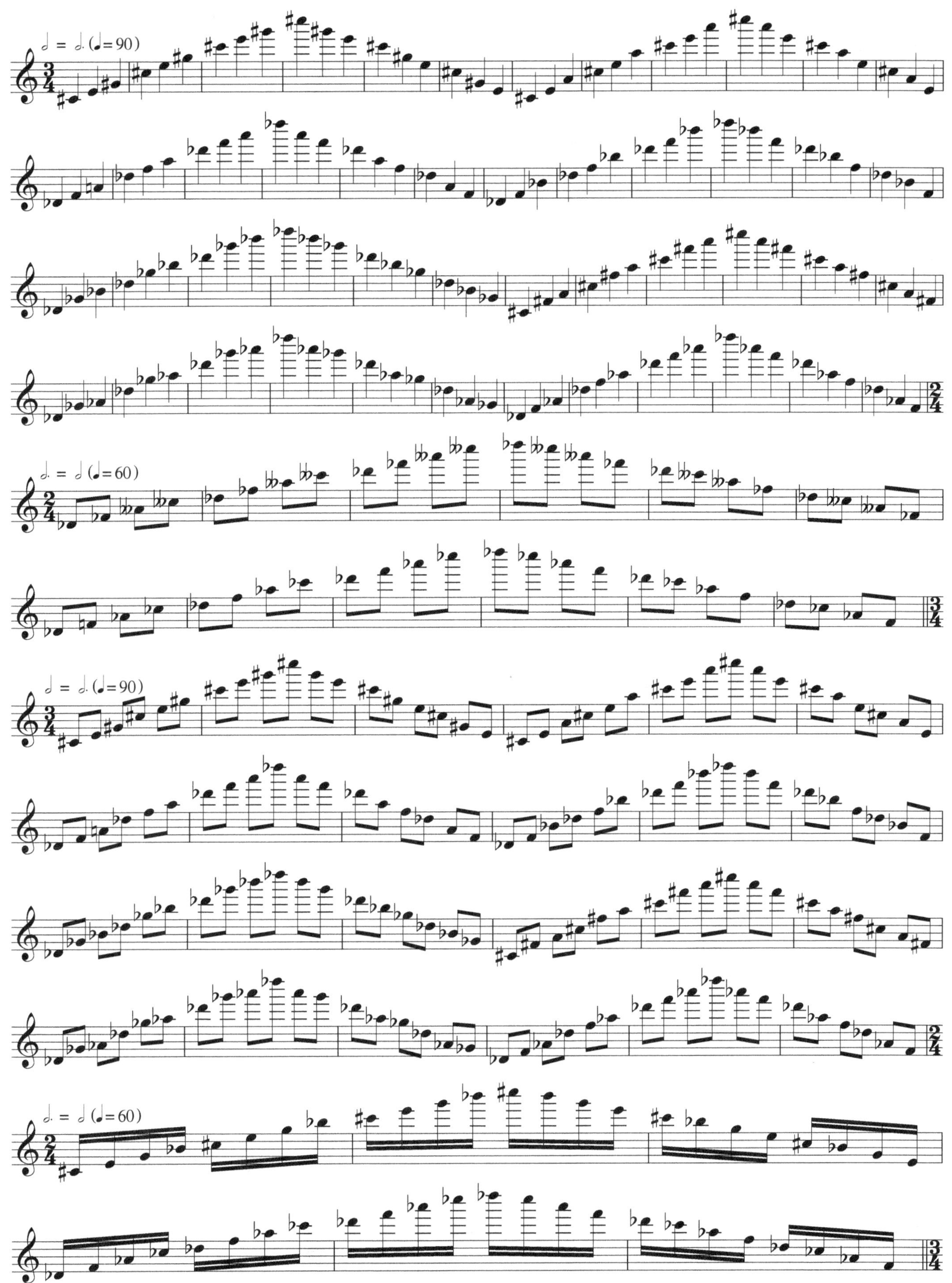

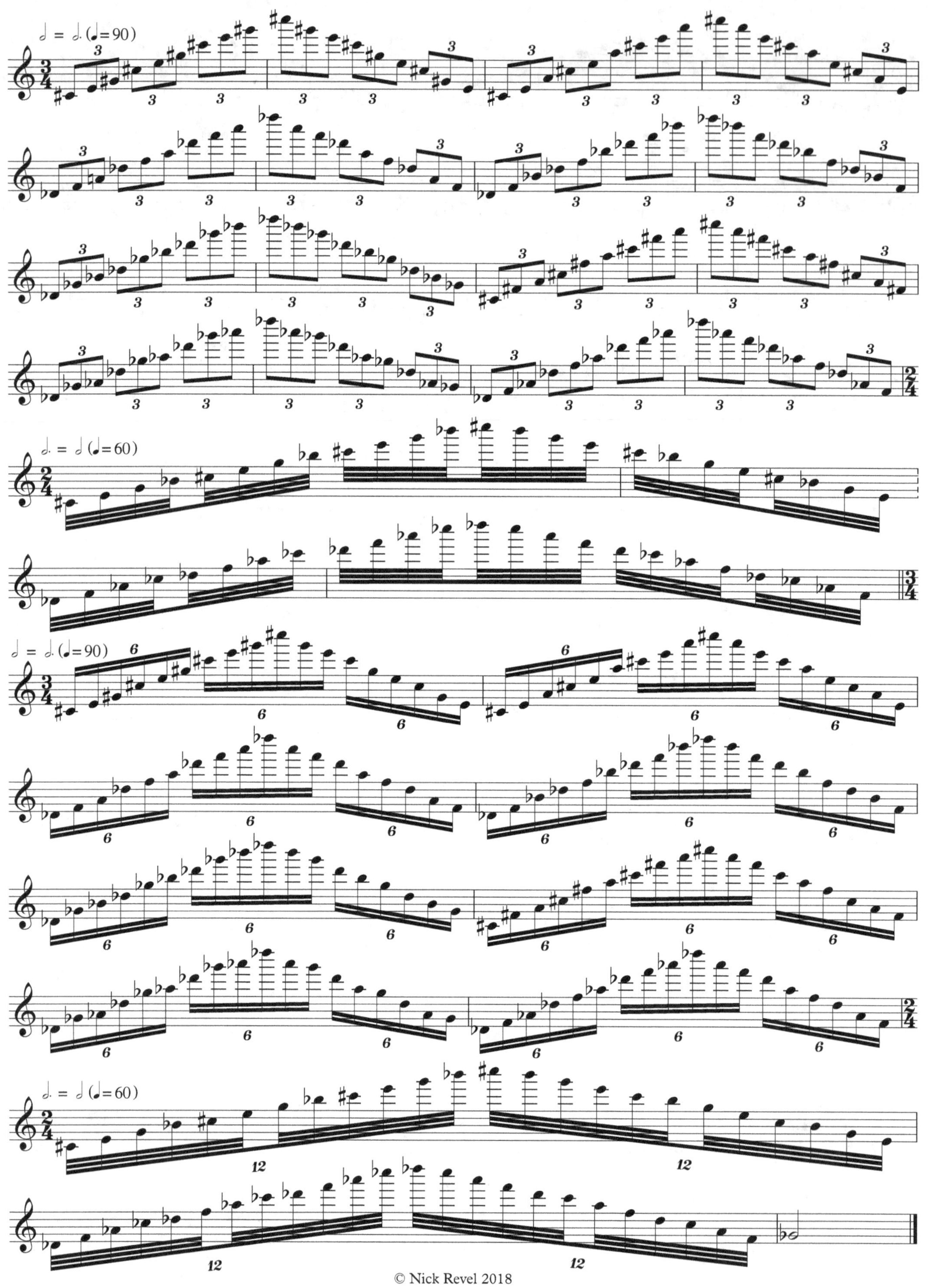

*This page left intentionally blank.*

## Arpeggios Version 2

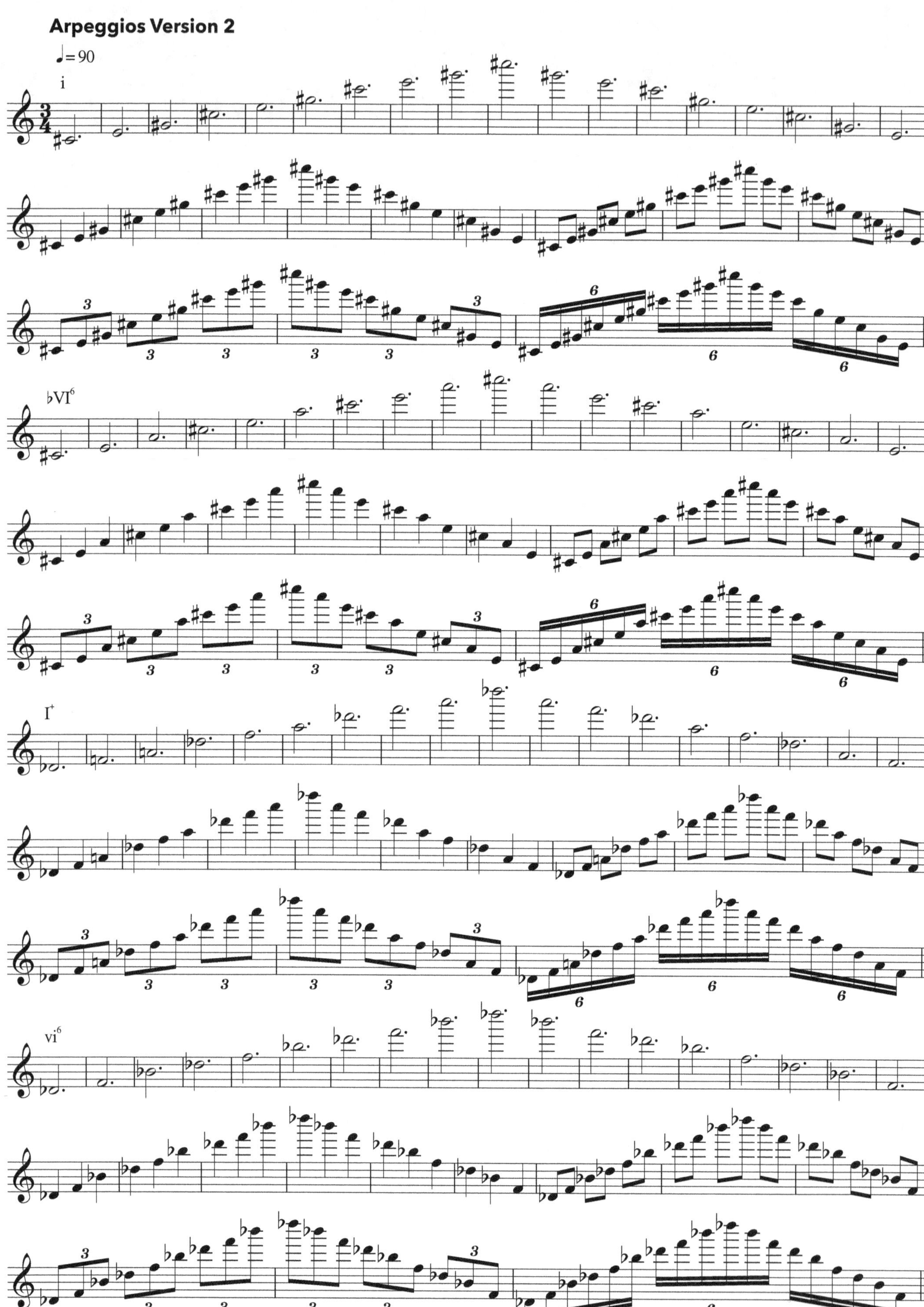


© Nick Revel 2018

IV6/4
iv6/4
Isus4
I
© Nick Revel 2018

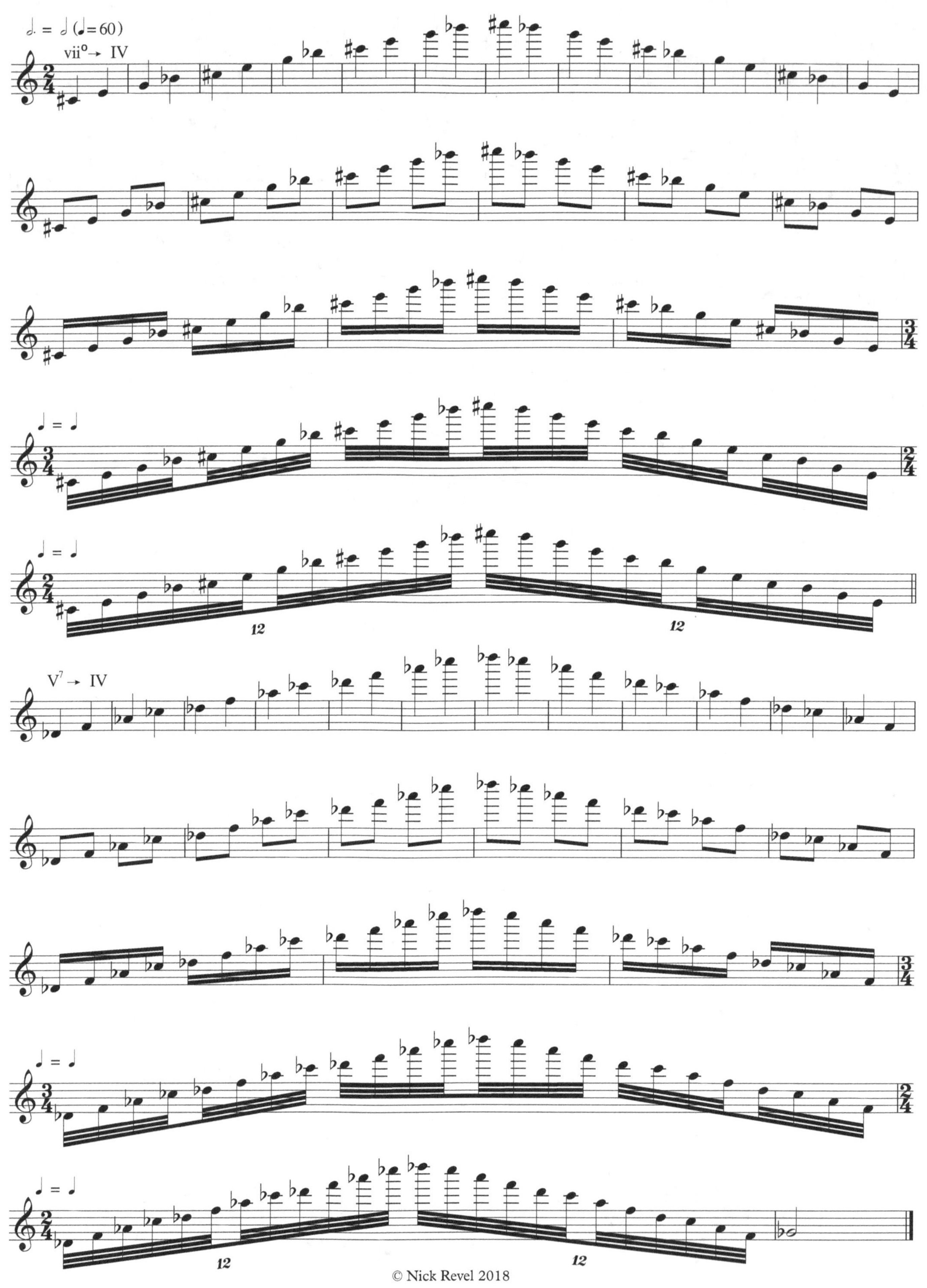

♩. = ♪ (♩ = 60)
vii° → IV
12
12
V⁷ → IV
12
12
vii° → IV
12
12
© Nick Revel 2018

# DRAGONSCALES

3-Octave Scales and Arpeggios
In Slow to Fast Rhythms
In All Keys

Nick Revel

# D

# DragonScales
## The Complete Set in D

© Nick Revel 2018

Minor

Whole Tone
© Nick Revel 2018

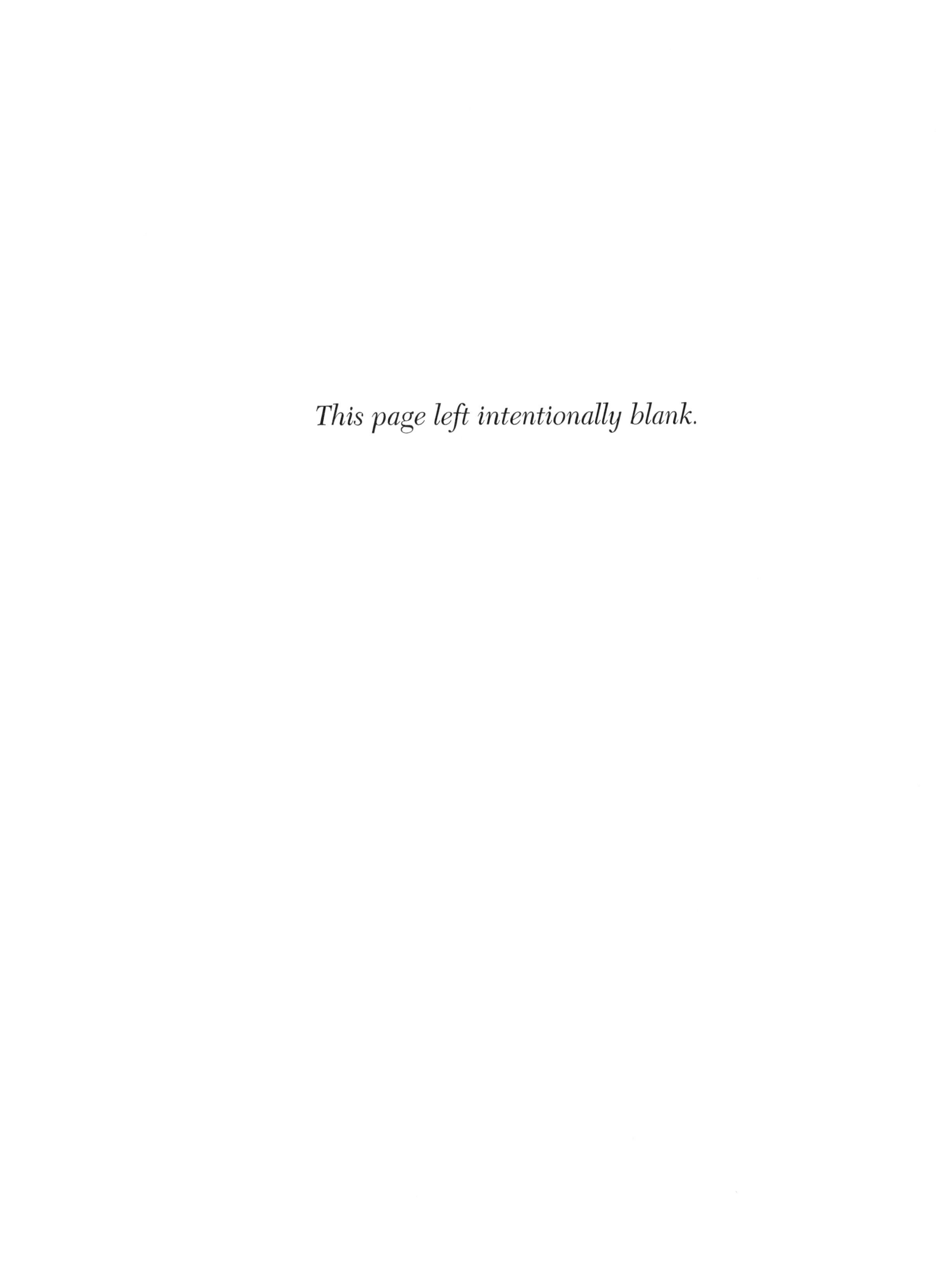


This page left intentionally blank.

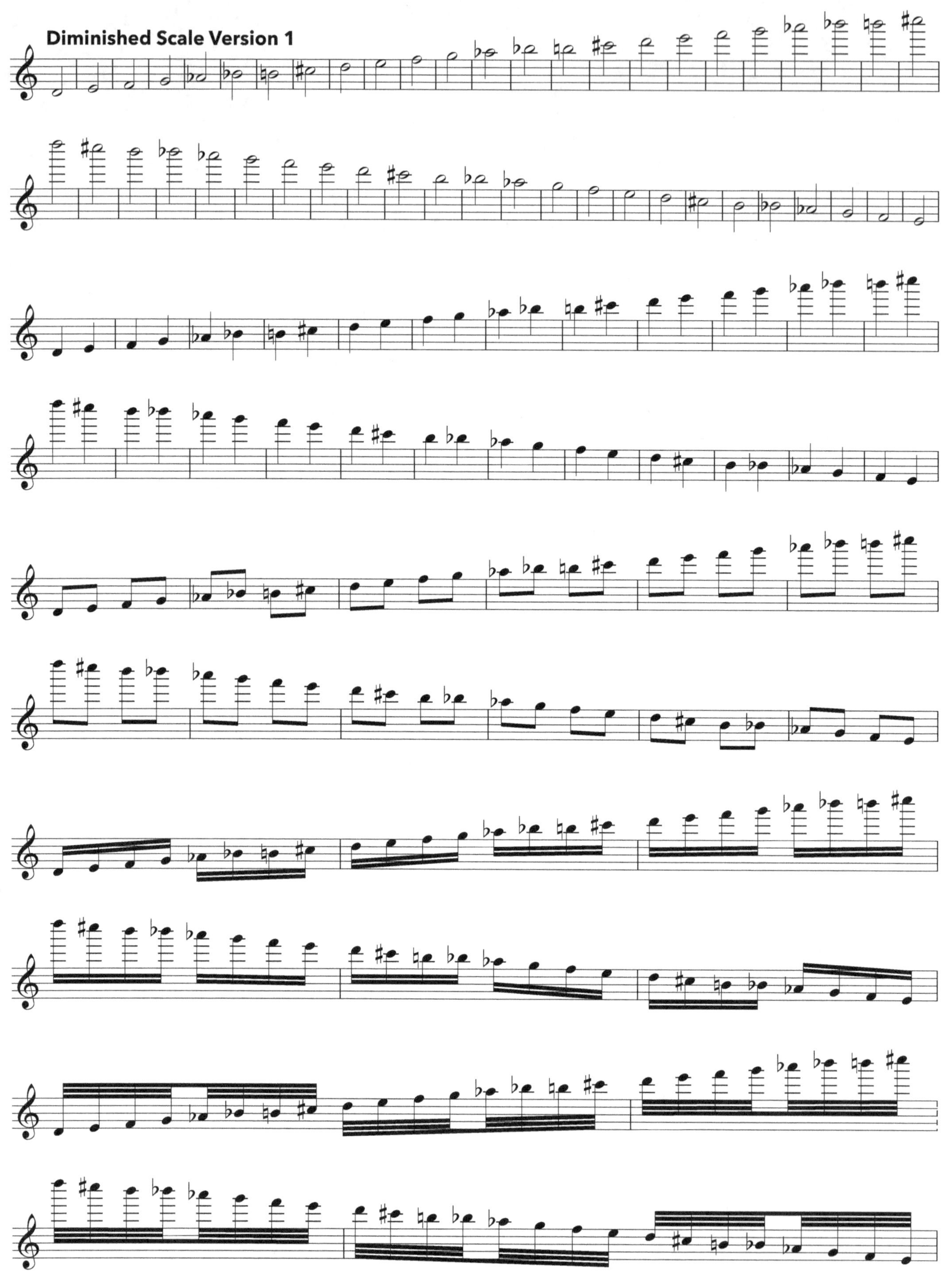

© Nick Revel 2018

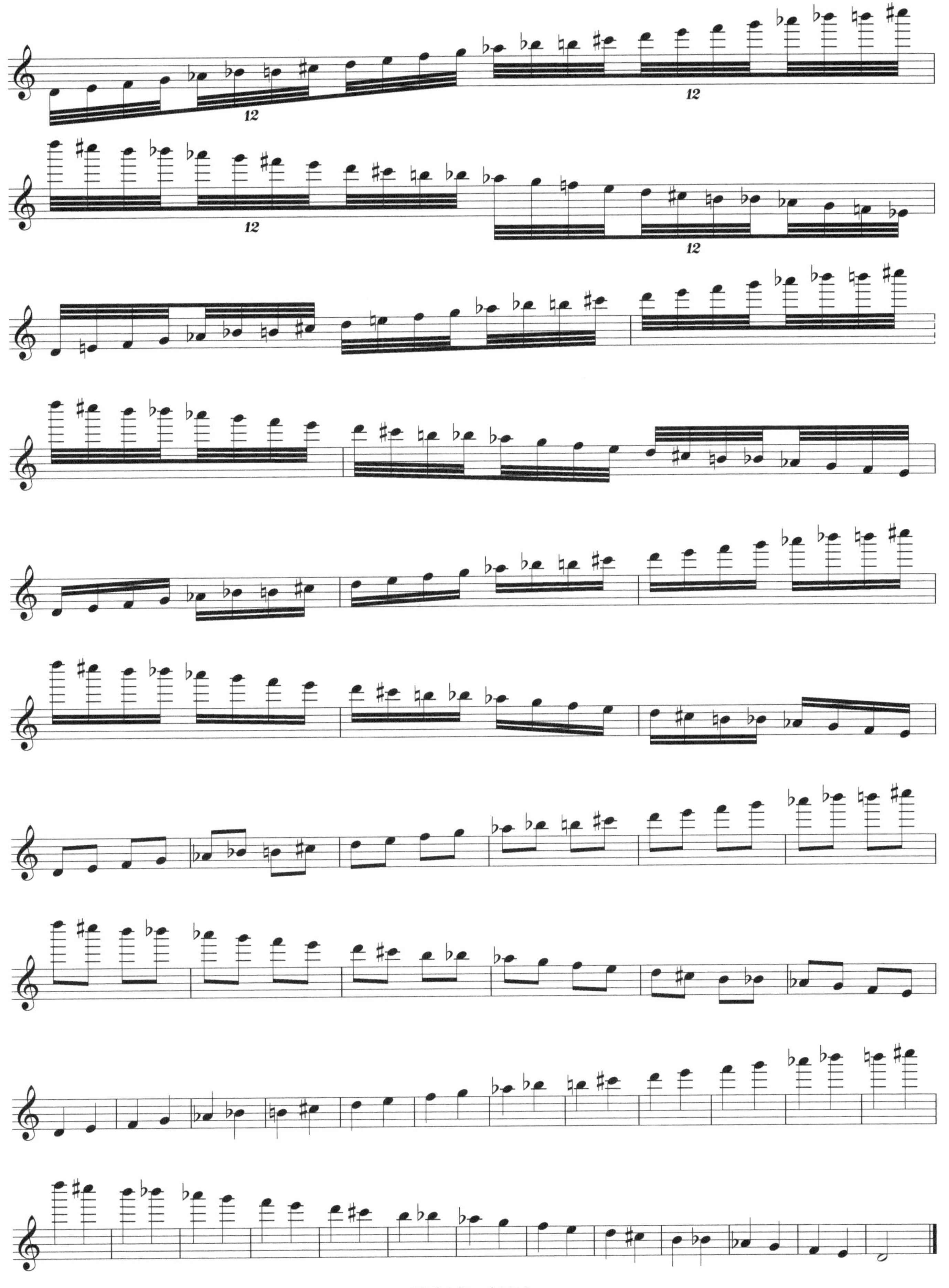


© Nick Revel 2018

Diminished Scale Version 2

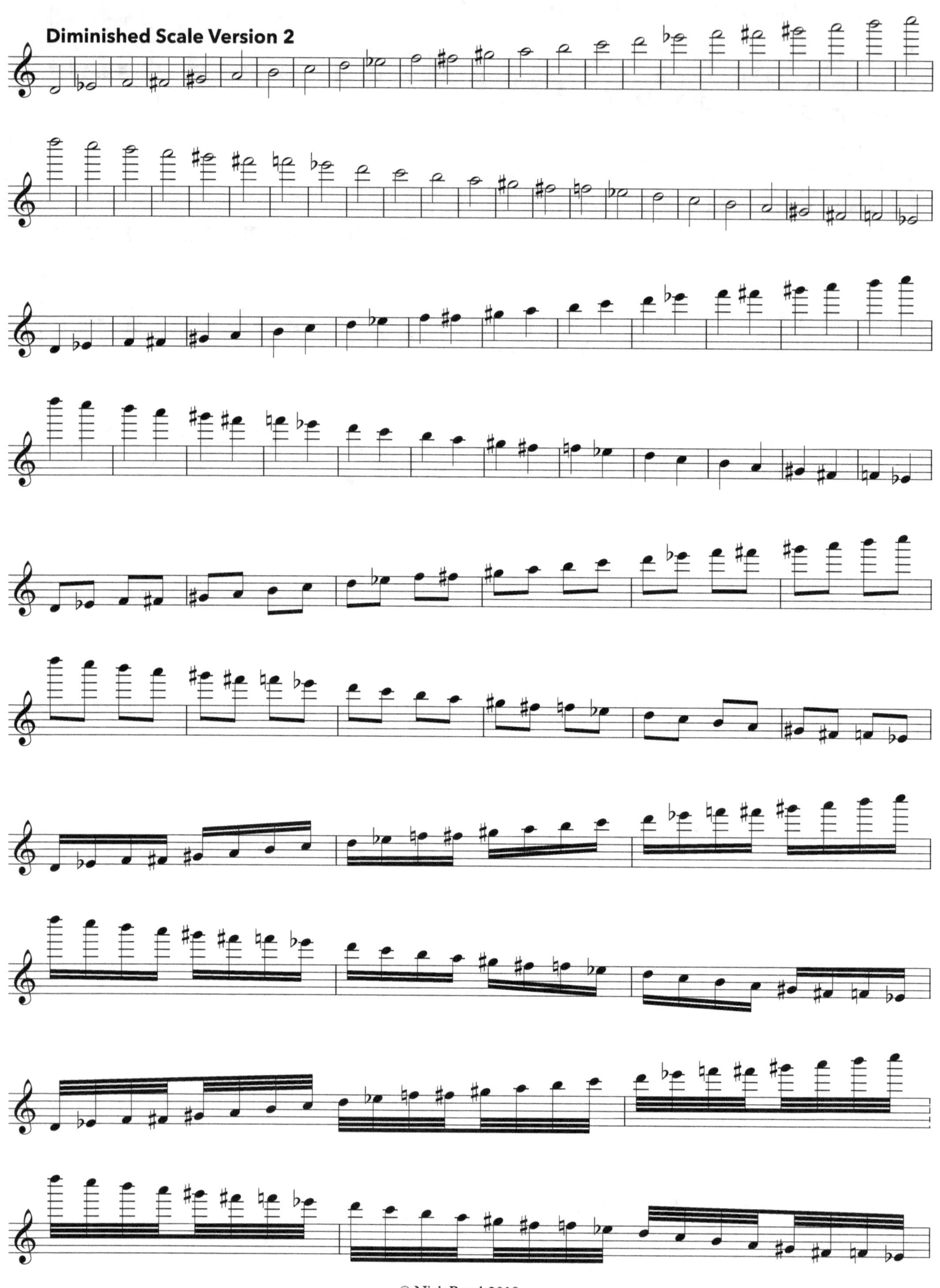

© Nick Revel 2018

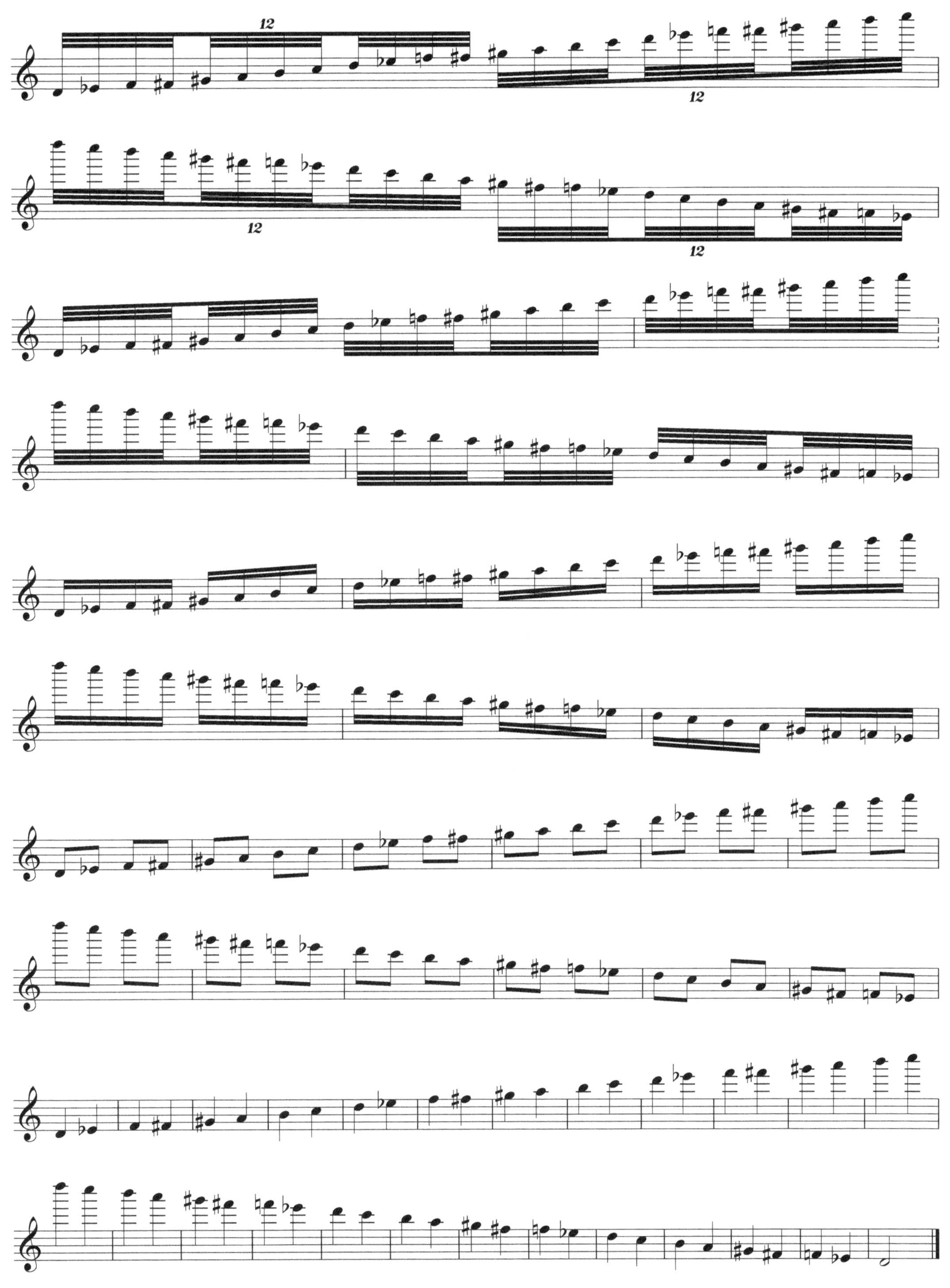

# Chromatic

© Nick Revel 2018

♩ = ♩
DRAGONSCALES – VIOLIN    153
© Nick Revel 2018

# Arpeggios Version 1

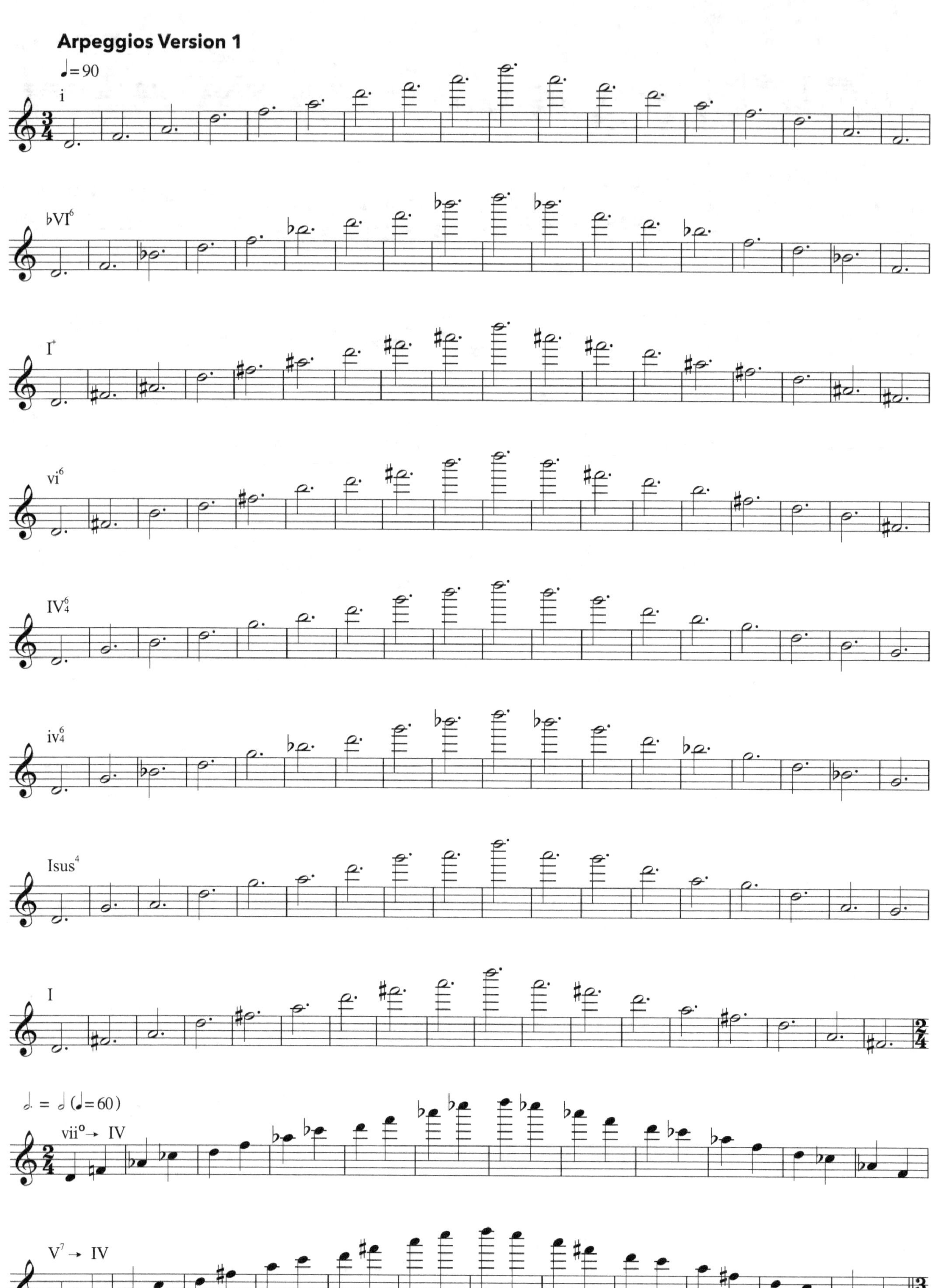


© Nick Revel 2018

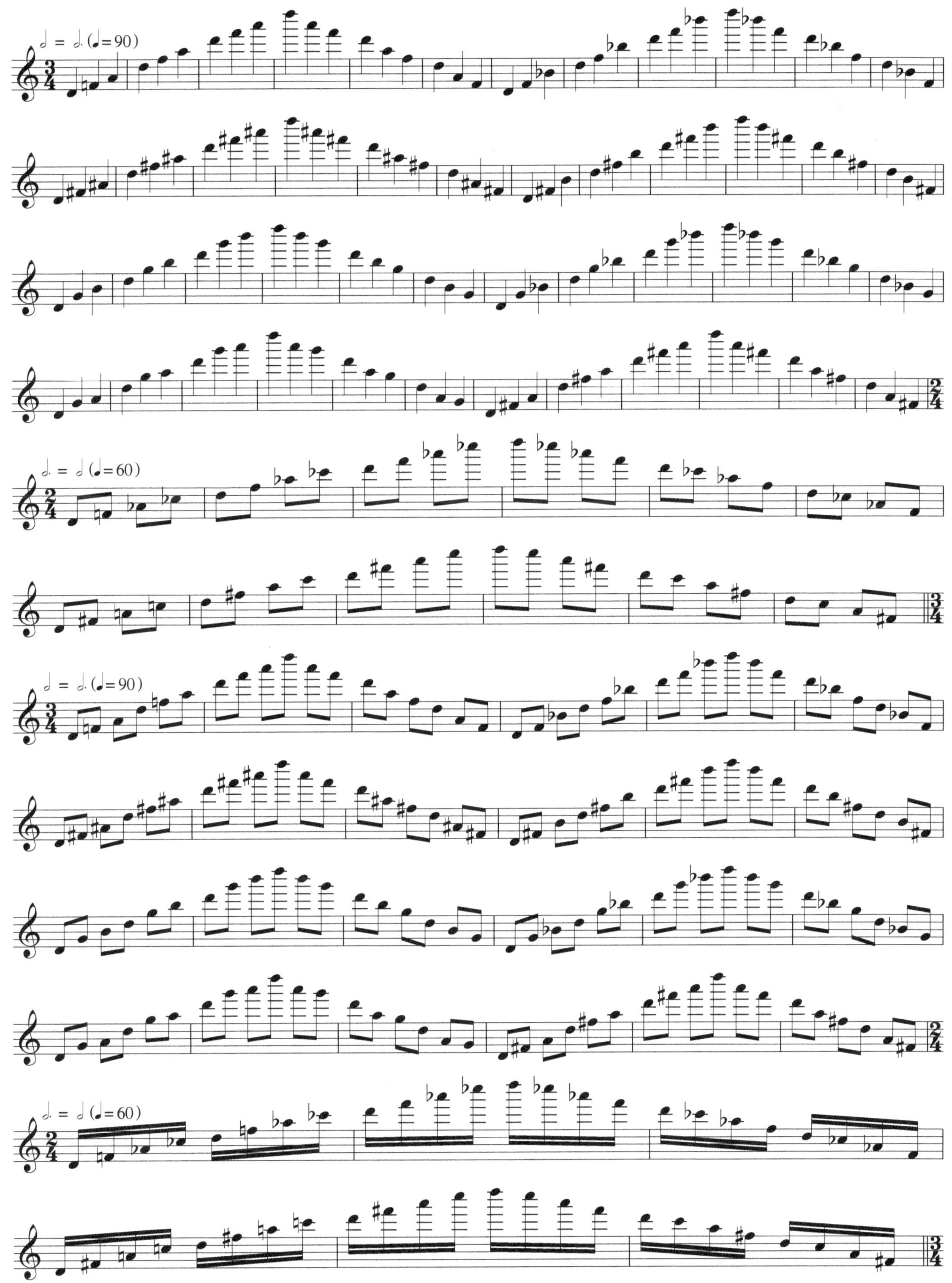

© Nick Revel 2018

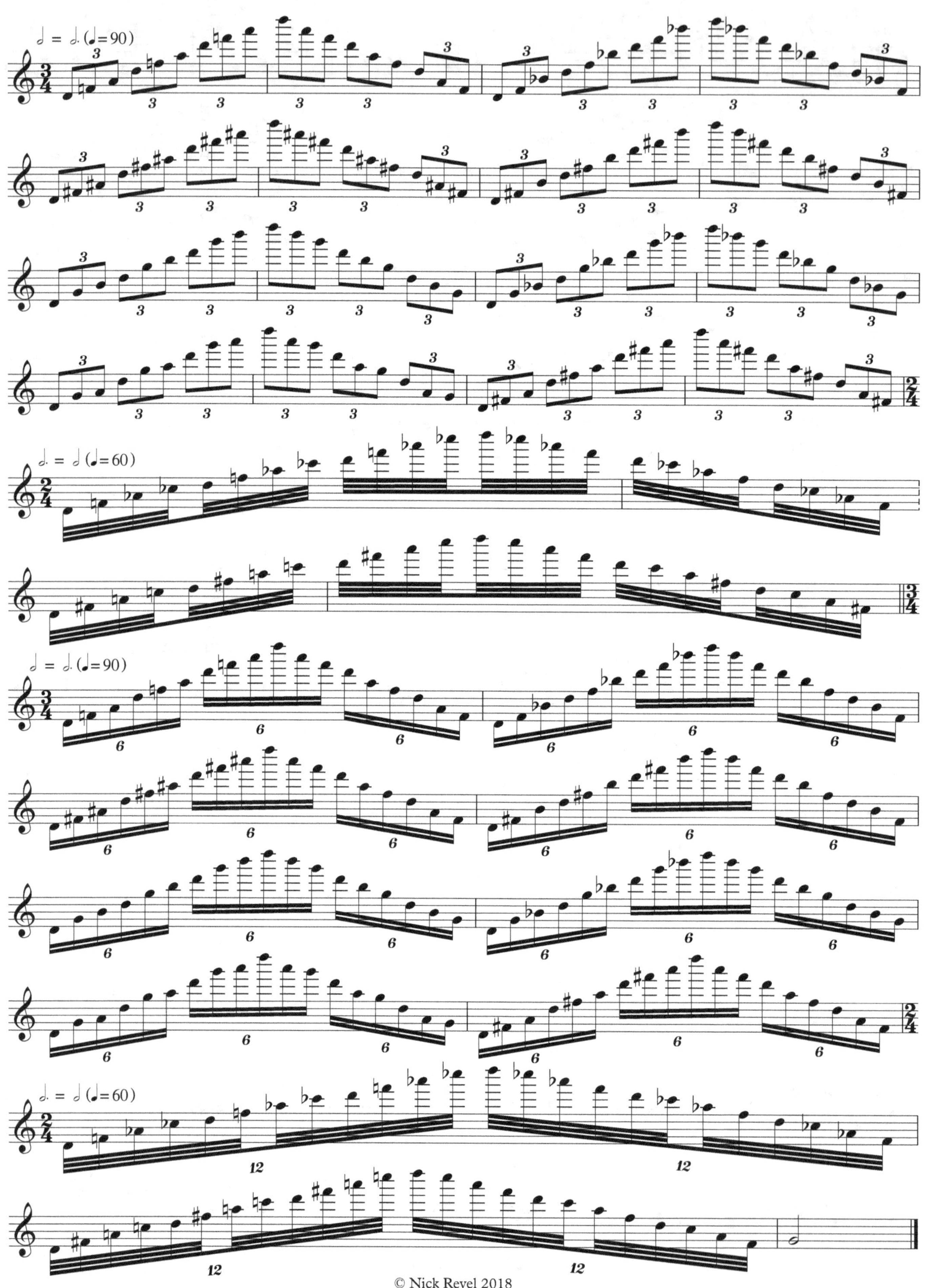

♩ = ♩. (♩=90)
♩. = ♩ (♩=60)
♩ = ♩. (♩=90)
♩. = ♩ (♩=60)
© Nick Revel 2018
156  DRAGONSCALES – VIOLIN

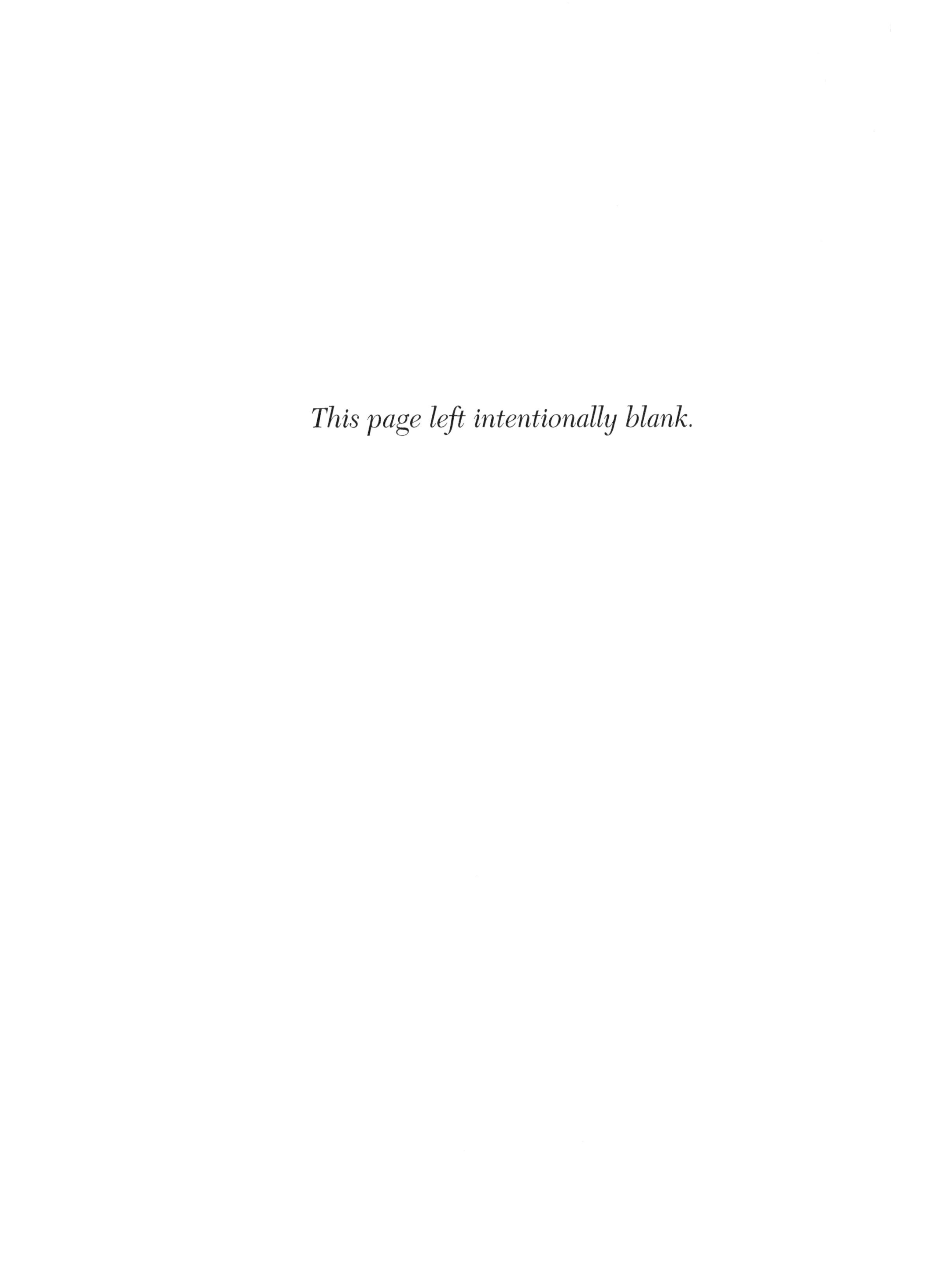


This page left intentionally blank.

# Arpeggios Version 2

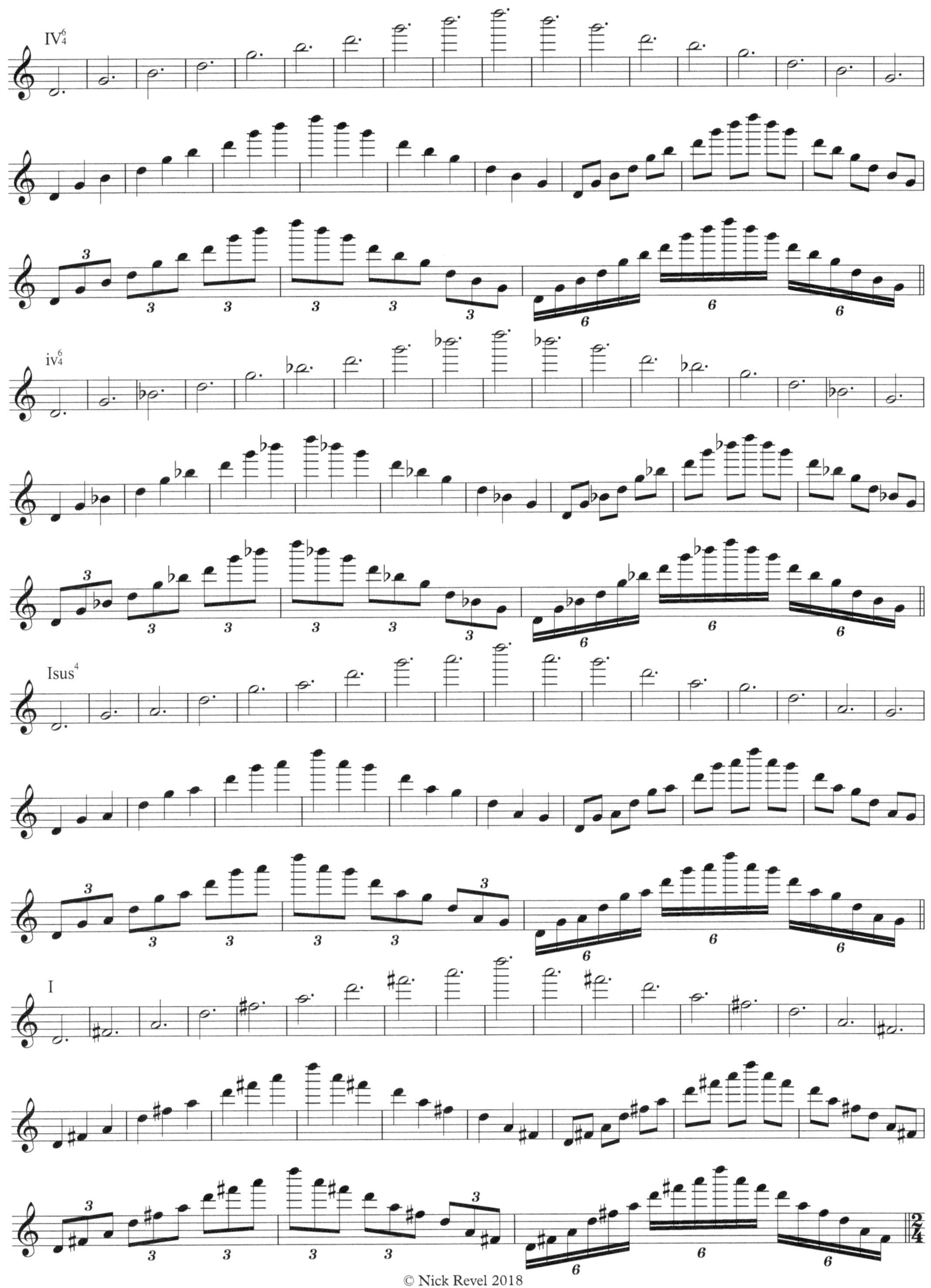

IV6/4
iv6/4
Isus4
I
© Nick Revel 2018
DRAGONSCALES – VIOLIN   159

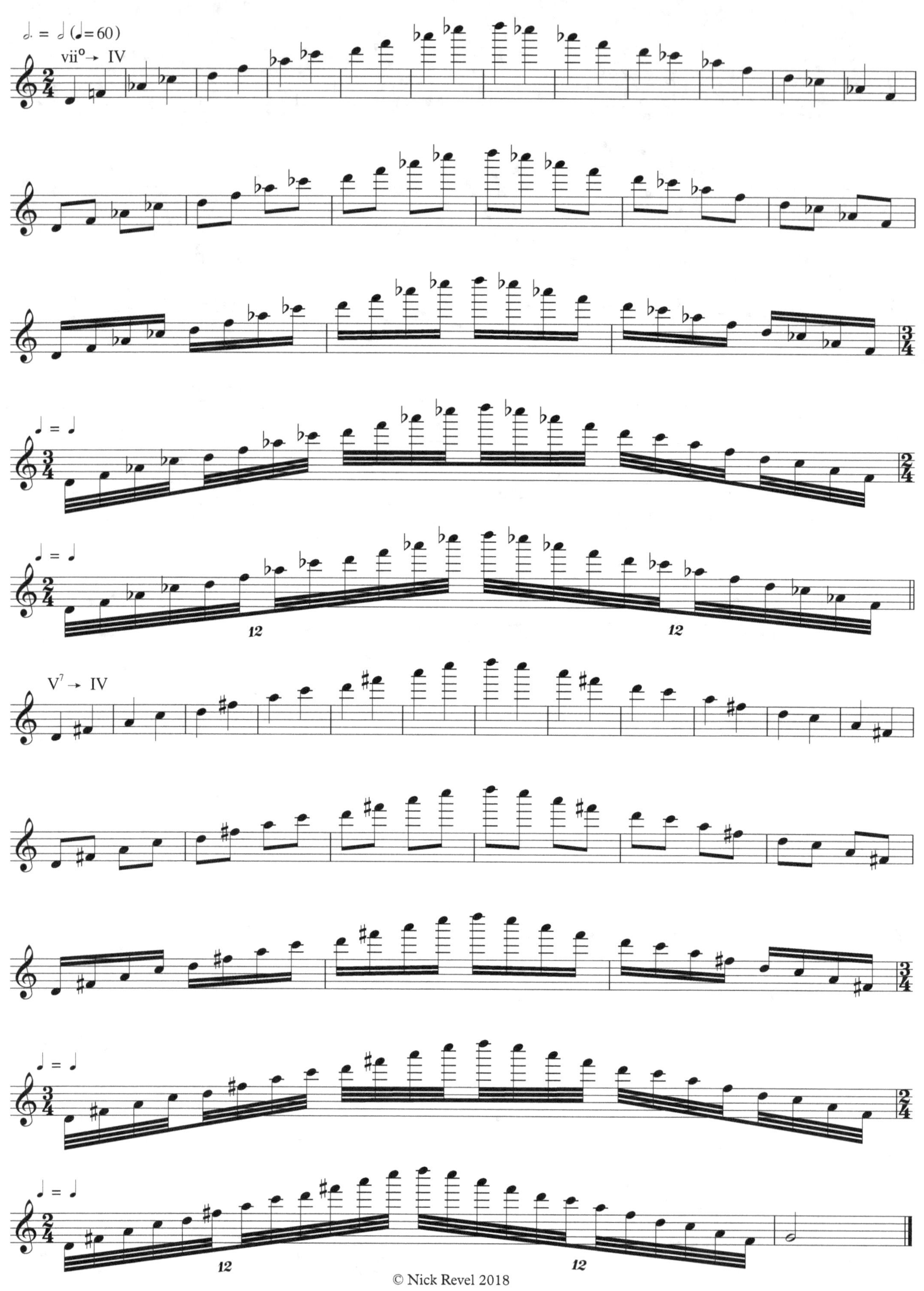

♩. = ♪ (♩ = 60)
vii° → IV
V⁷ → IV
© Nick Revel 2018

# DRAGONSCALES

3-Octave Scales and Arpeggios
In Slow to Fast Rhythms
In All Keys

Nick Revel

# Eb

# DragonScales
## The Complete Set in D#Eb

Nick Revel

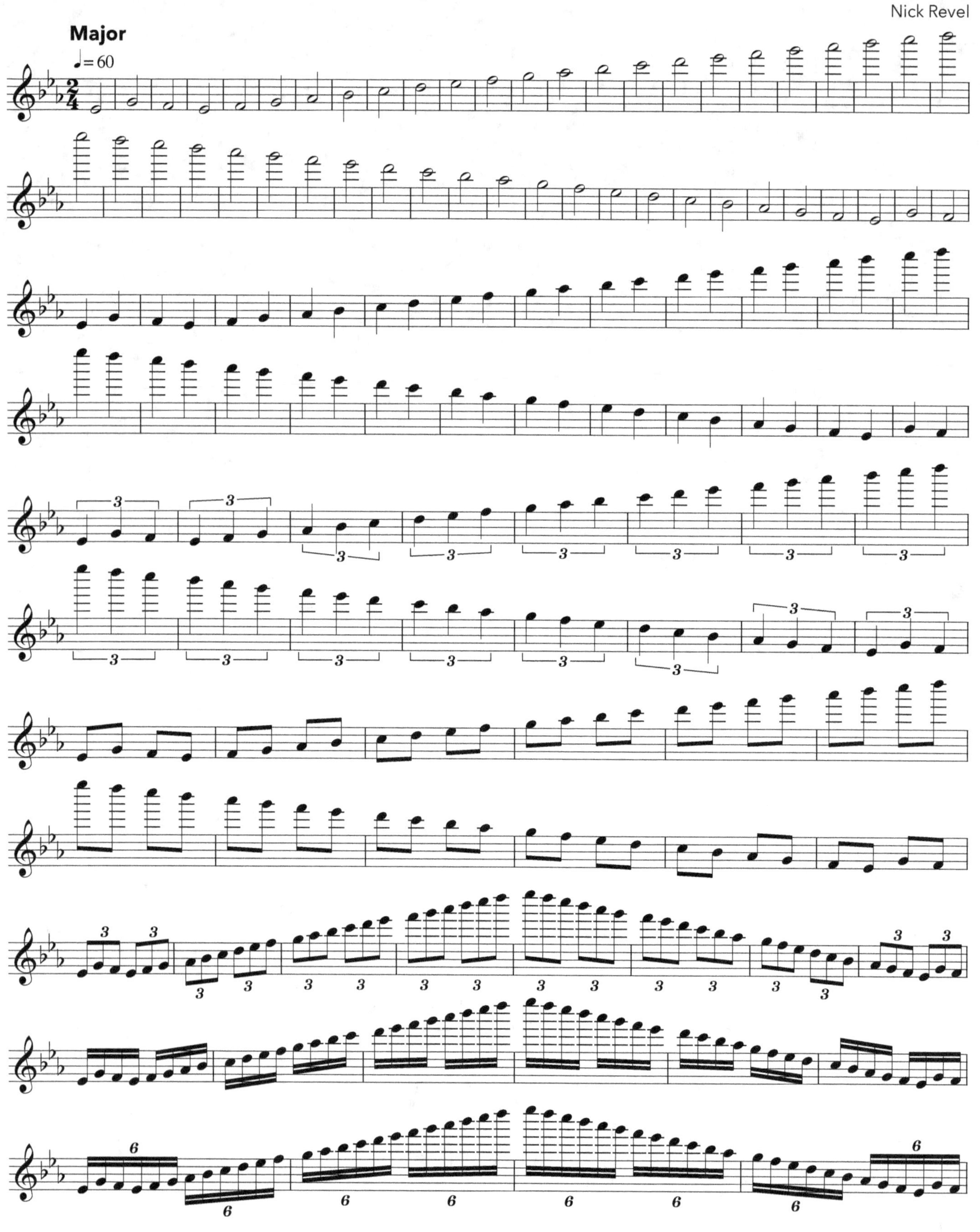

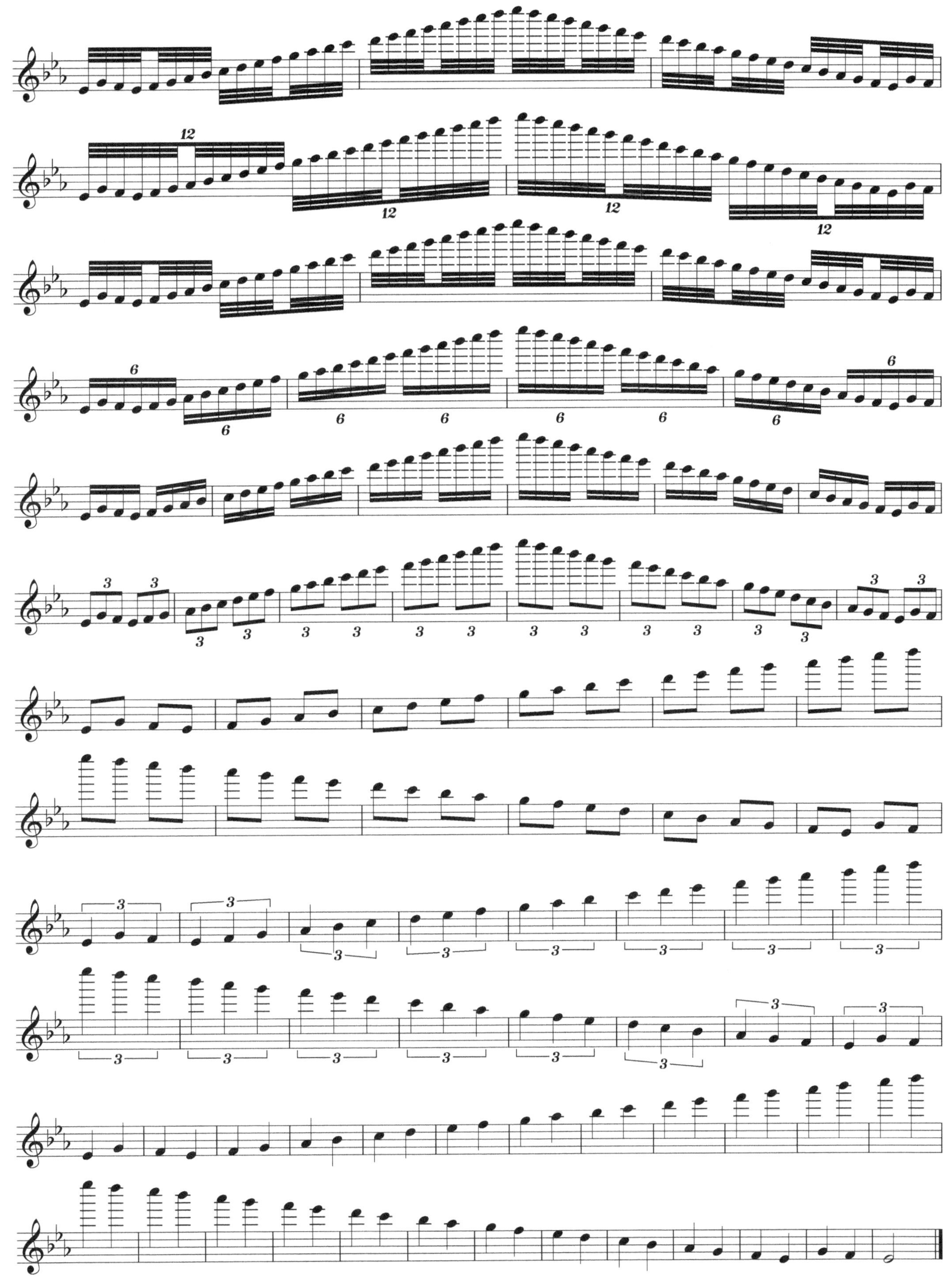


12
12
12
12
6
6
6
6
6
6
6
3
3
3
3
3
3
3
3
3
3
3
3
3
3
3
3
3
3
3
3
3
3
3
3
3
3
3
3
3
3
3
© Nick Revel 2018

© Nick Revel 2018

Whole Tone


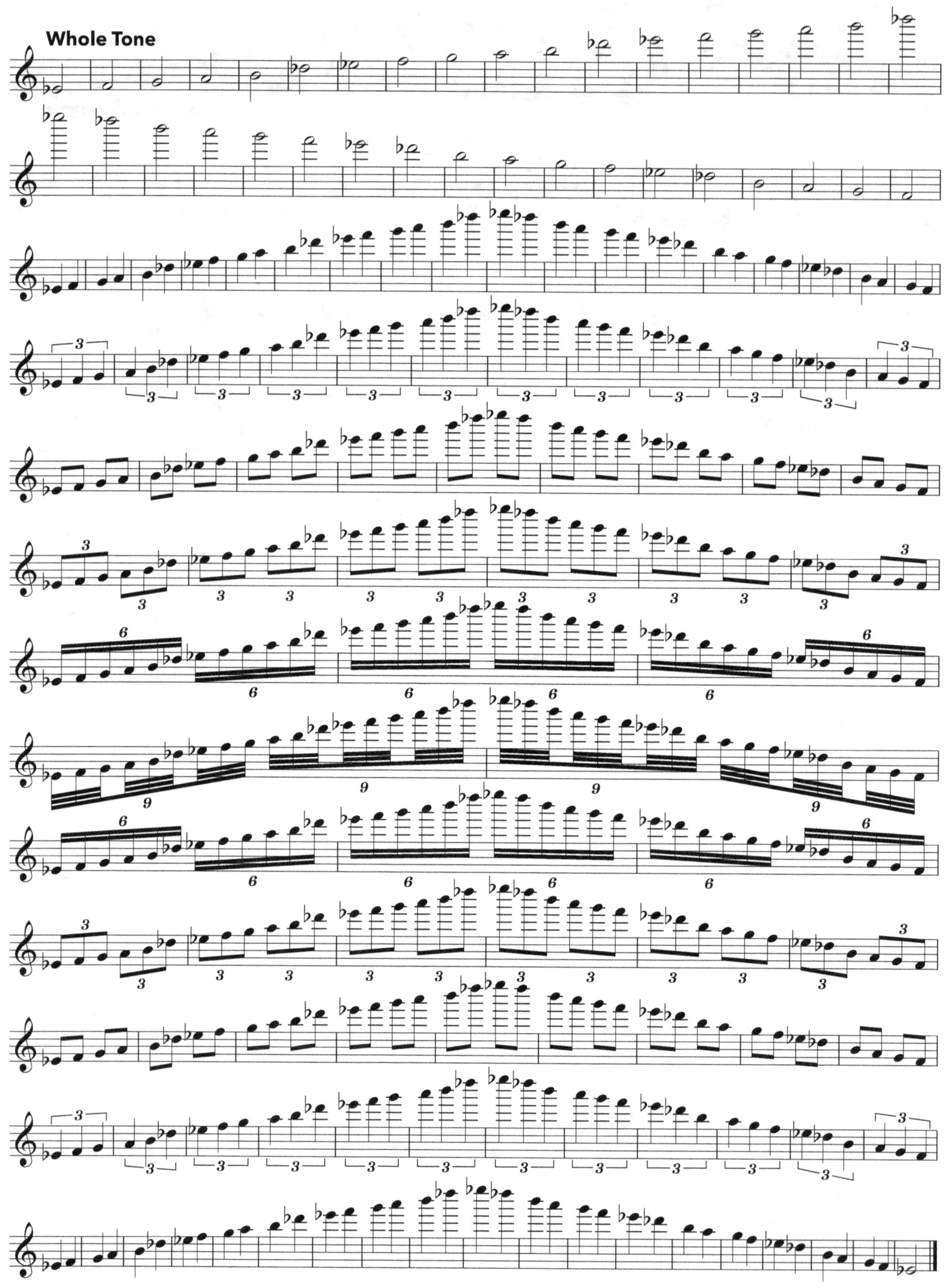

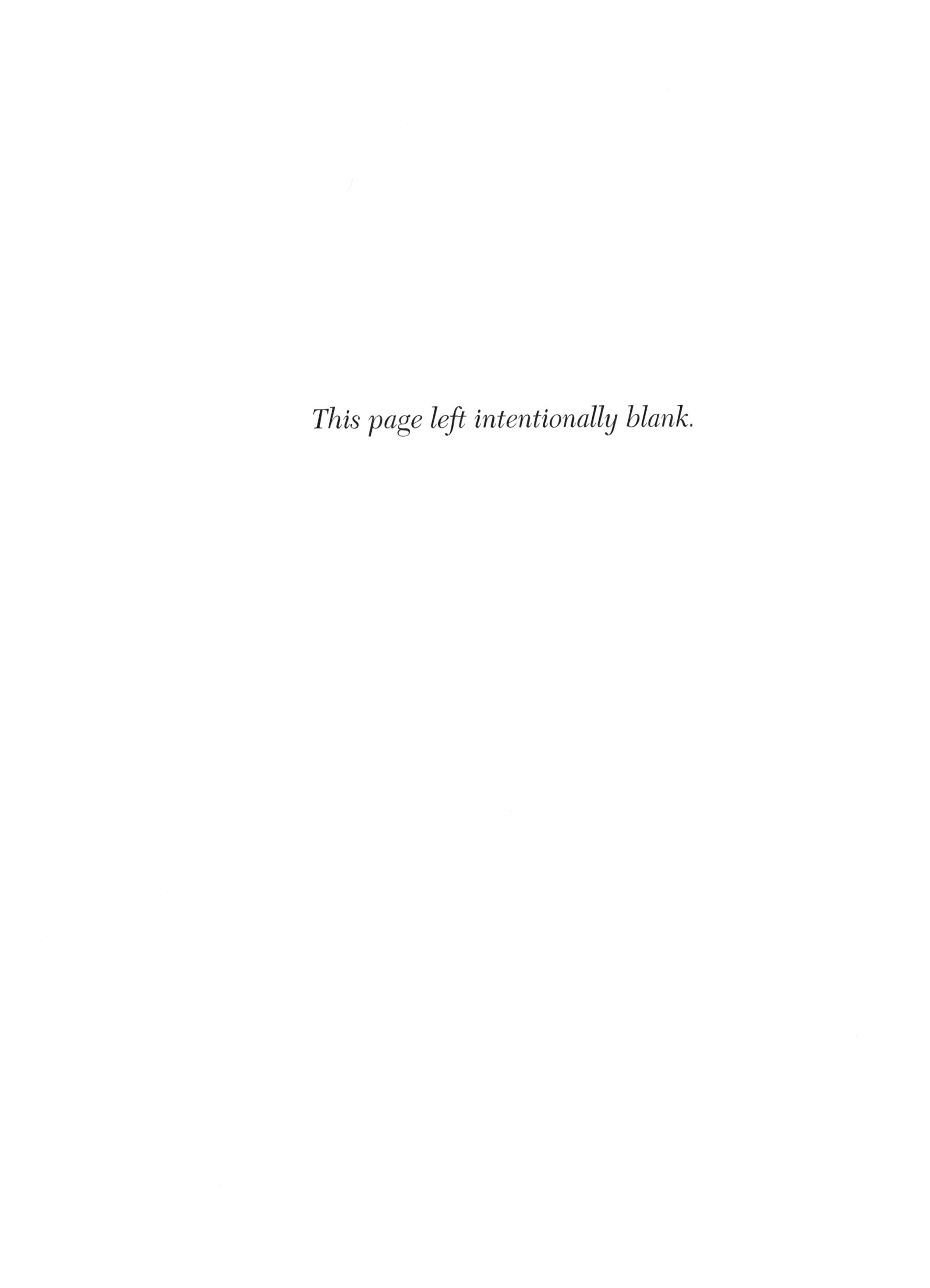

*This page left intentionally blank.*

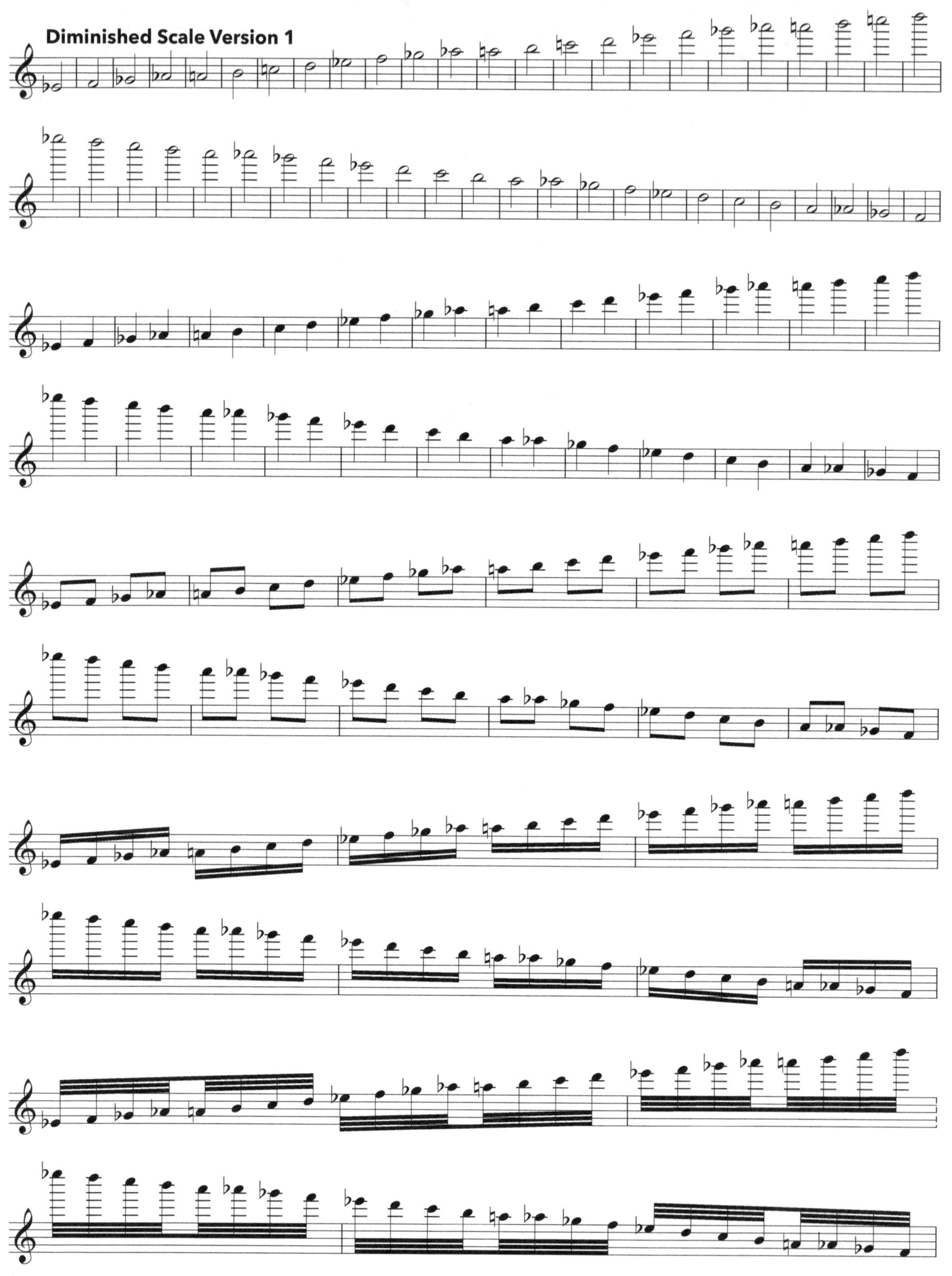


© Nick Revel 2018

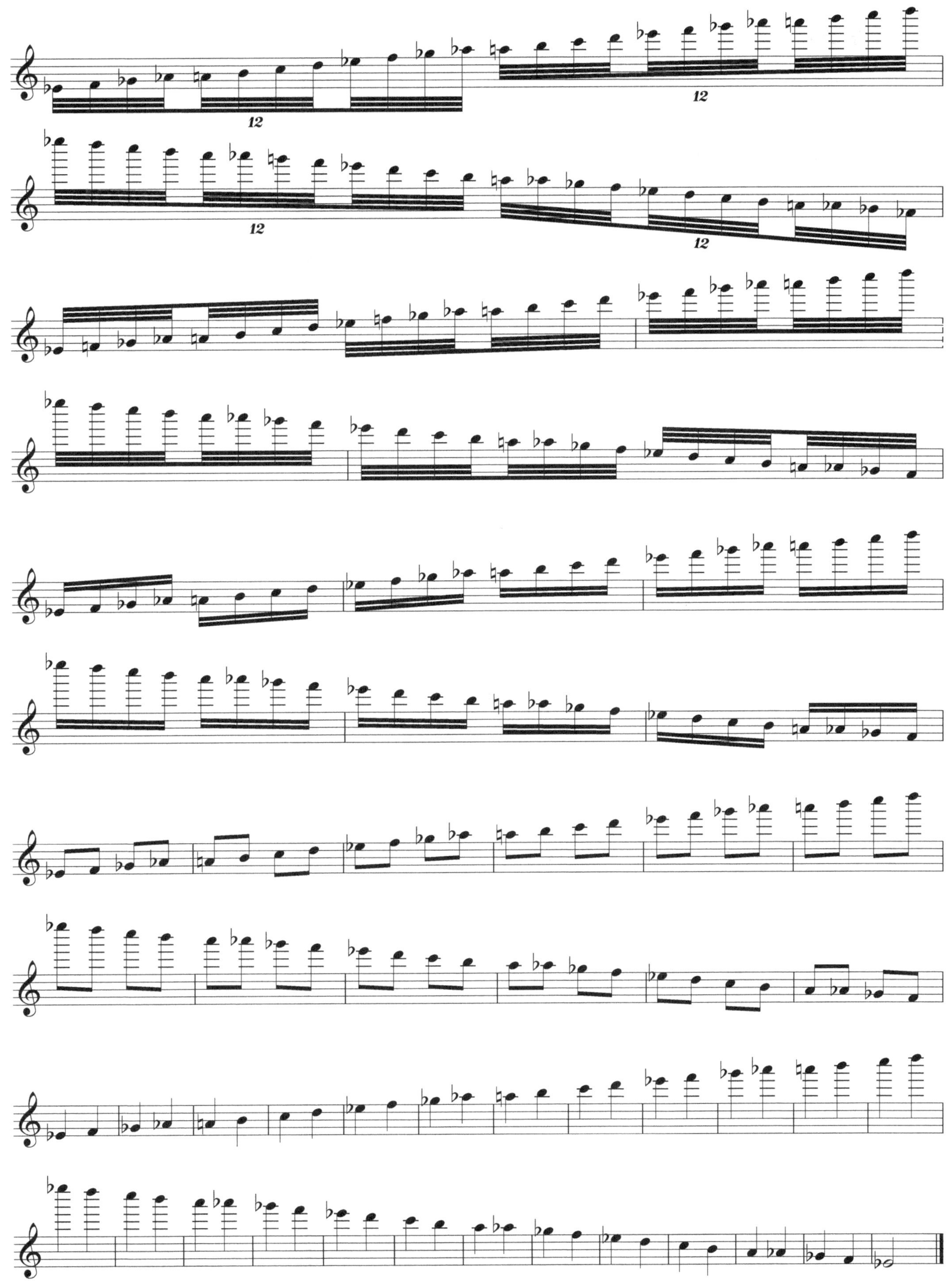

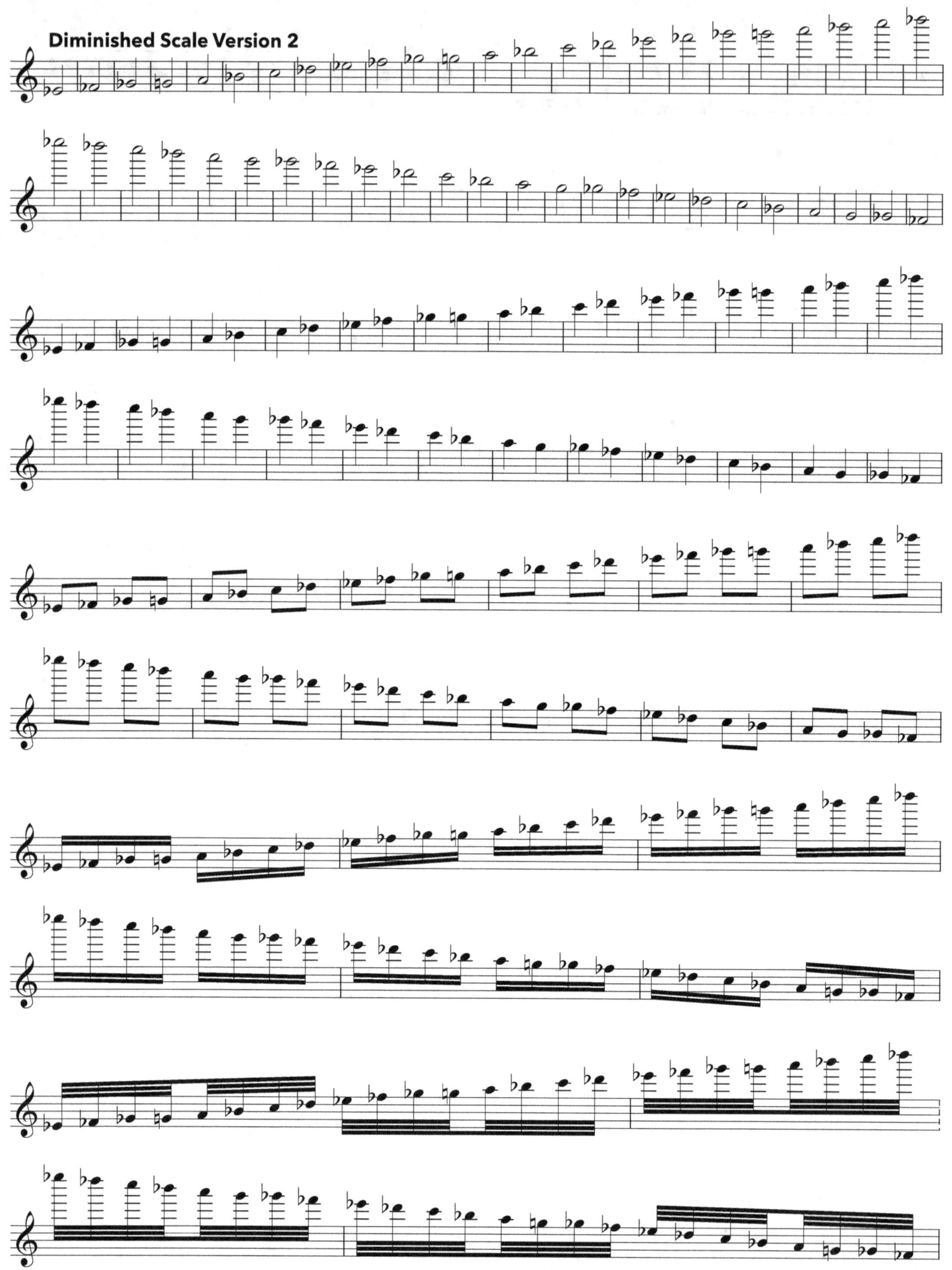



© Nick Revel 2018

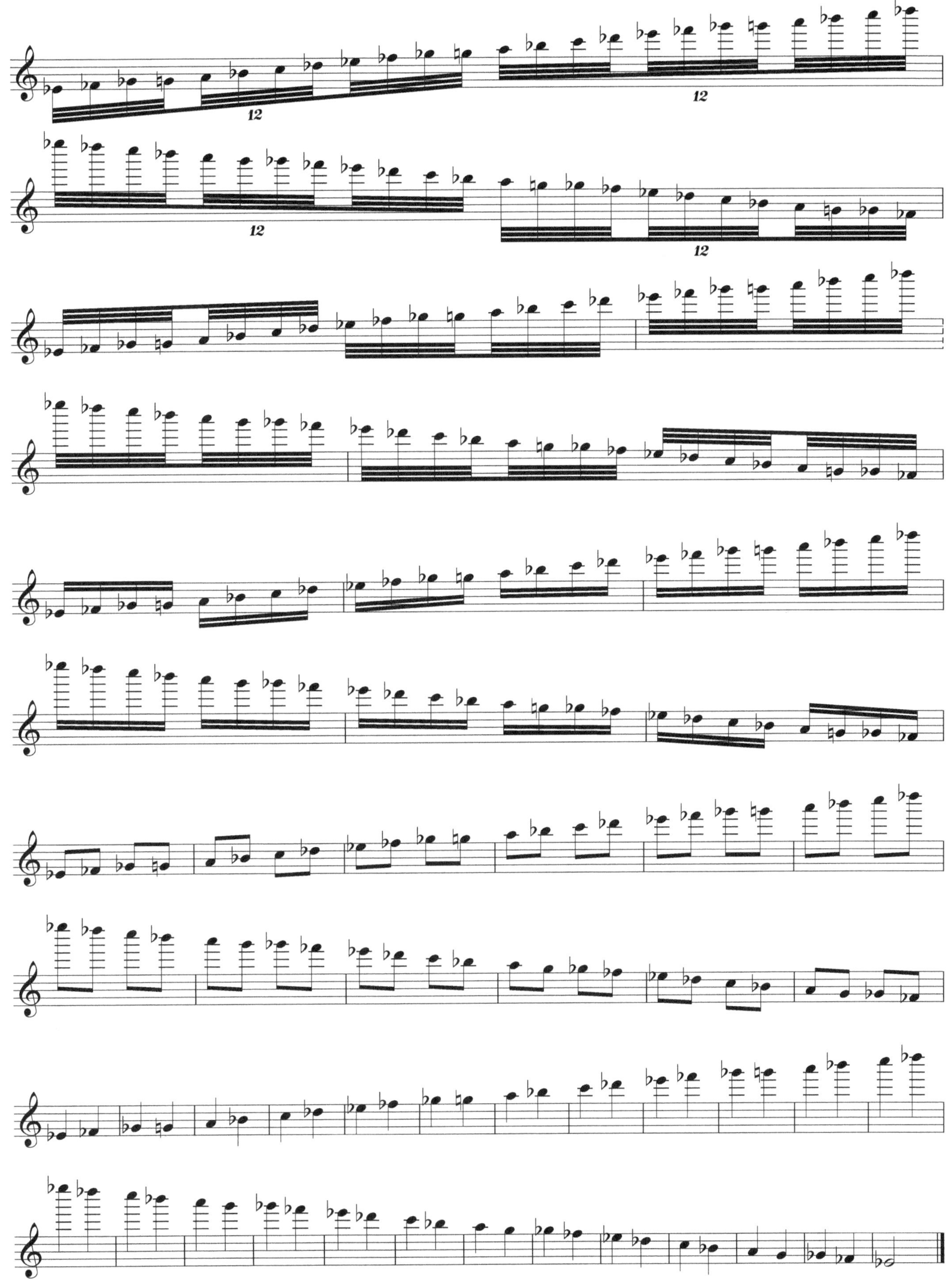


12
12
12
12
© Nick Revel 2018

# Chromatic

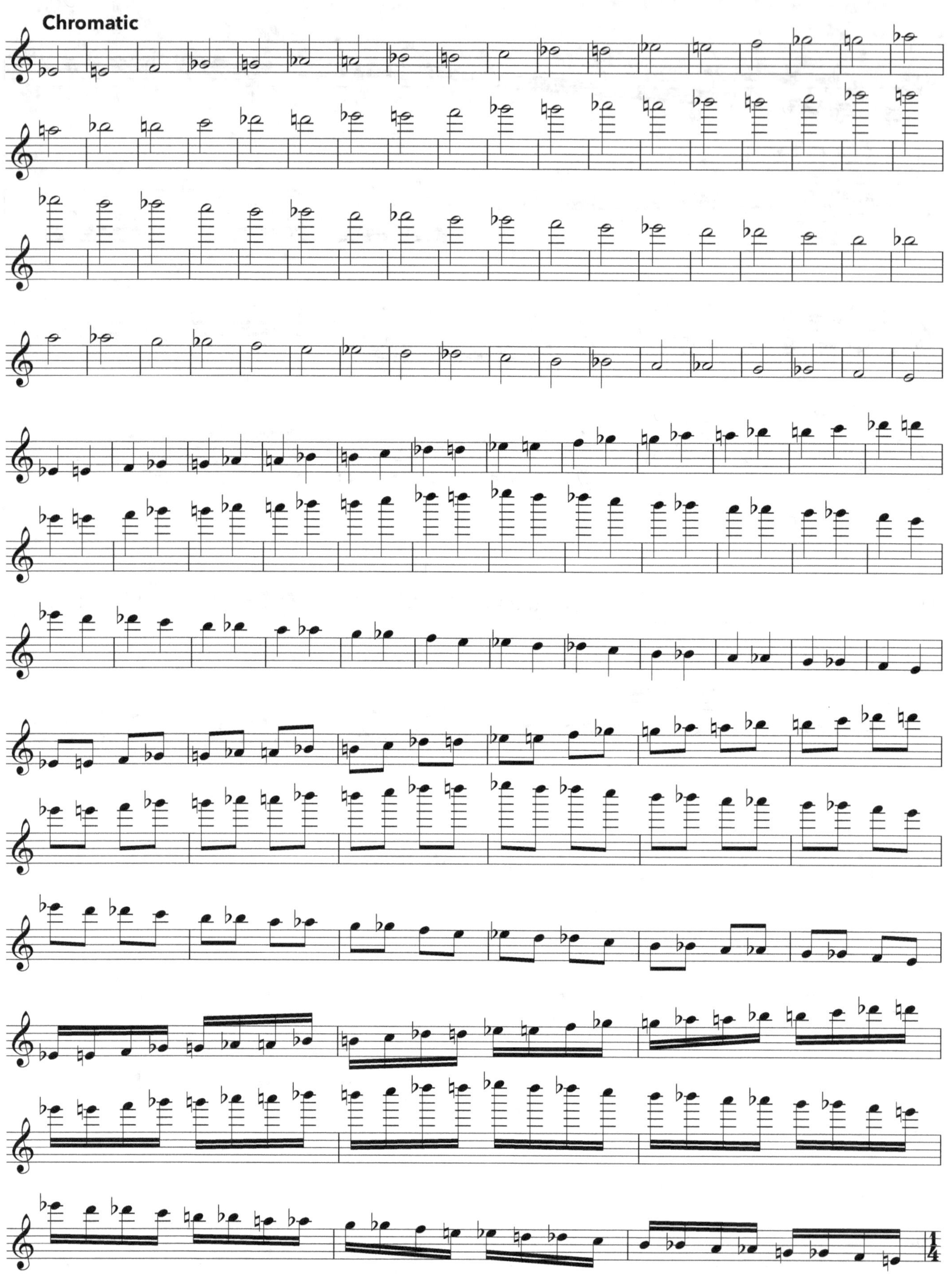

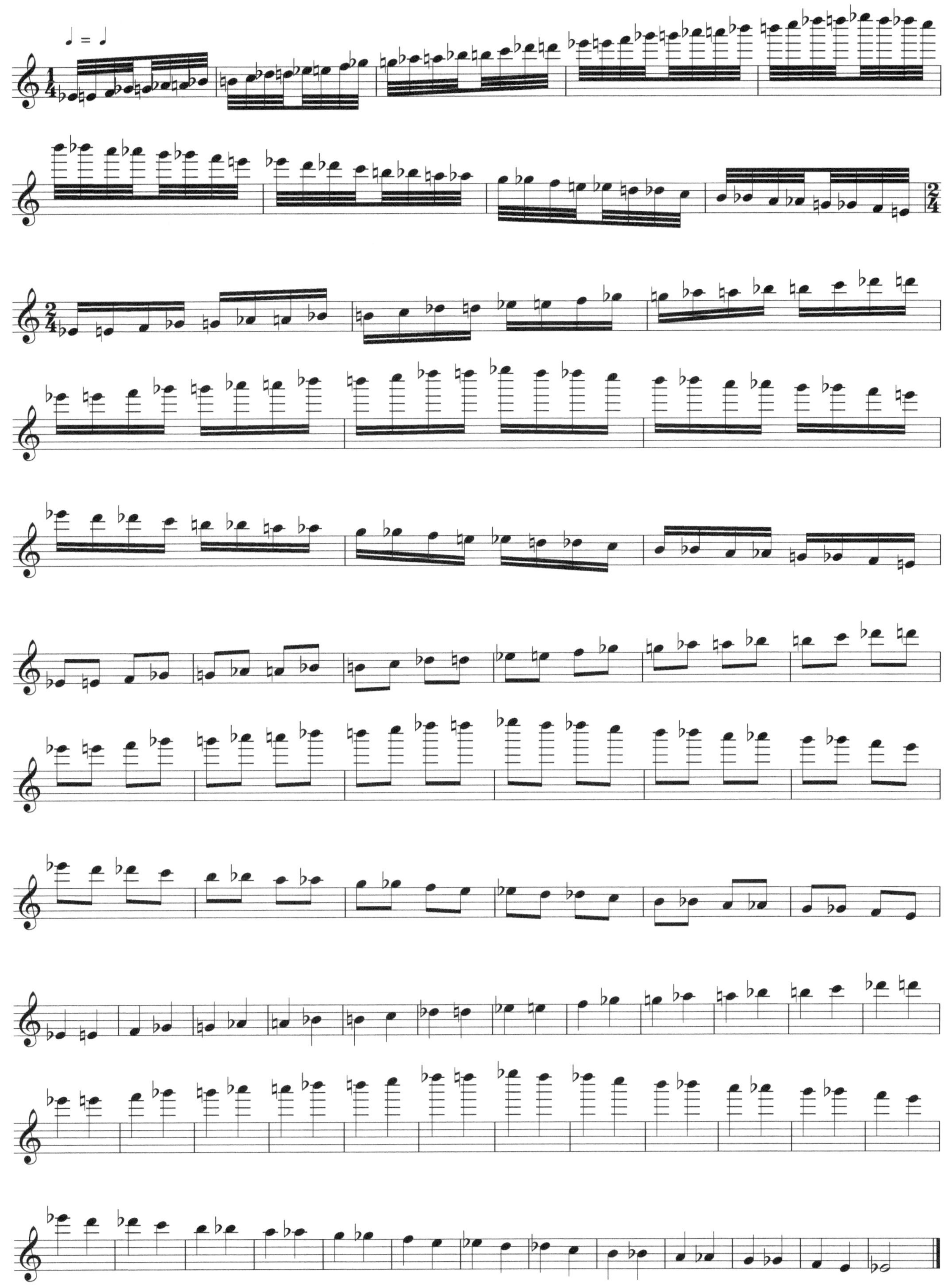

© Nick Revel 2018

# Arpeggios Version 1

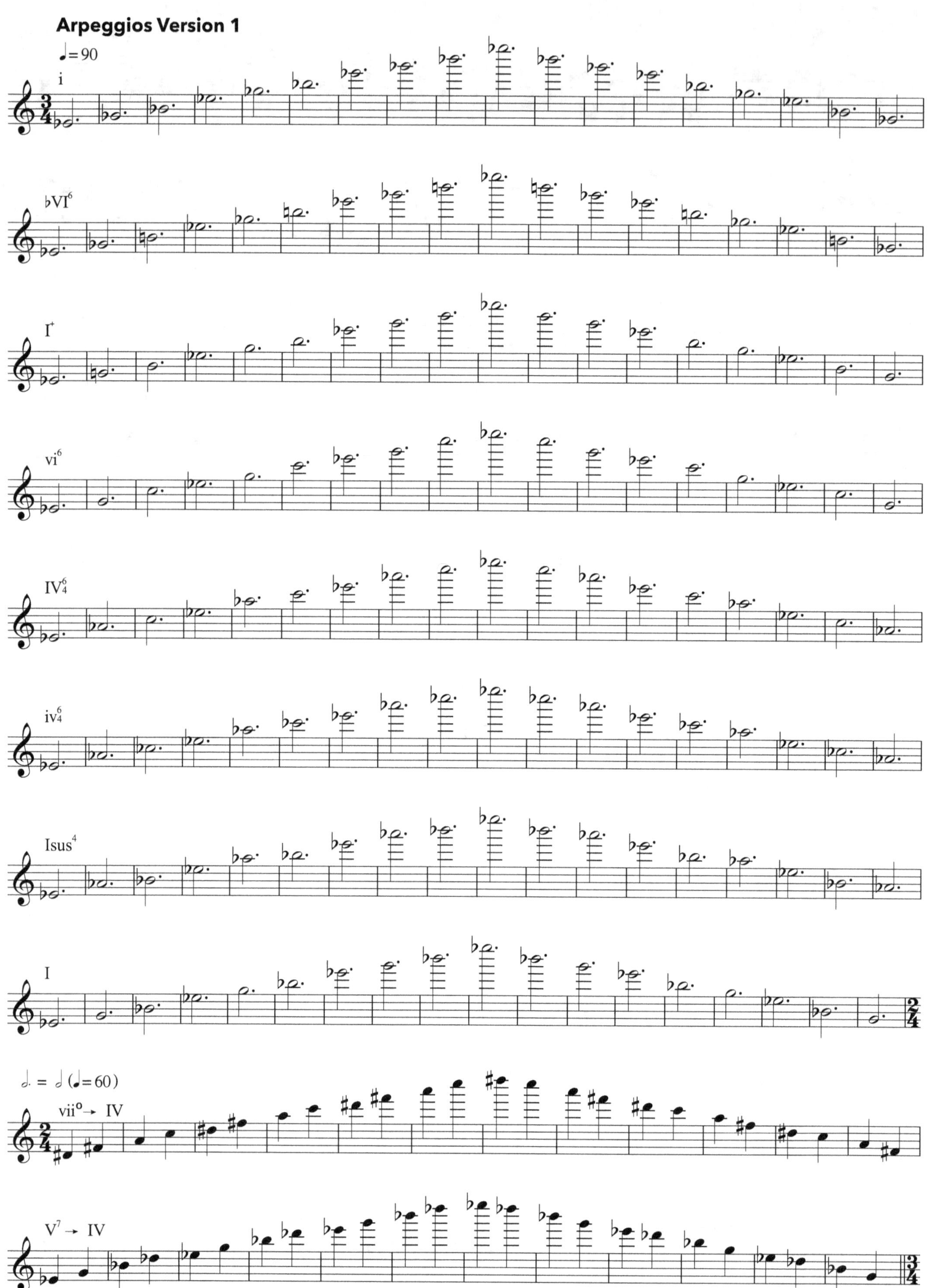

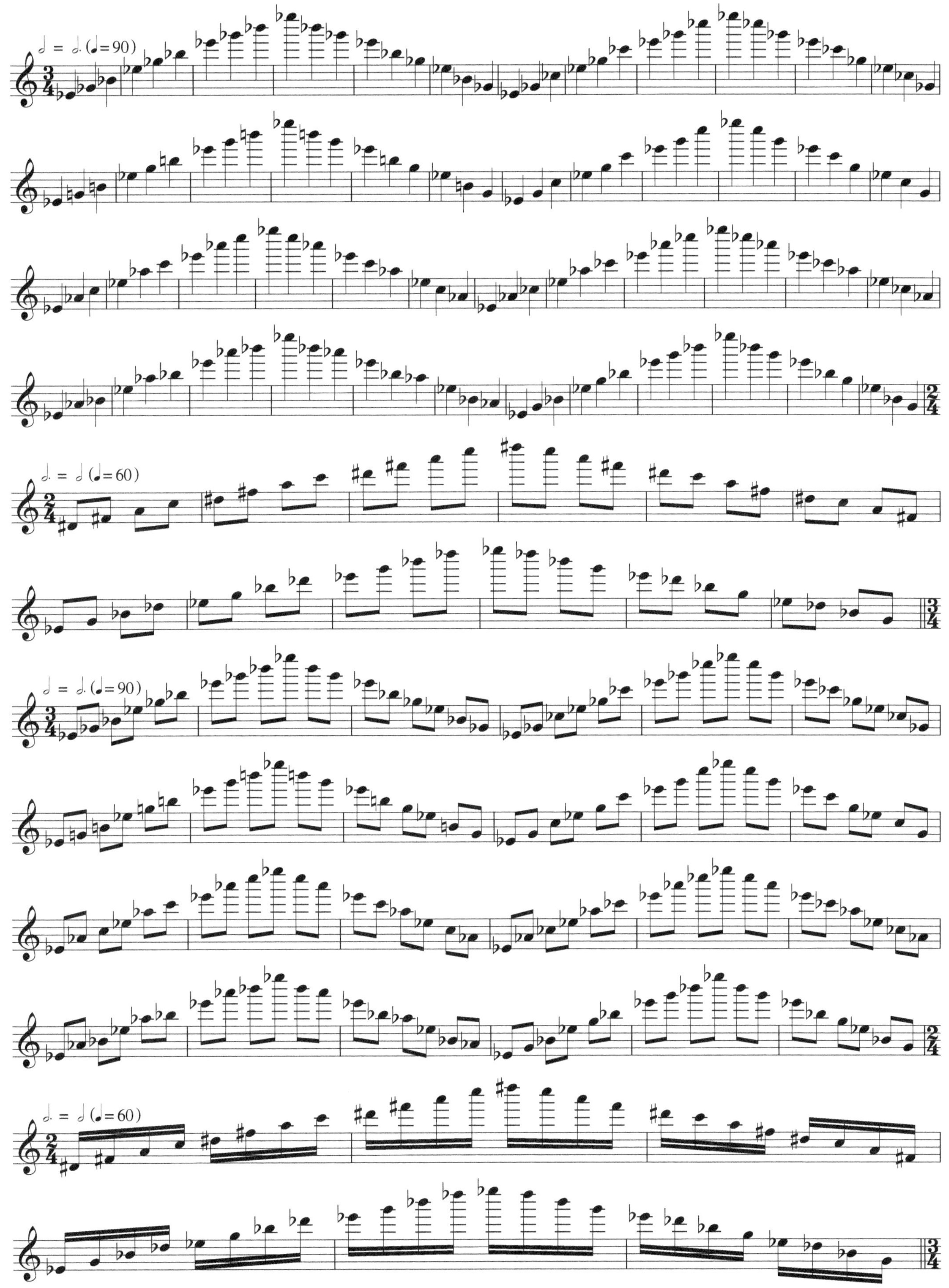

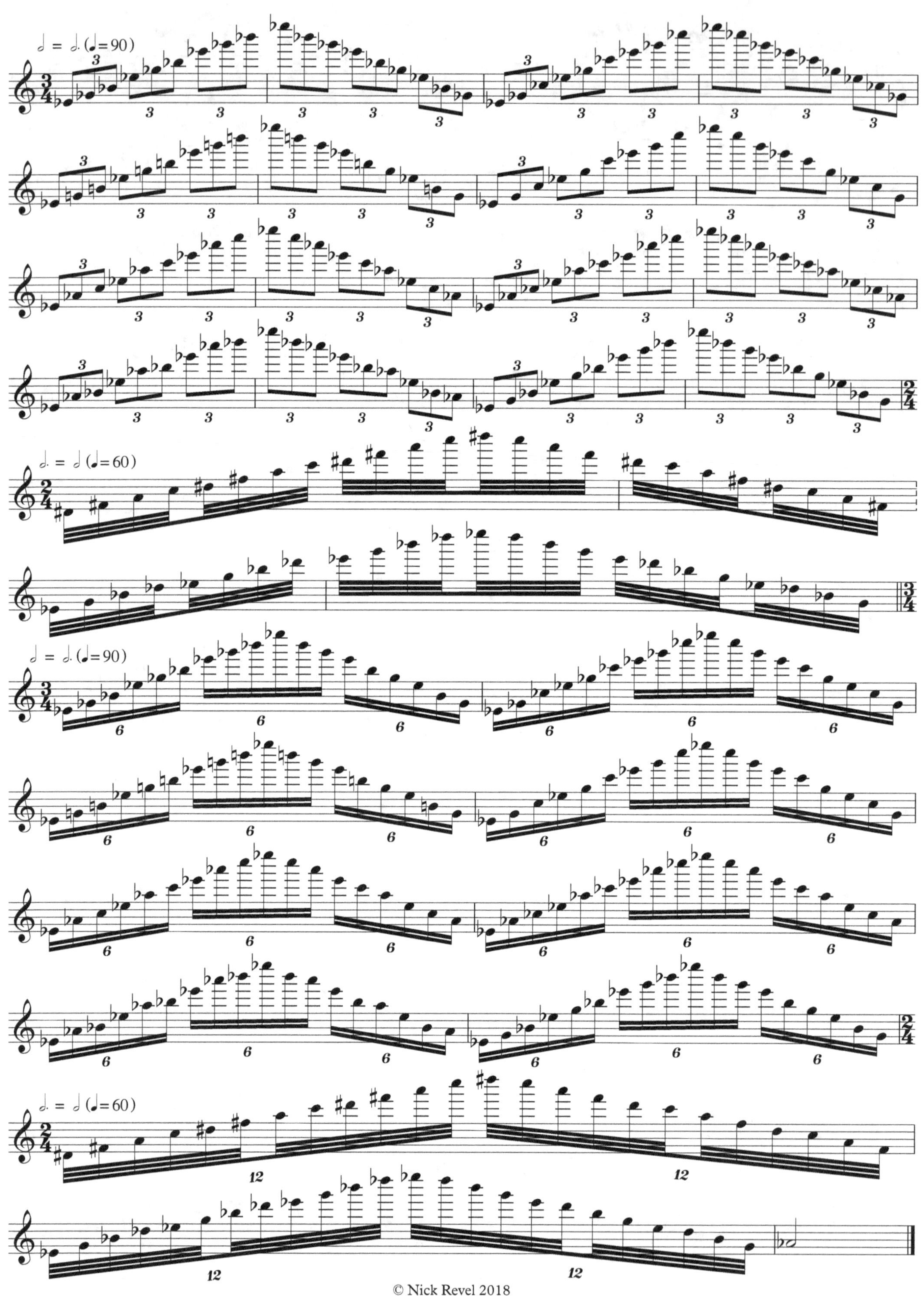

♩ = ♩. (♩=90)
♩. = ♩ (♩=60)
♩. = ♩. (♩=90)
♩. = ♩ (♩=60)
© Nick Revel 2018
176  DRAGONSCALES – VIOLIN

*This page left intentionally blank.*

# Arpeggios Version 2

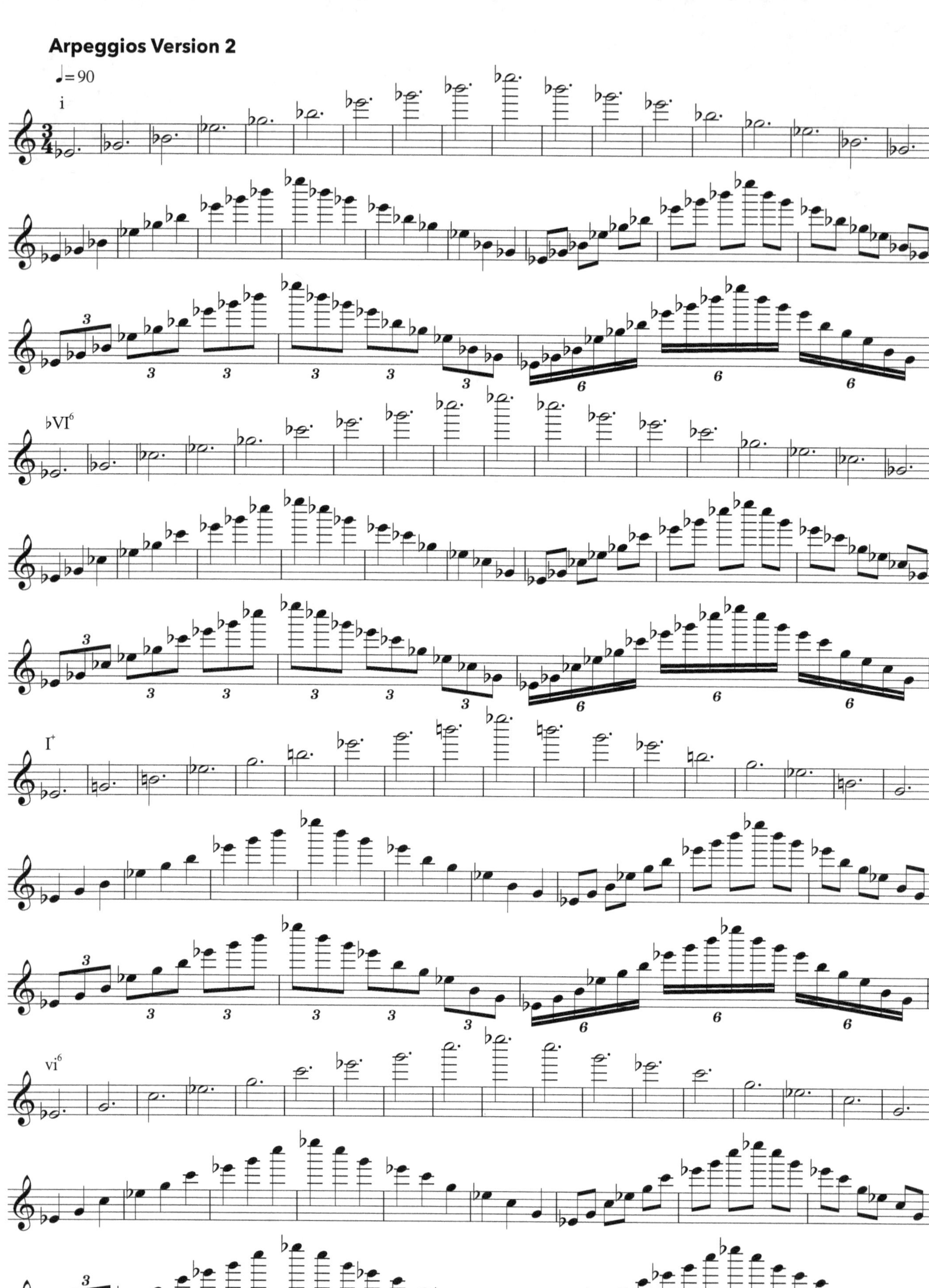

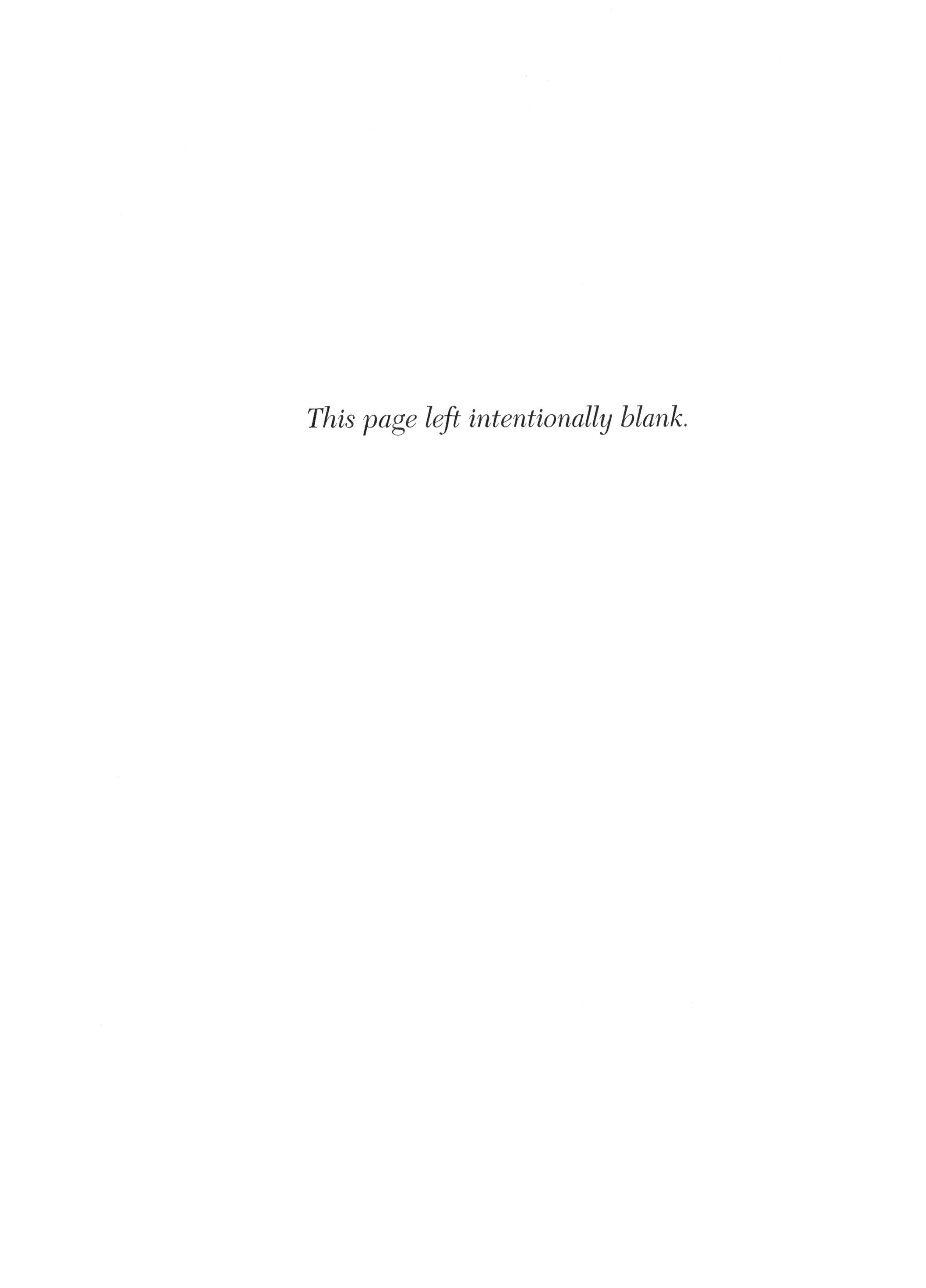
*This page left intentionally blank.*

# Arpeggios Version 2

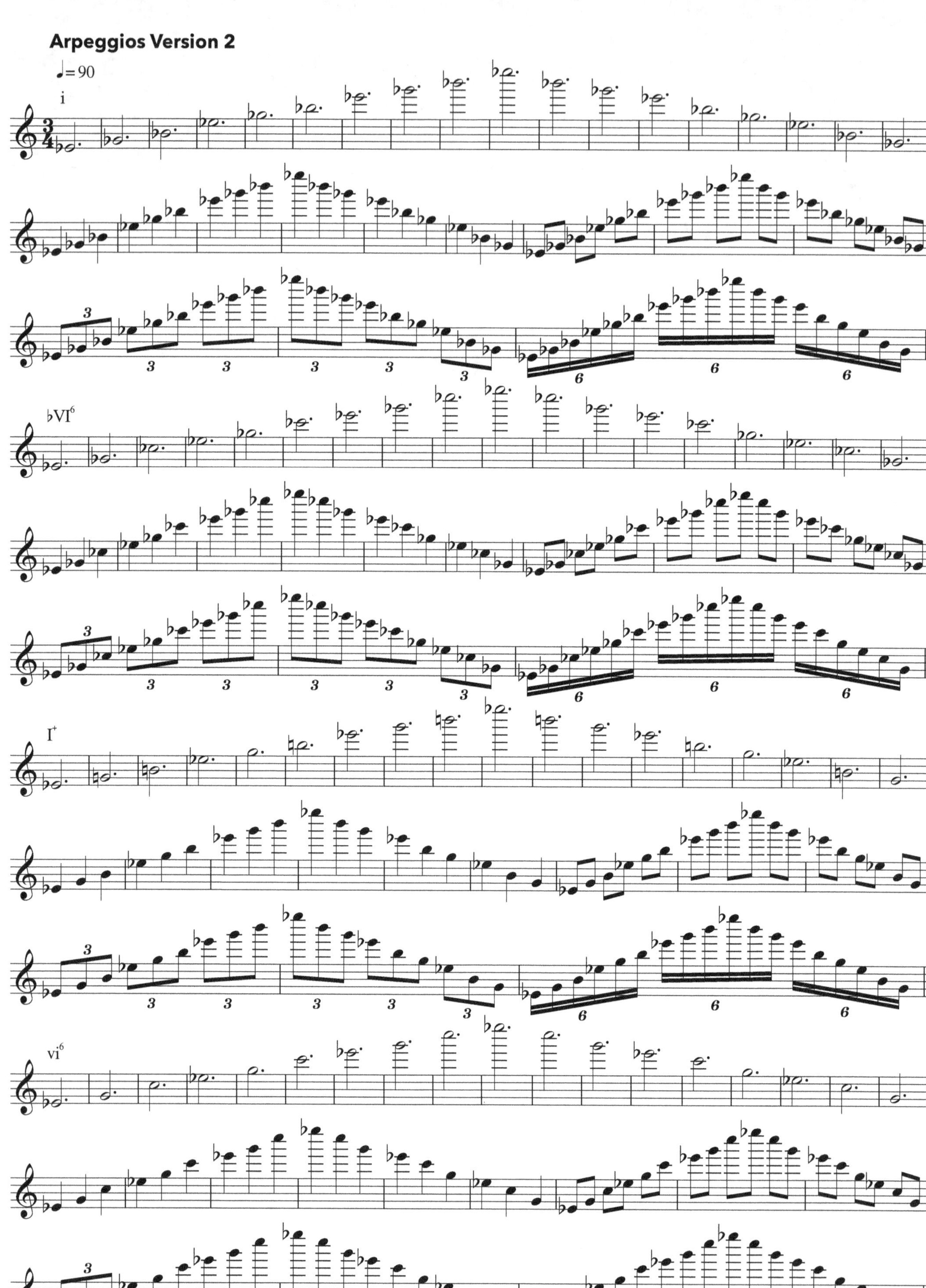

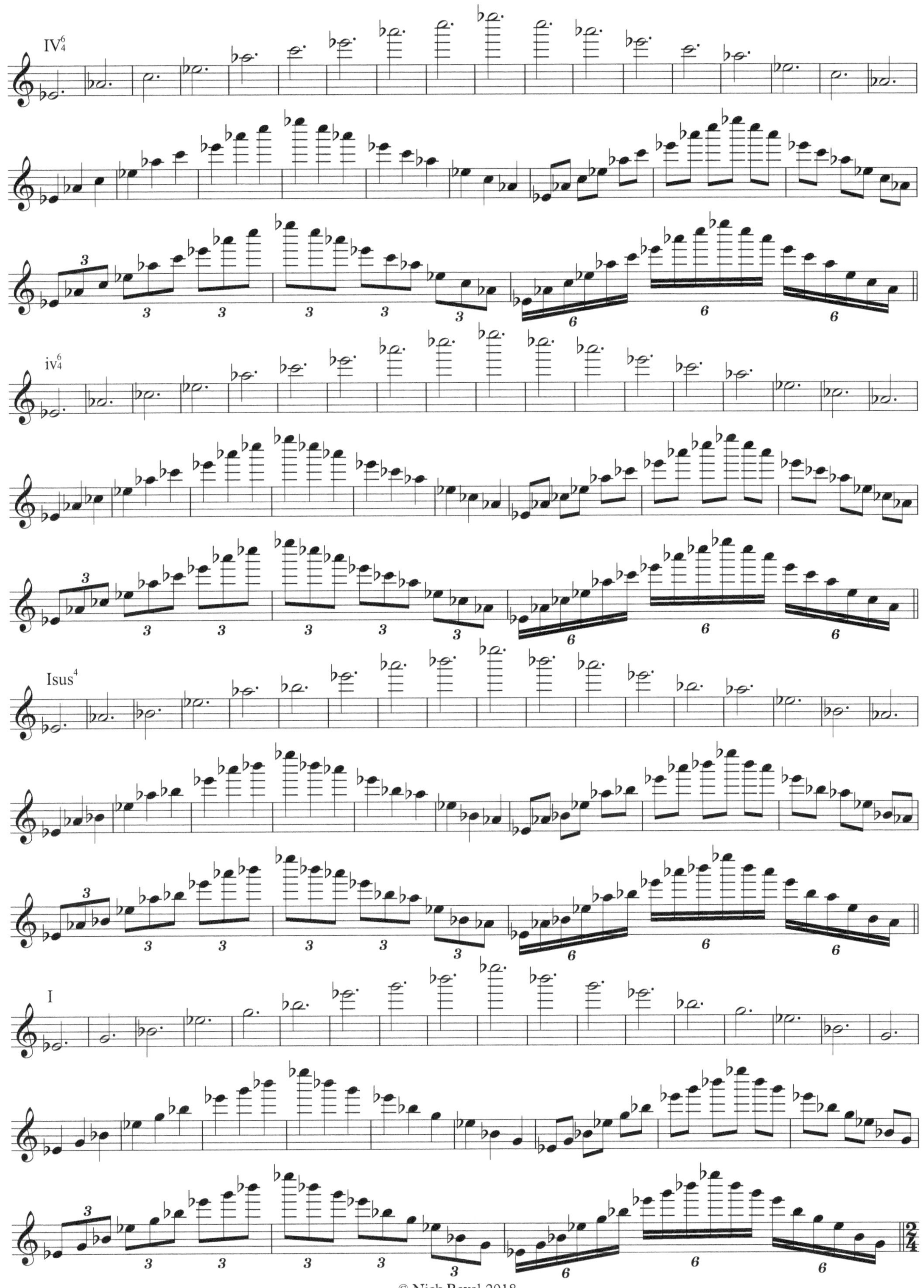

IV6/4
iv6/4
Isus4
I
3 3 3 3 3 6 6 6
© Nick Revel 2018

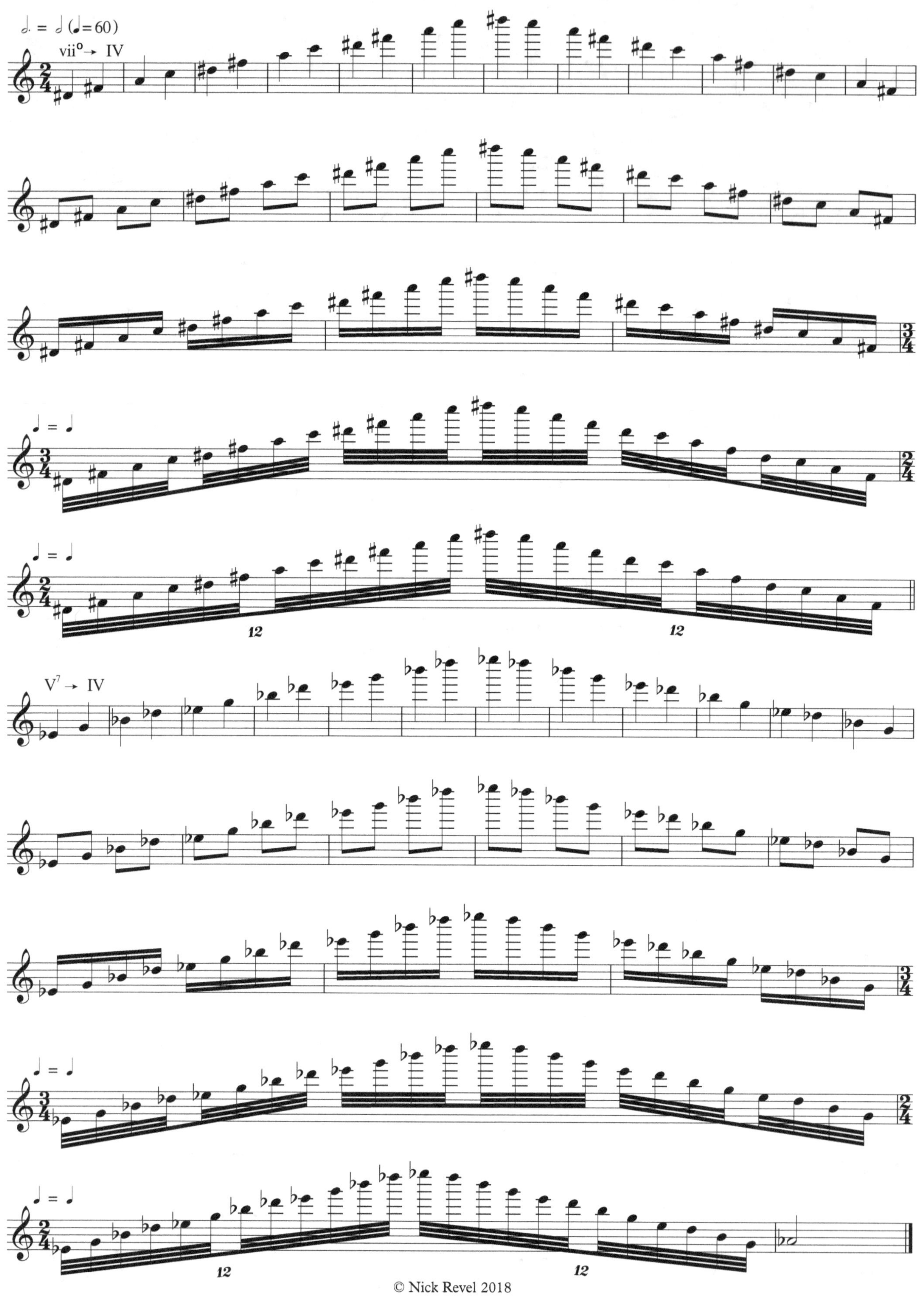

♩. = ♩ (♩ = 60)
vii° → IV
V⁷ → IV
12
12
12
12
© Nick Revel 2018

# DRAGONSCALES

3-Octave Scales and Arpeggios
In Slow to Fast Rhythms
In All Keys

Nick Revel

# E

# DragonScales
## The Complete Set in E

Nick Revel

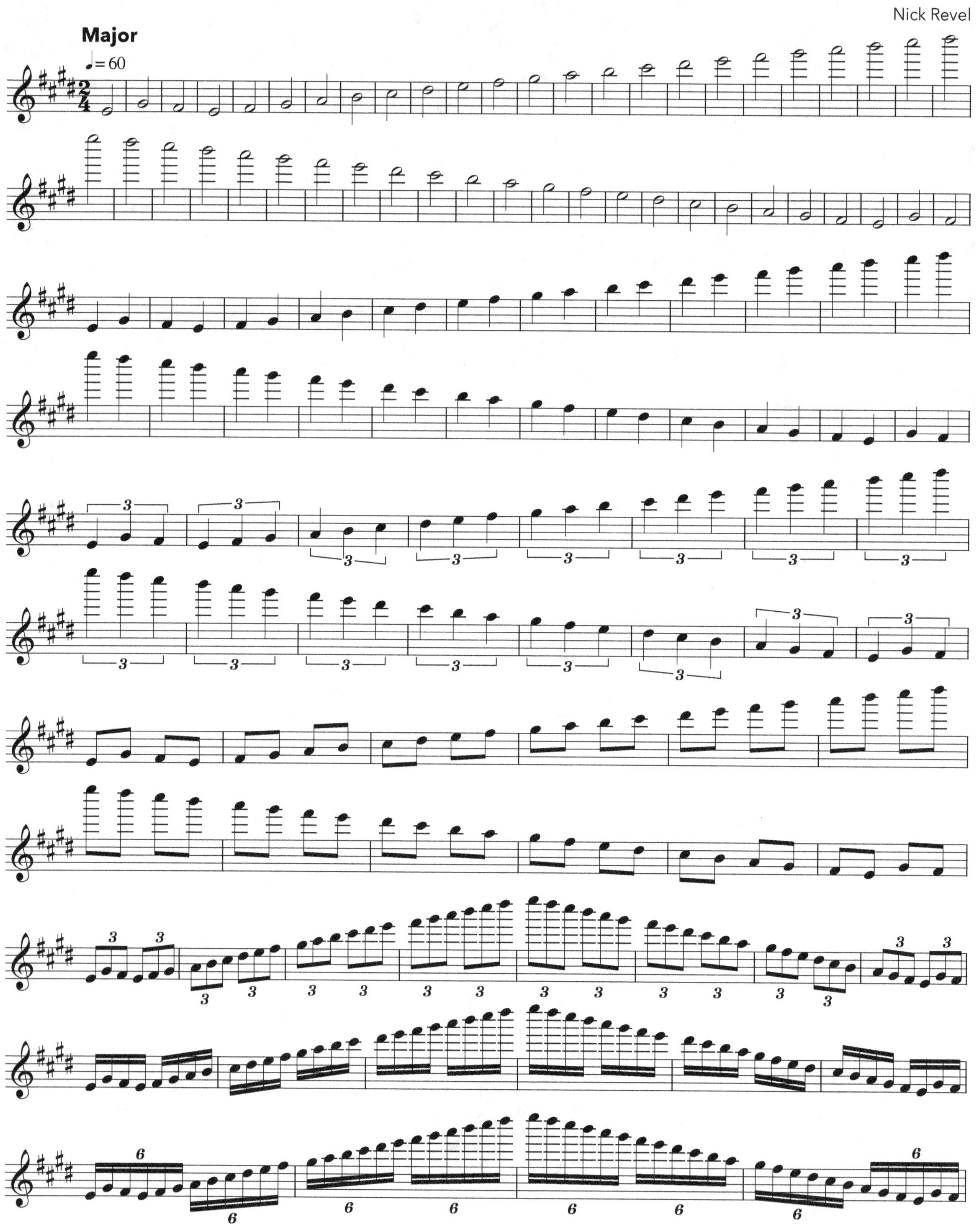


© Nick Revel 2018

Minor

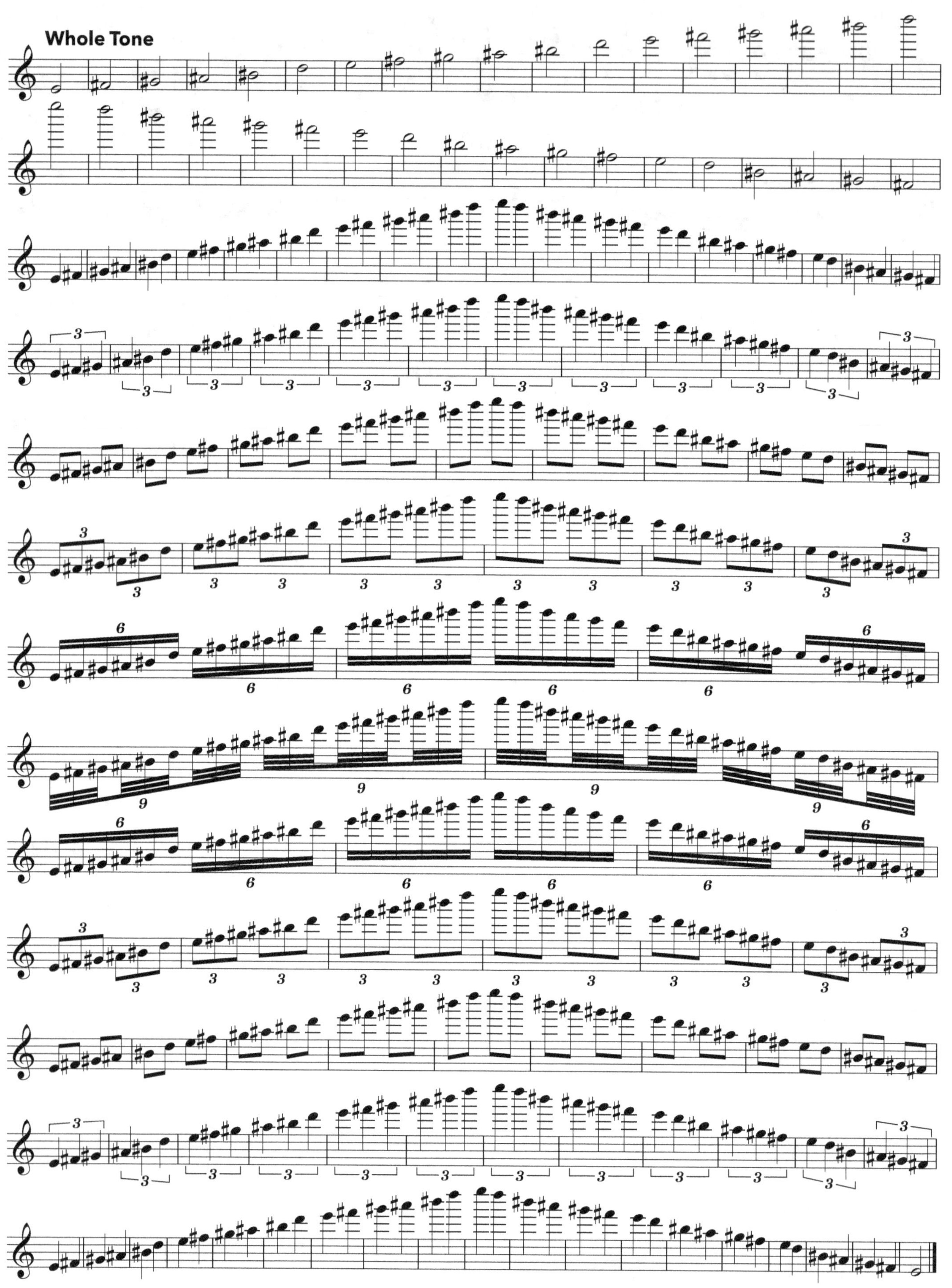

© Nick Revel 2018

*This page left intentionally blank.*

# Diminished Scale Version 1

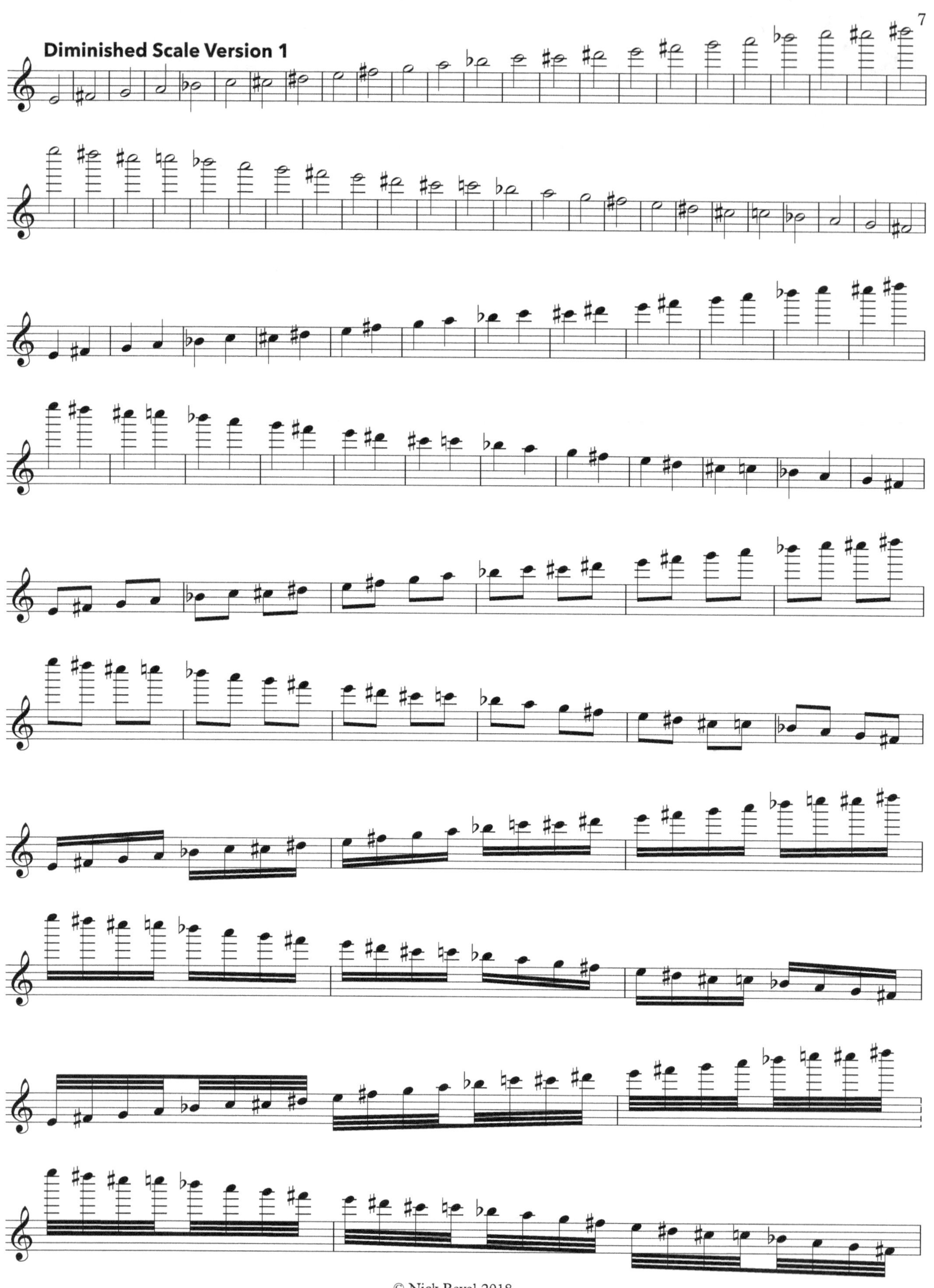

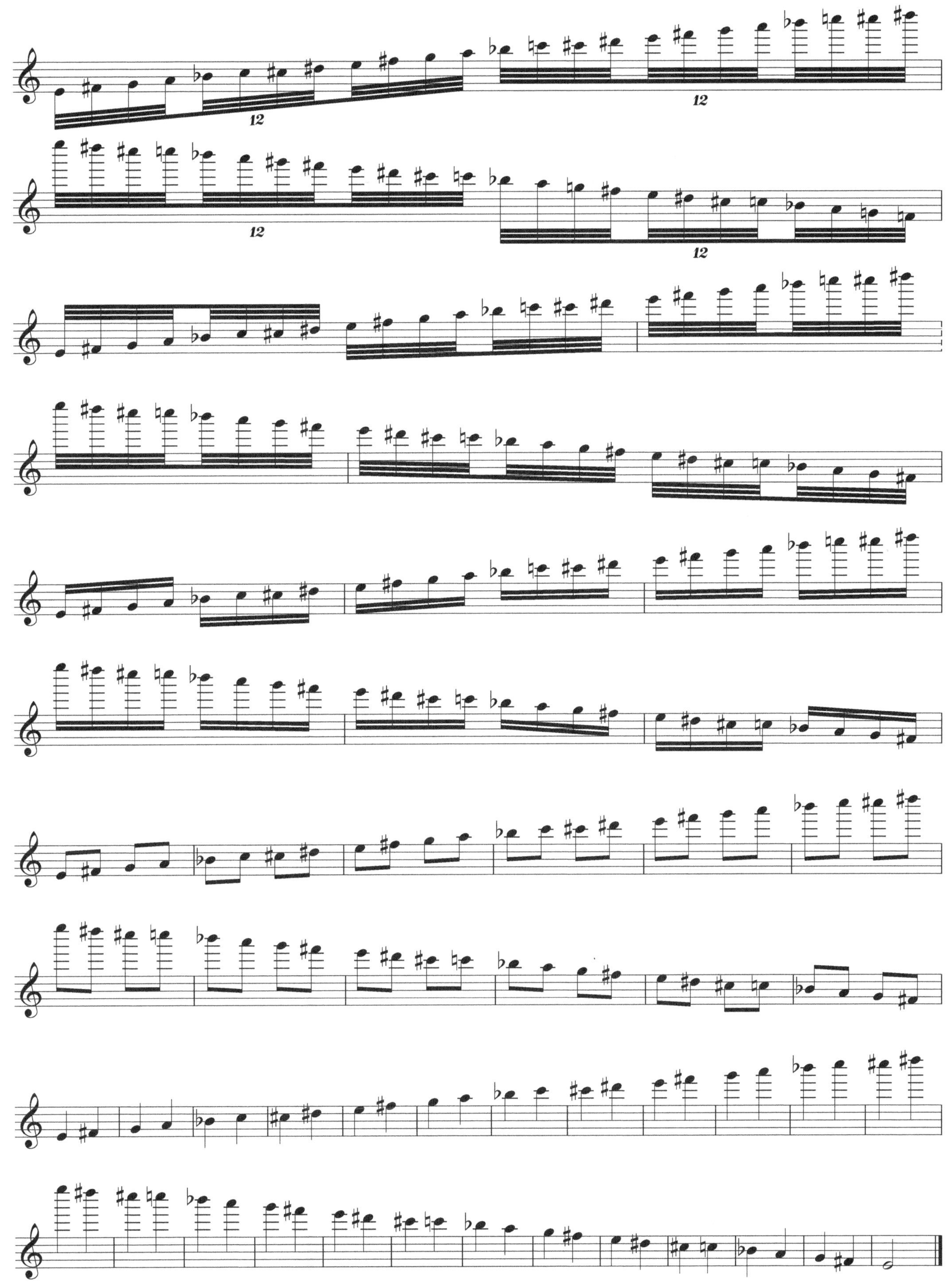



© Nick Revel 2018

# Diminished Scale Version 2

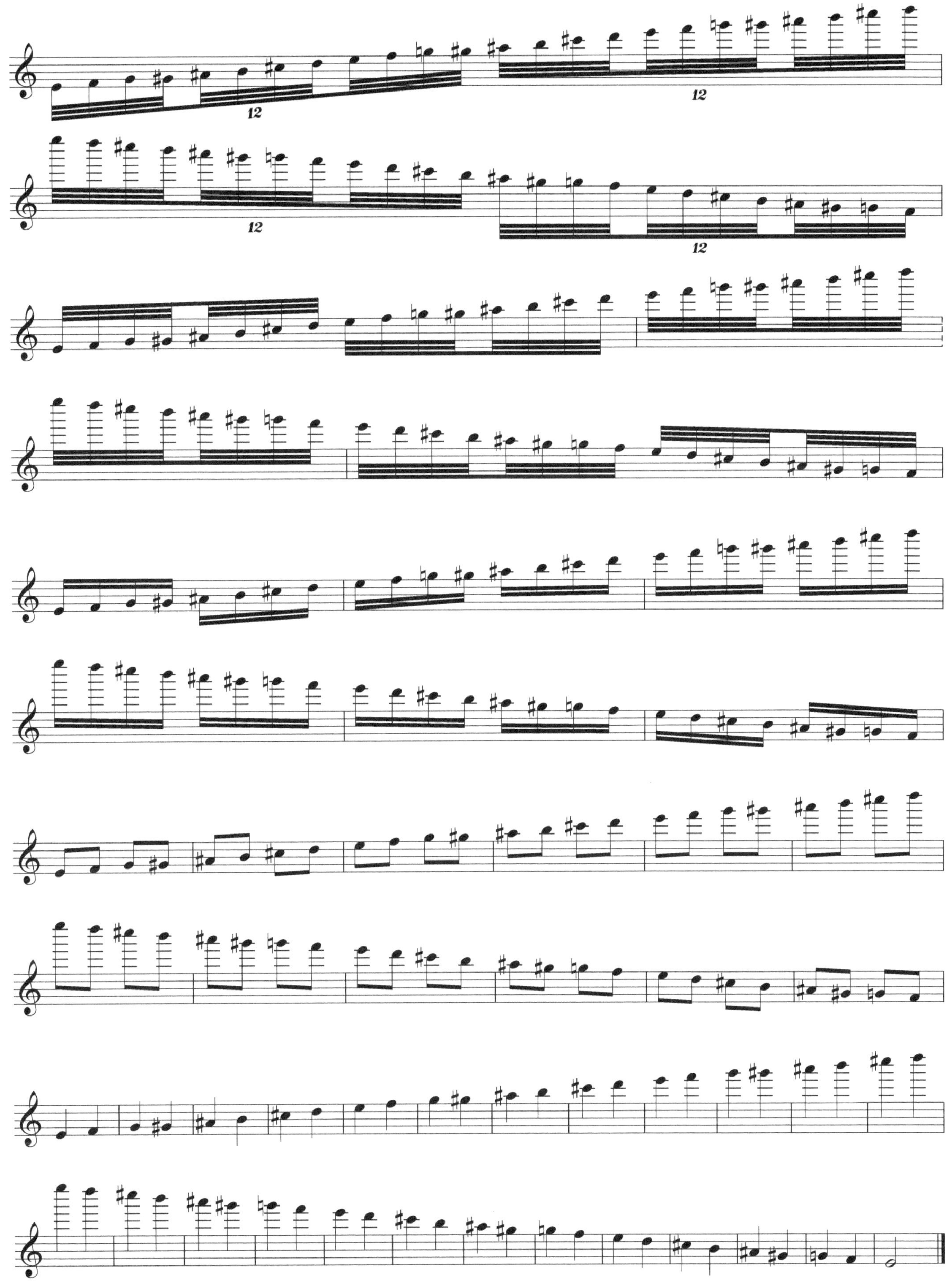



© Nick Revel 2018

# Chromatic

© Nick Revel 2018

# Arpeggios Version 1

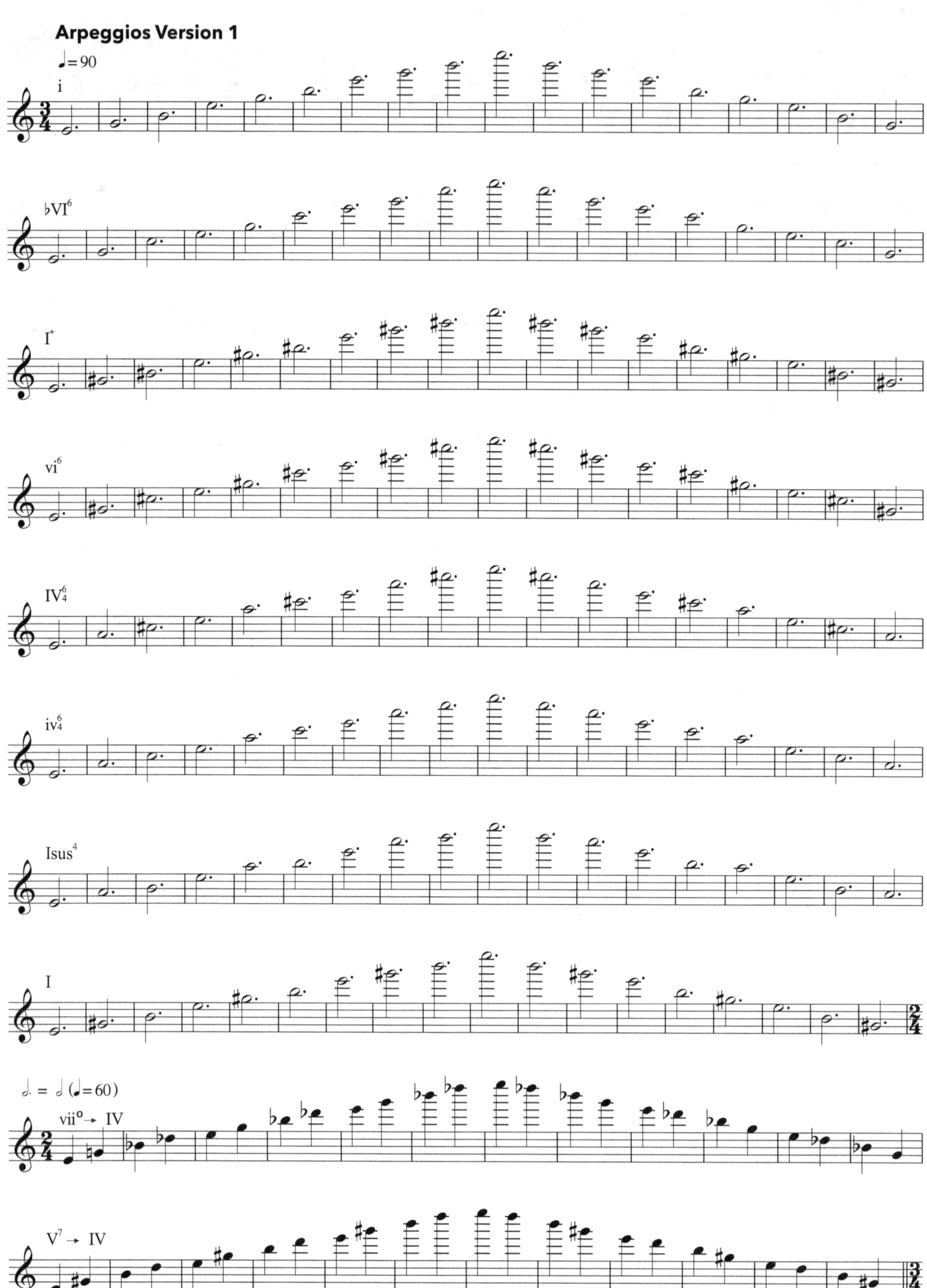


© Nick Revel 2018

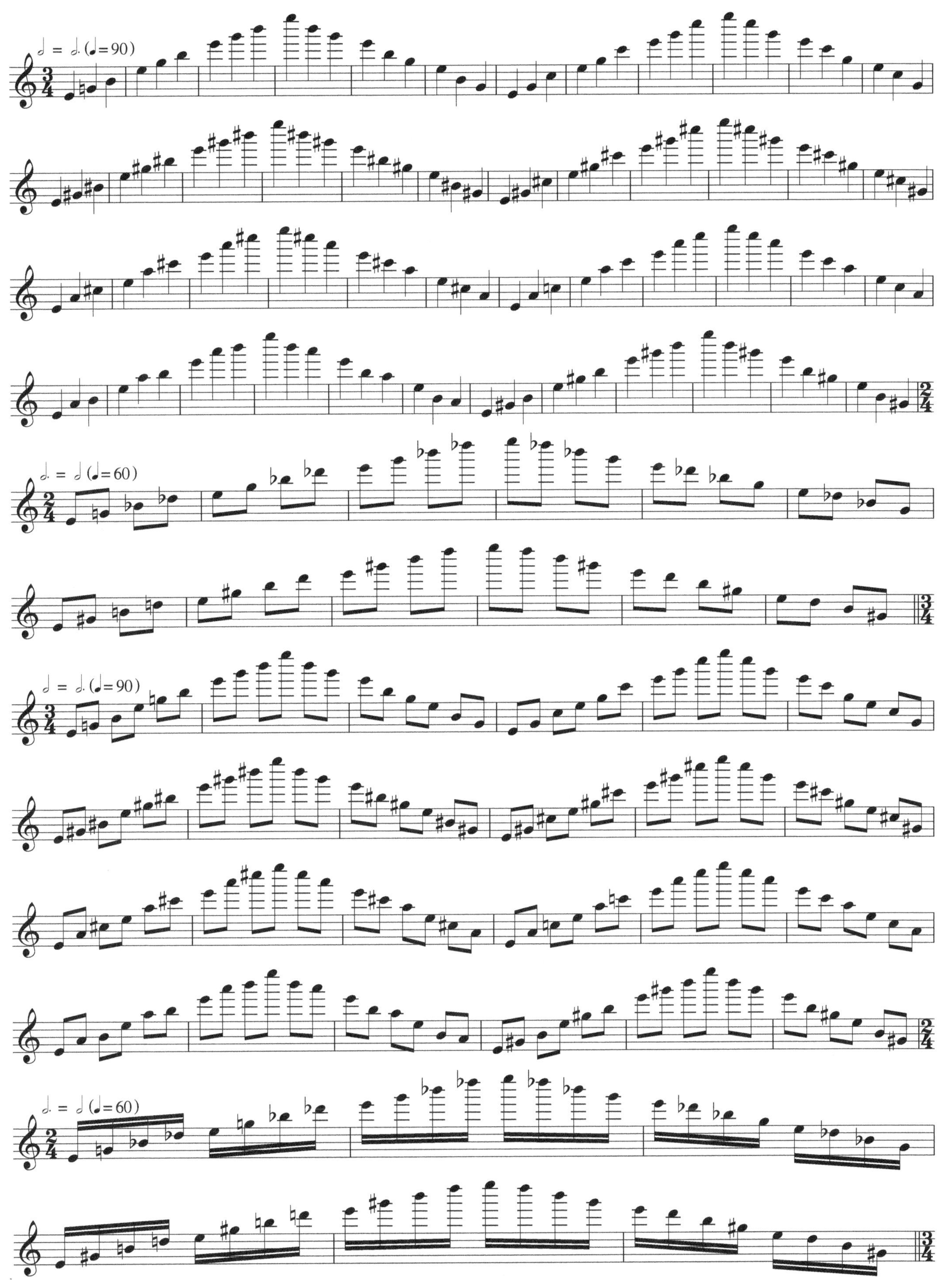

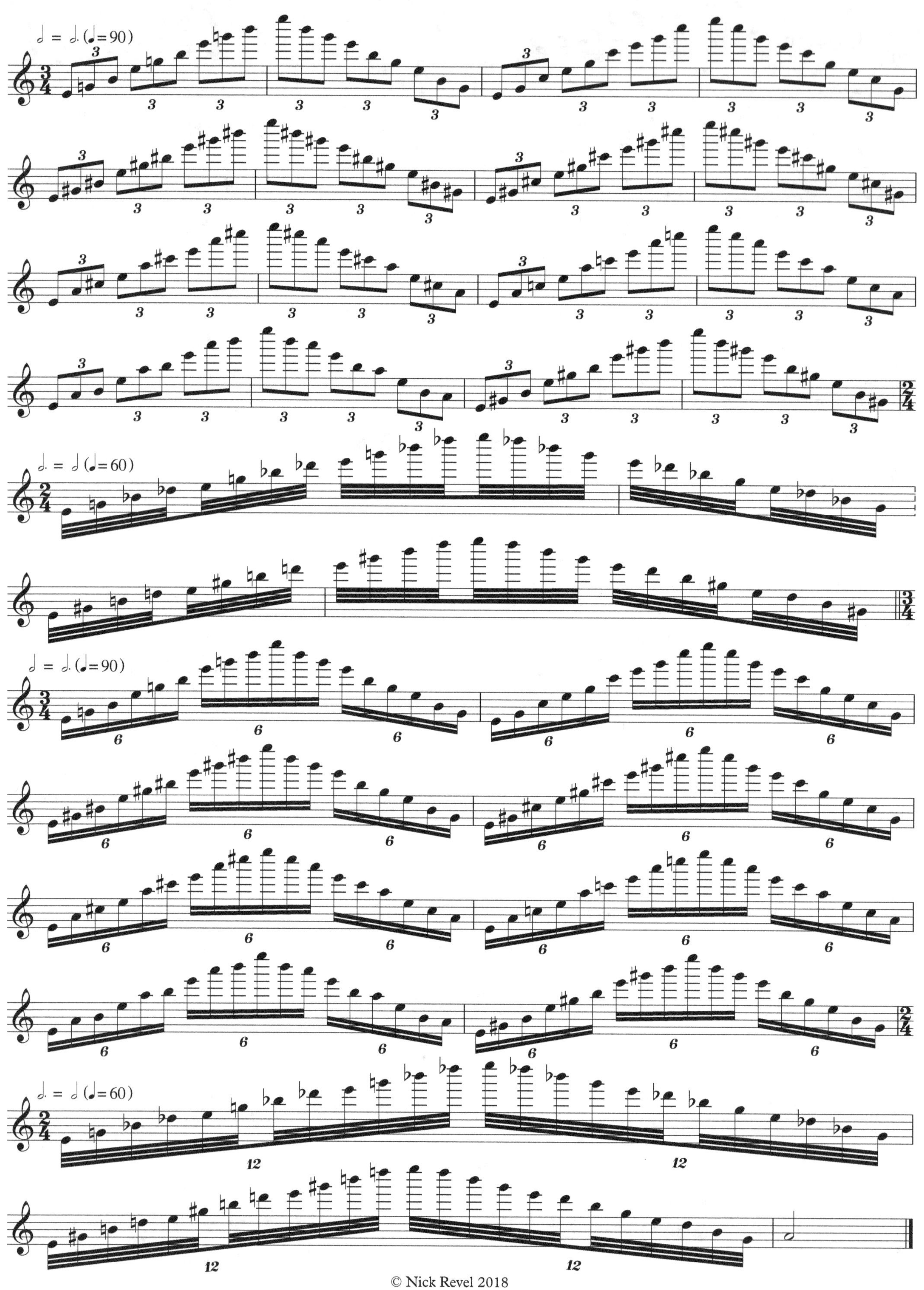
© Nick Revel 2018

*This page left intentionally blank.*

# Arpeggios Version 2

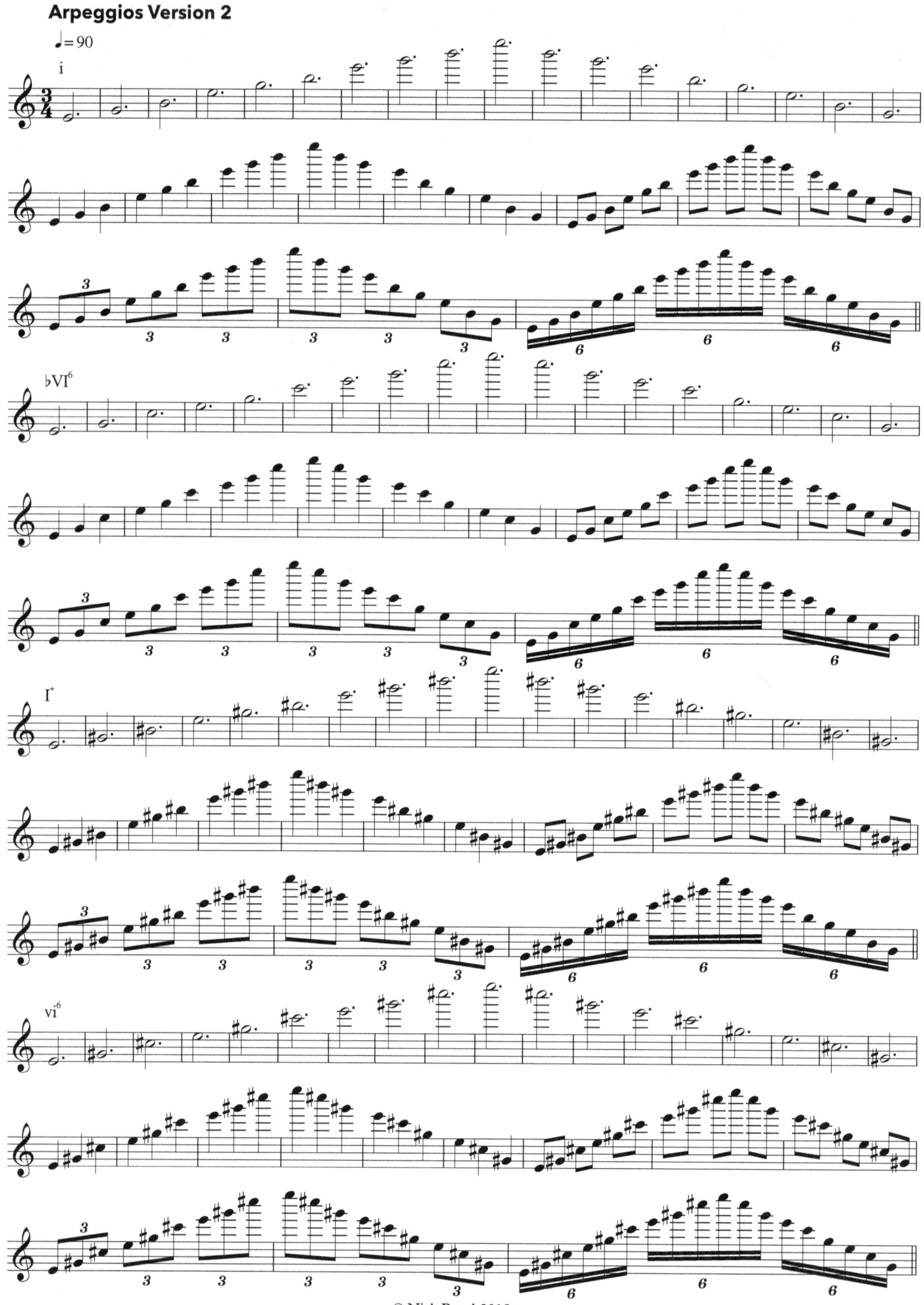


© Nick Revel 2018

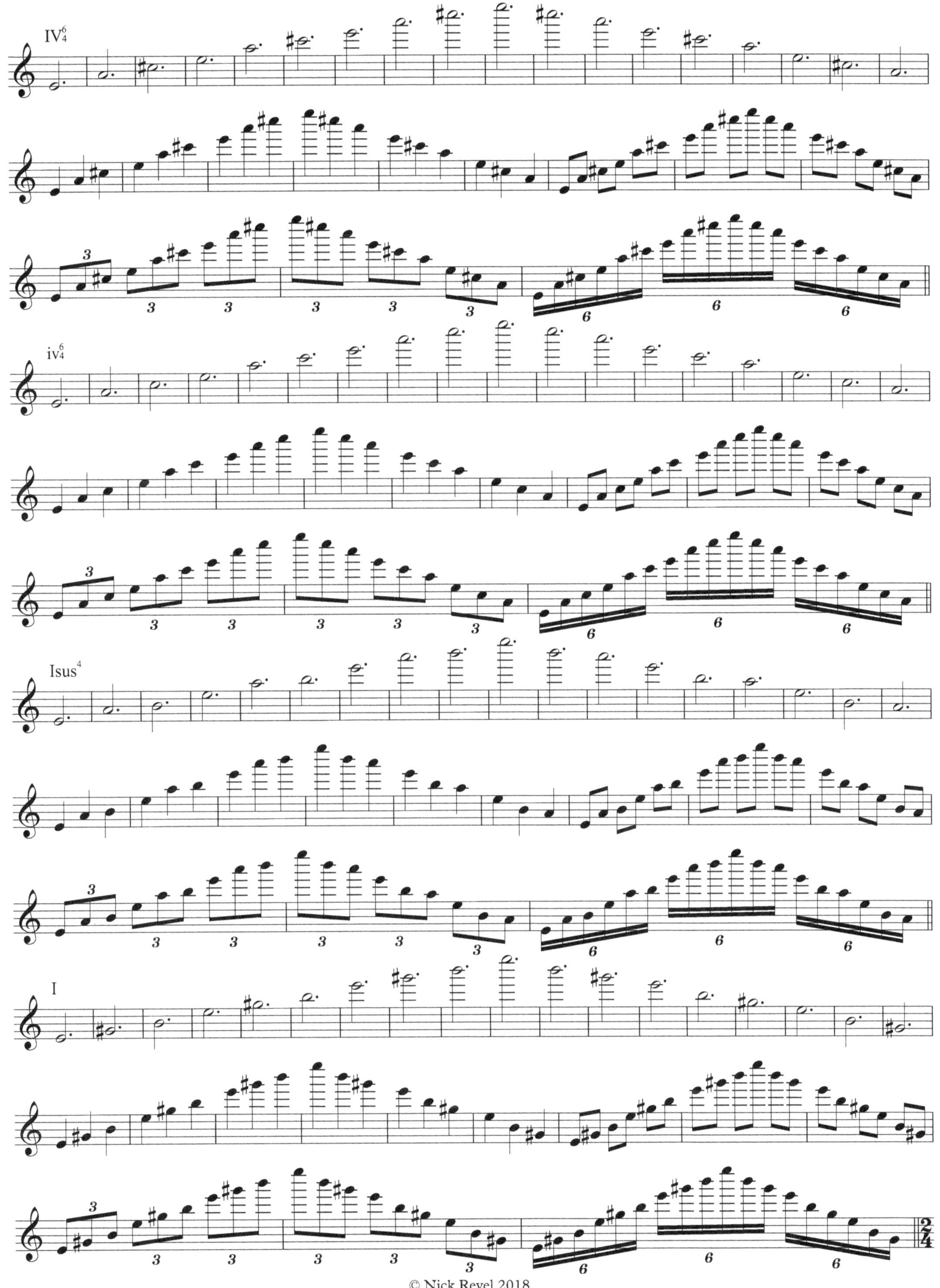

IV6/4
iv6/4
Isus4
I
© Nick Revel 2018
DRAGONSCALES – VIOLIN   199

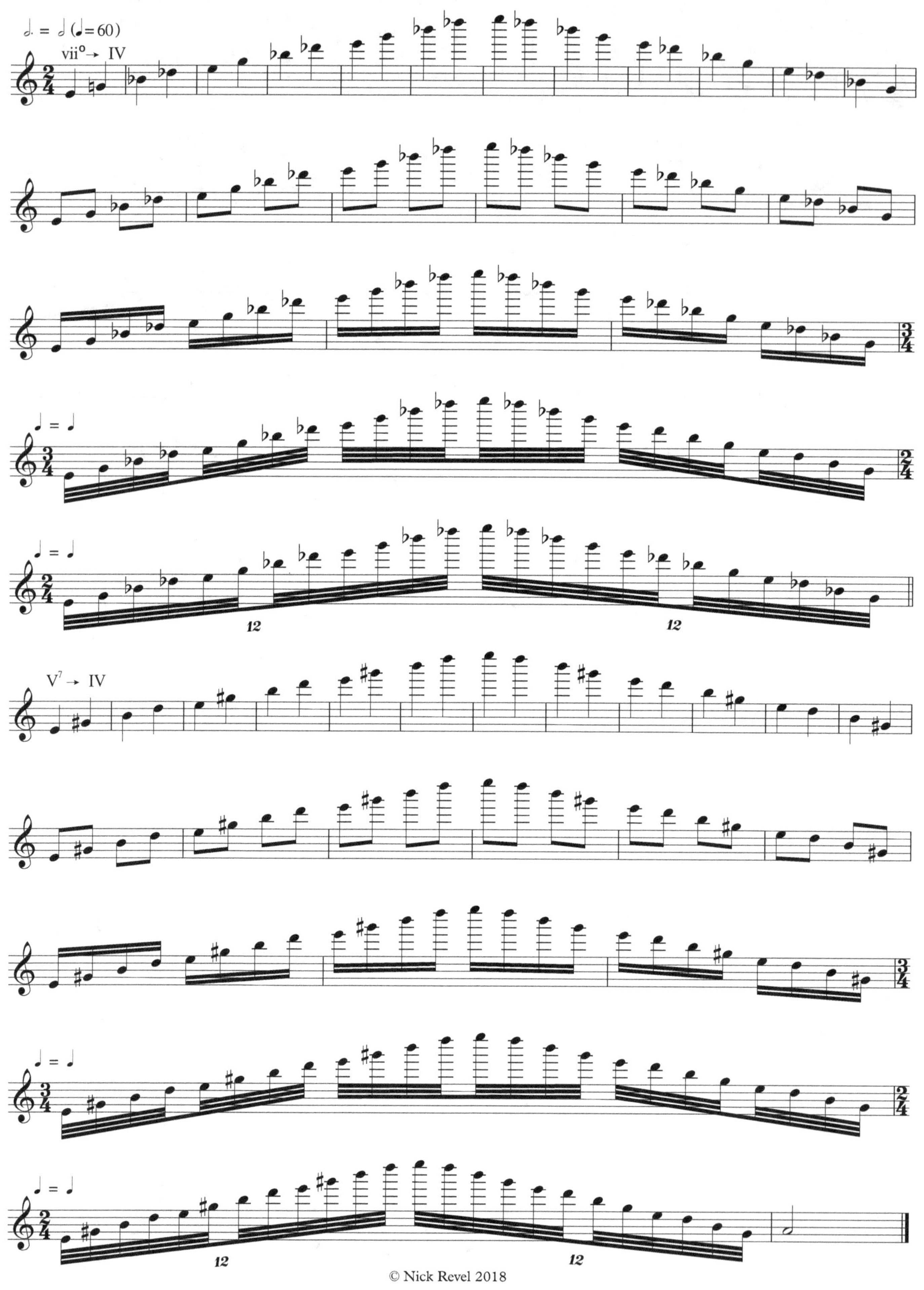

vii°→ IV
V⁷ → IV
vii°→ IV
© Nick Revel 2018

# DRAGONSCALES

3-Octave Scales and Arpeggios
In Slow to Fast Rhythms
In All Keys

Nick Revel

F

# DragonScales
## The Complete Set in F

Nick Revel

© Nick Revel 2018

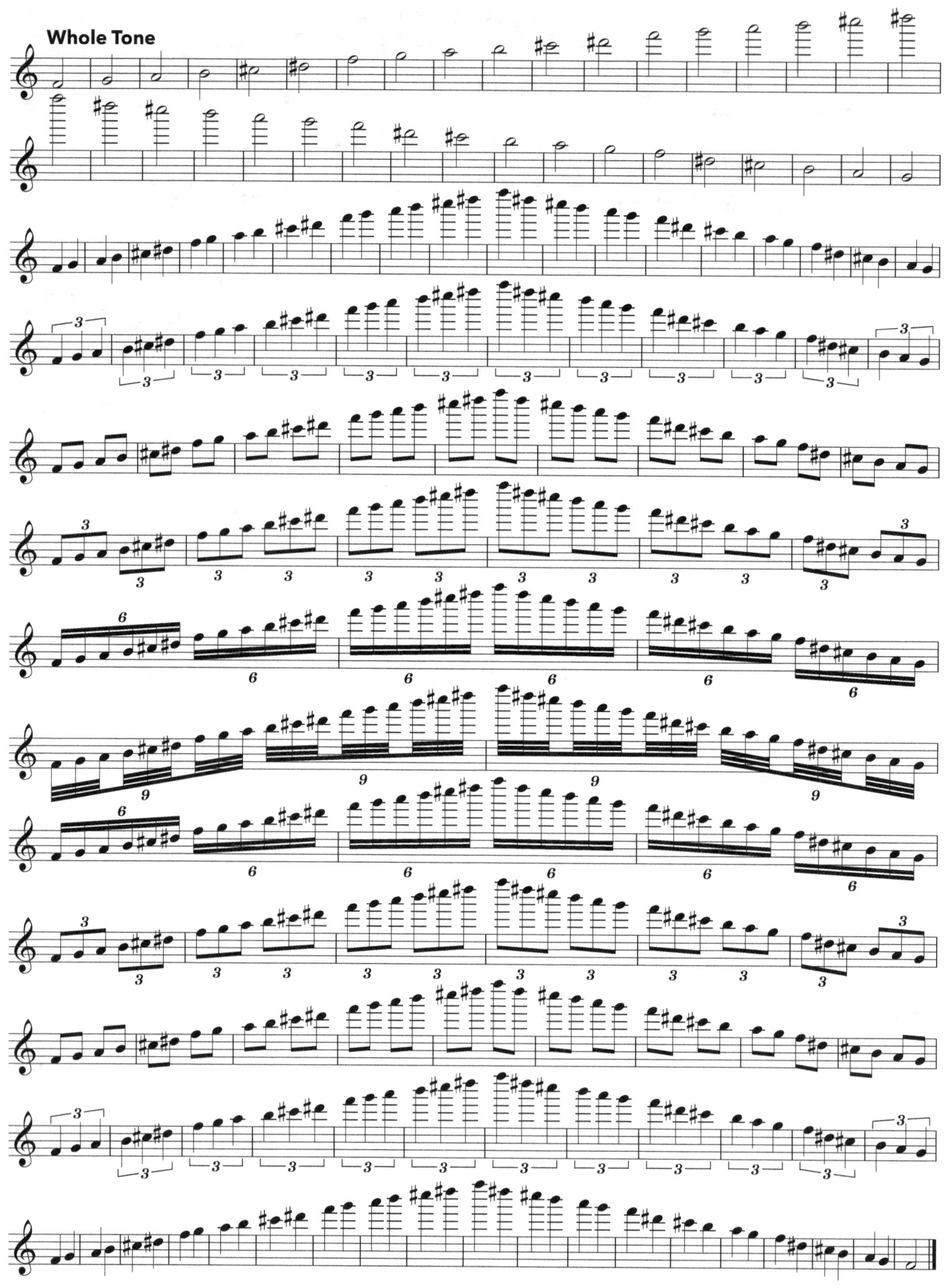


© Nick Revel 2018

*This page left intentionally blank.*

Diminished Scale Version 1

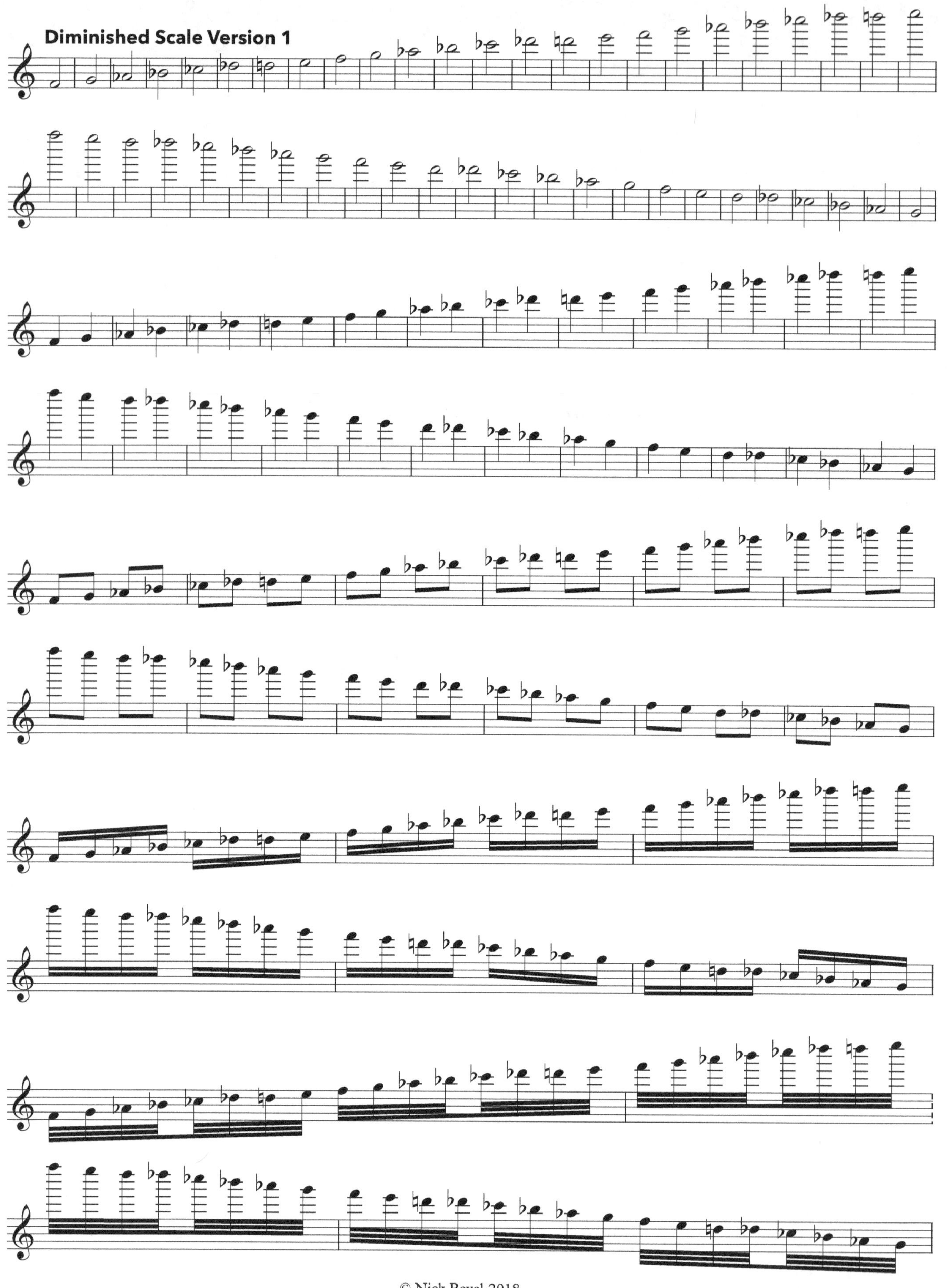

© Nick Revel 2018

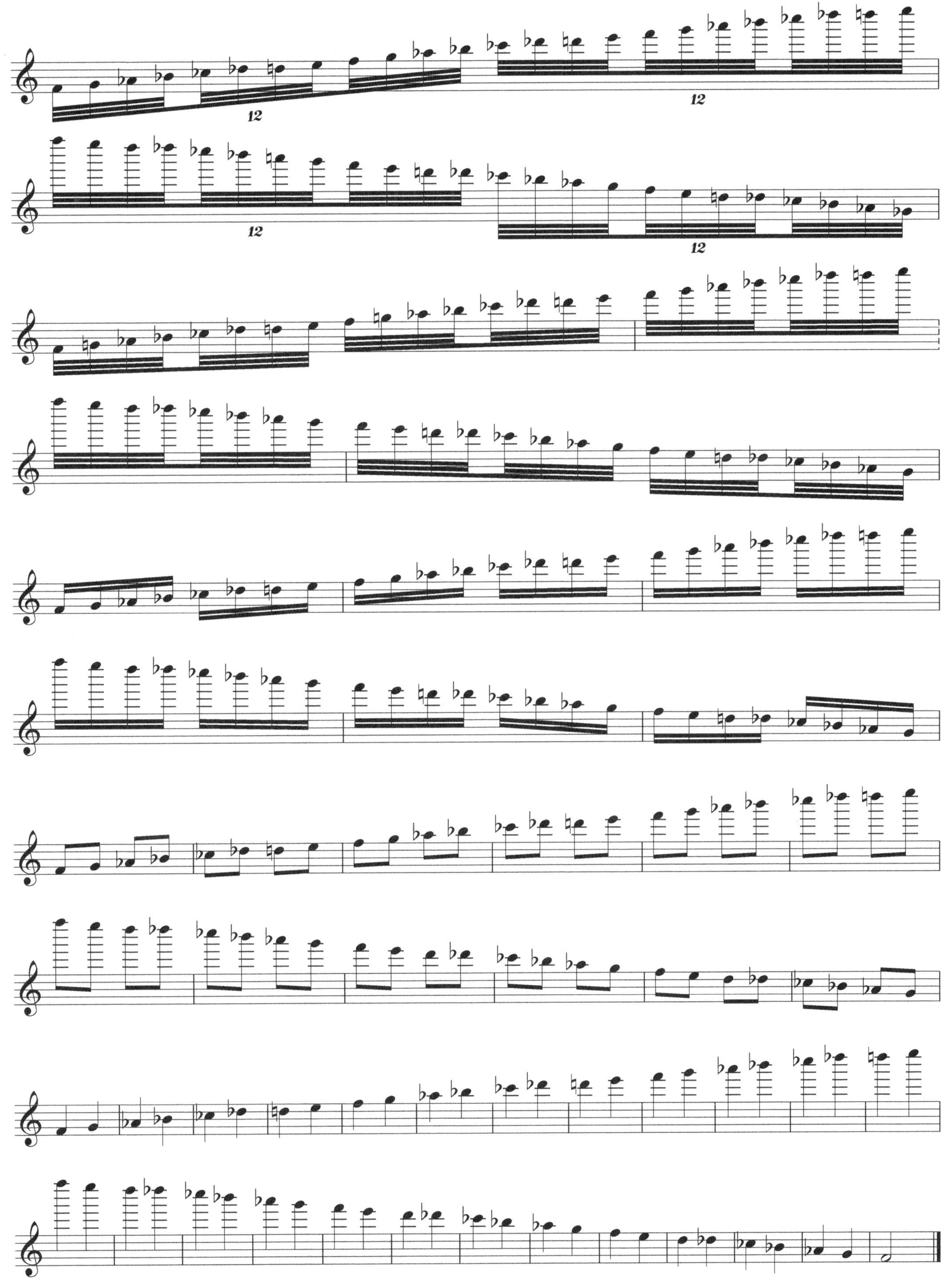

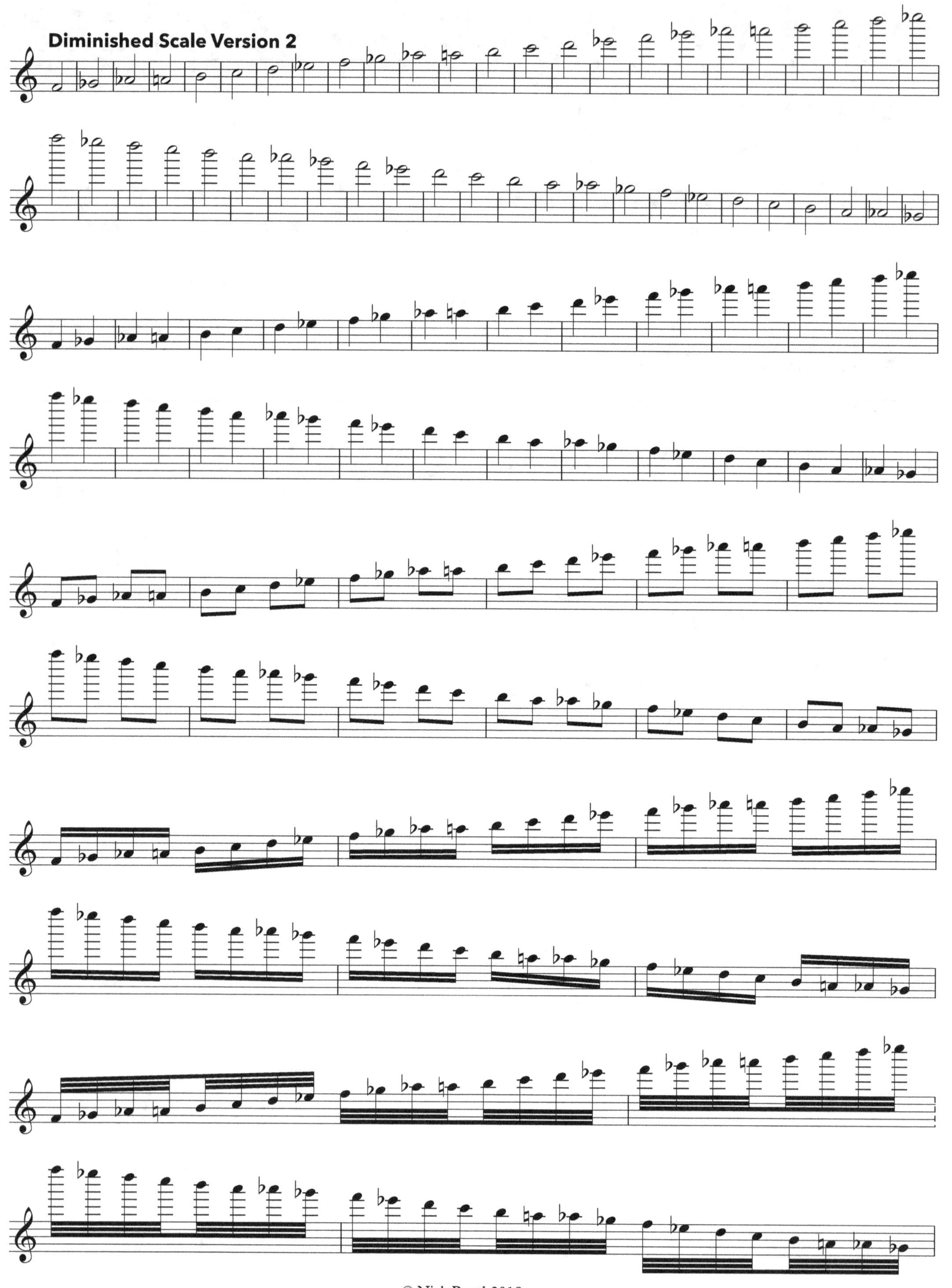


© Nick Revel 2018

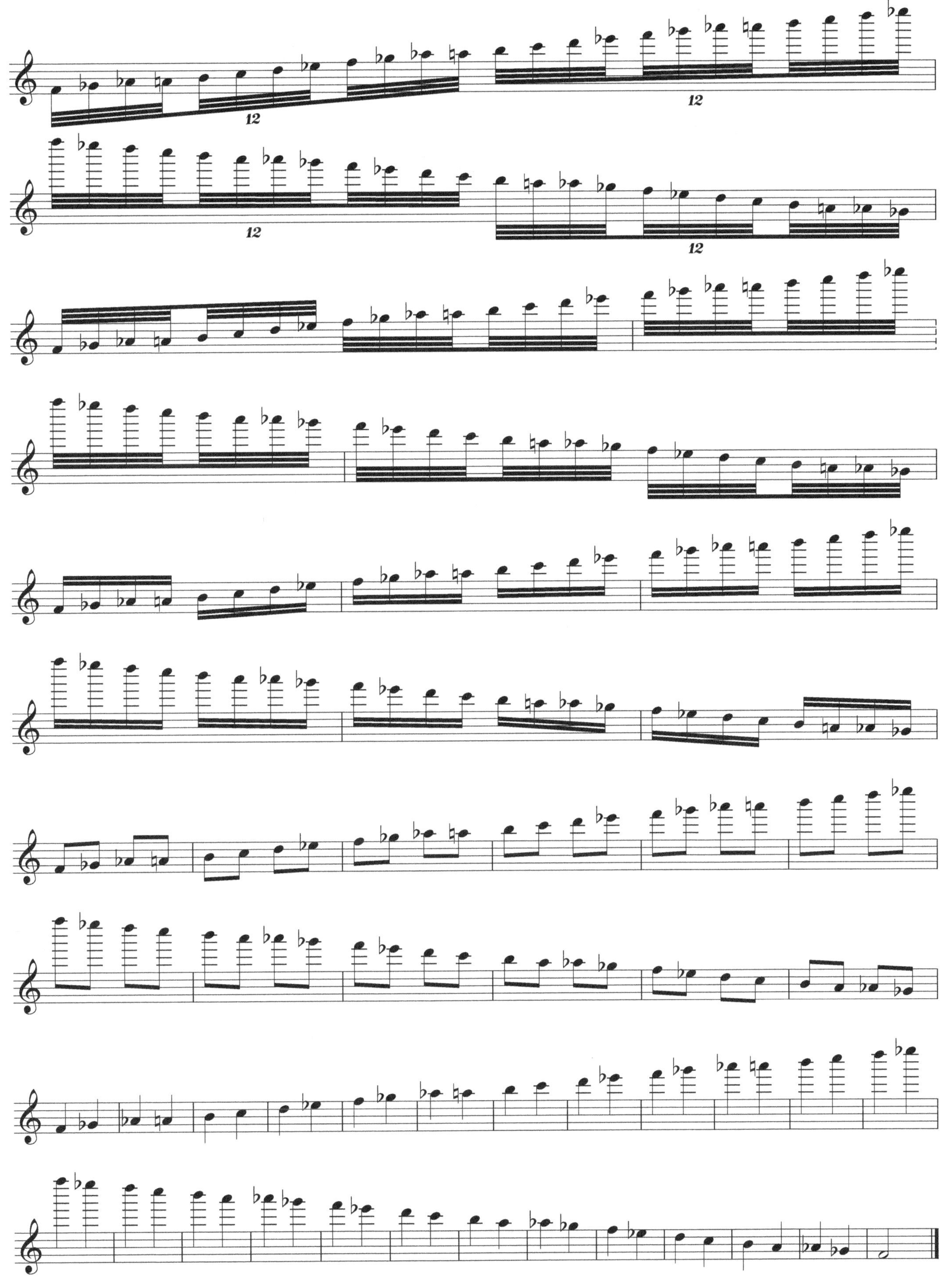

© Nick Revel 2018

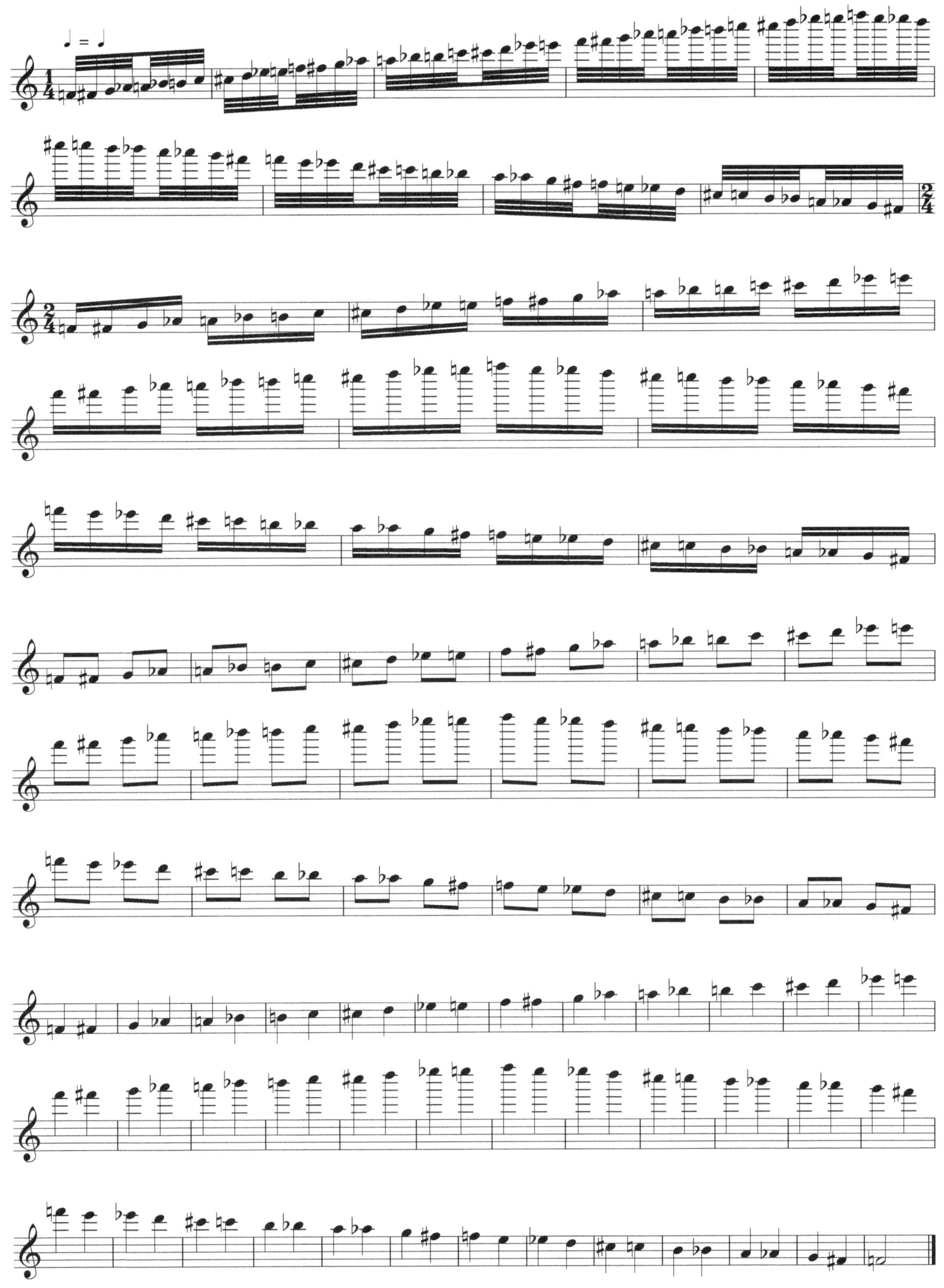

Arpeggios Version 1

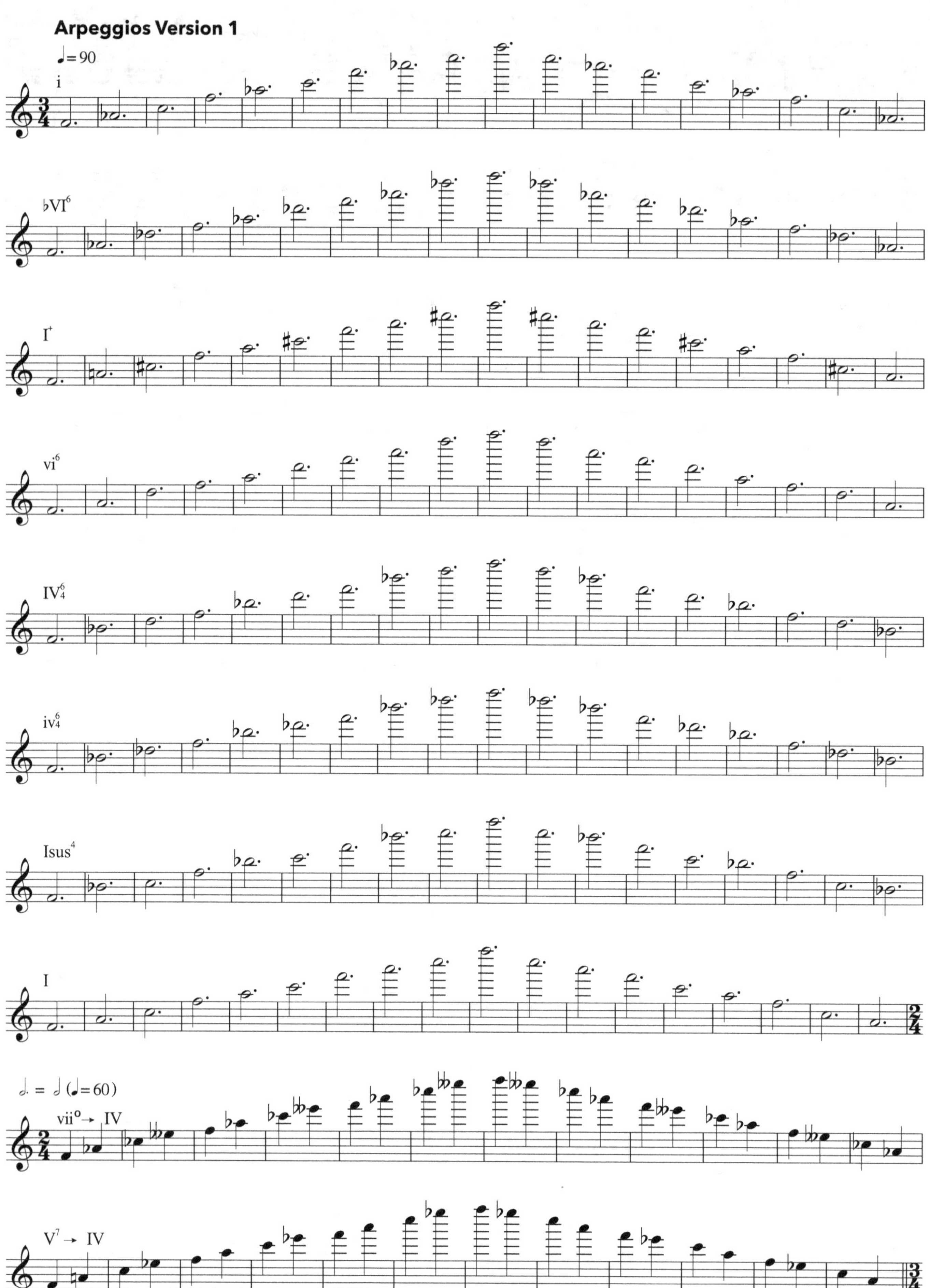
Arpeggios Version 1
♩ = 90
© Nick Revel 2018

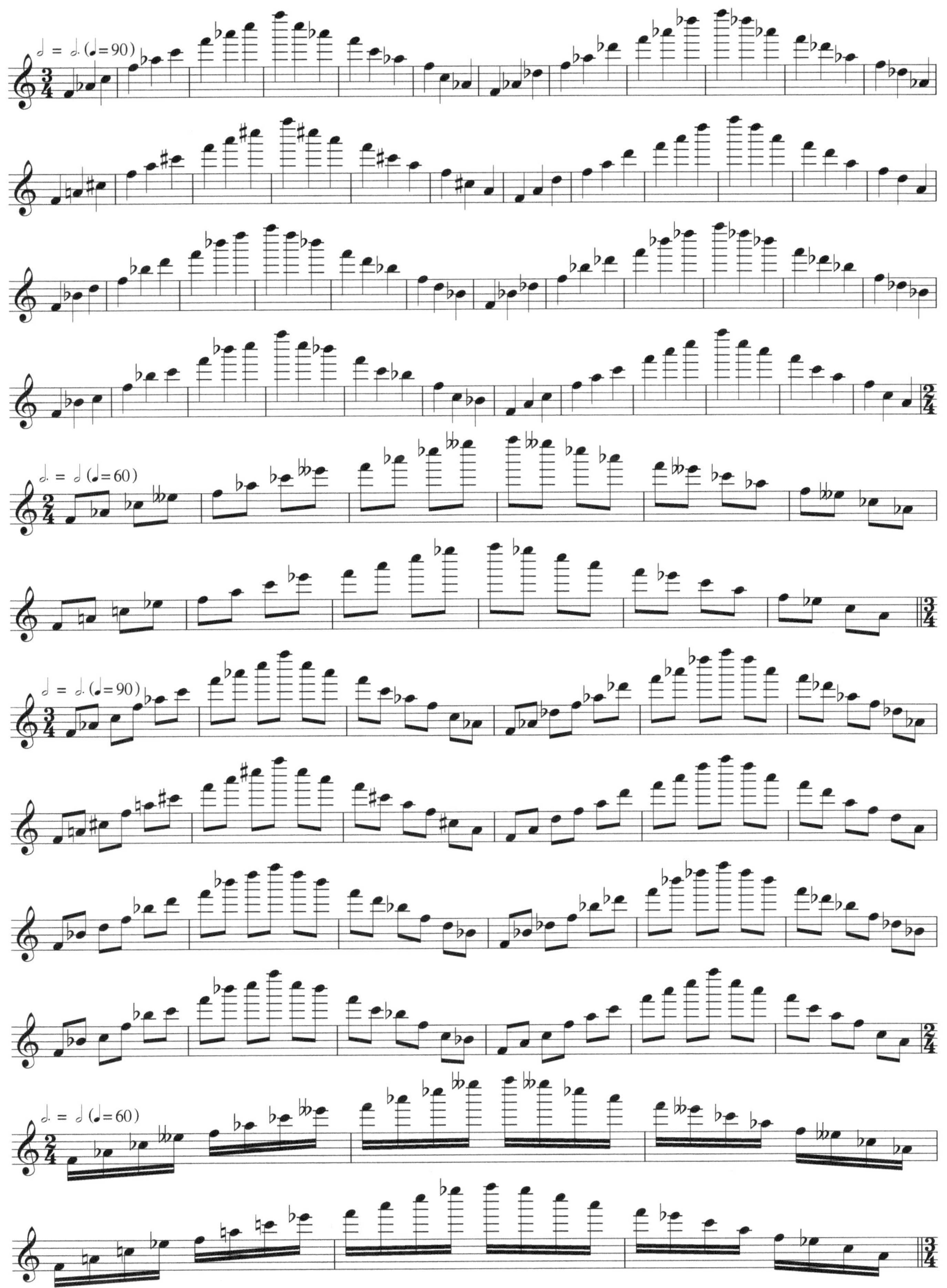

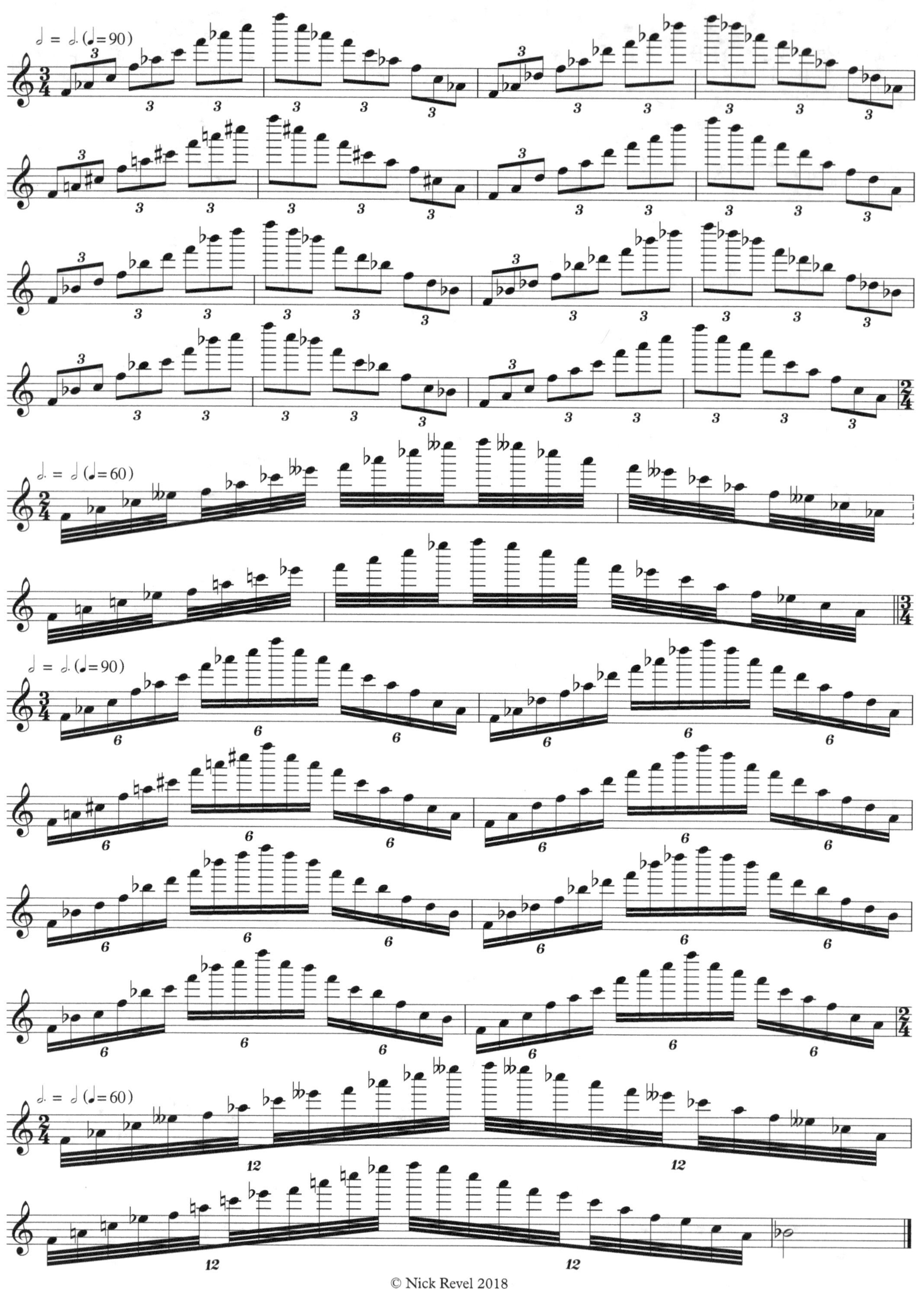

© Nick Revel 2018

*This page left intentionally blank.*

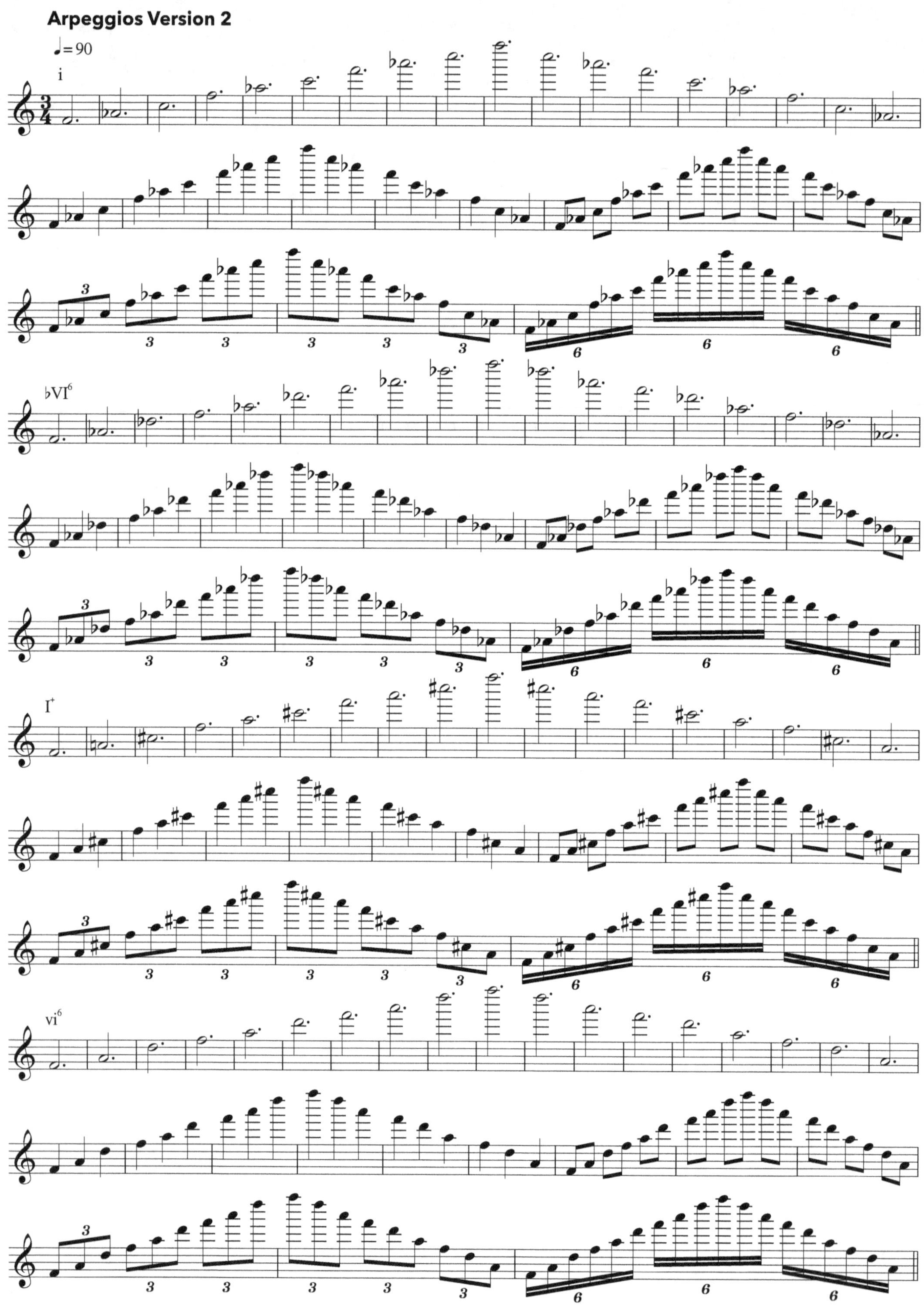

© Nick Revel 2018

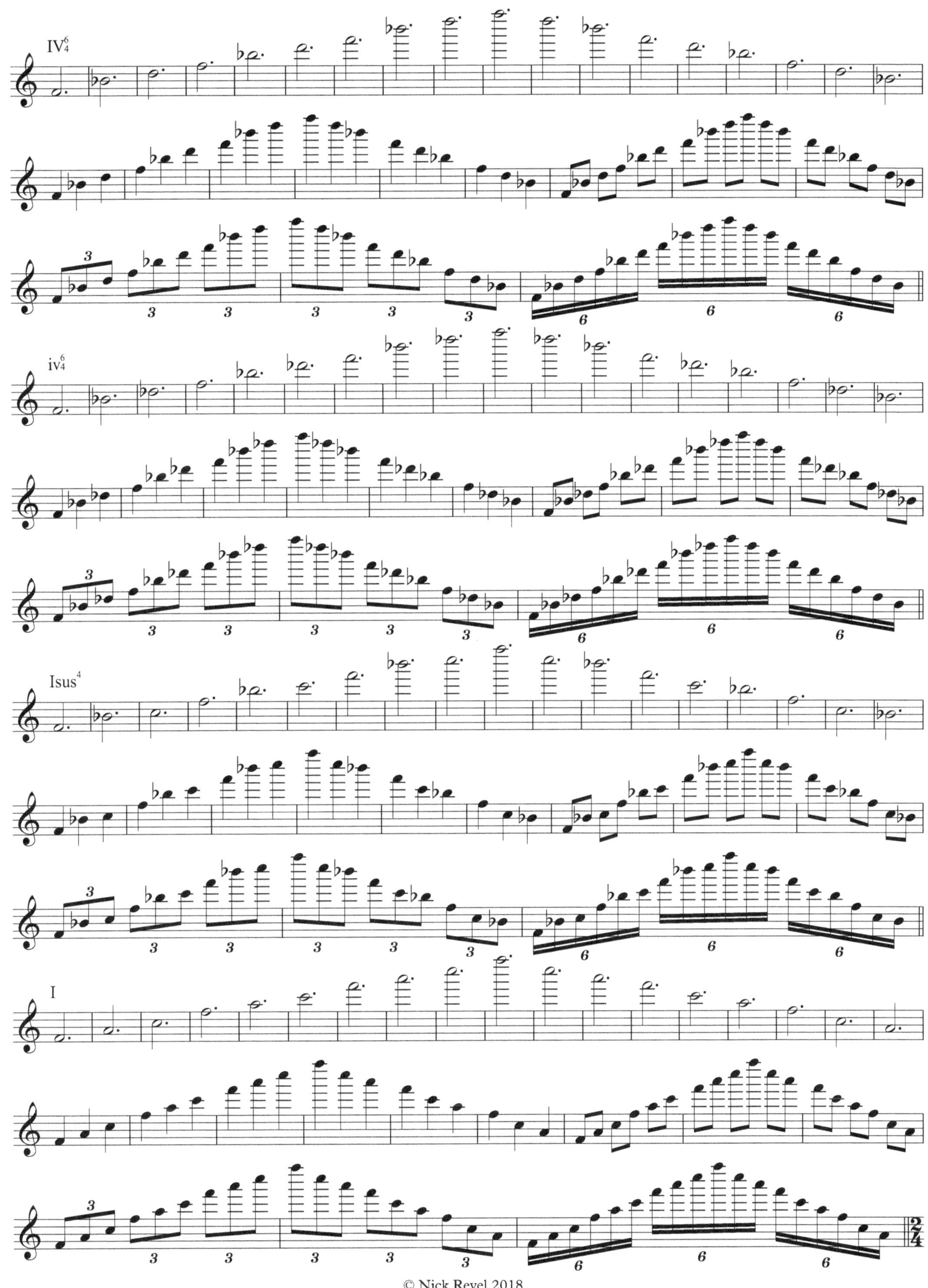

IV⁶₄
iv⁶₄
Isus⁴
I

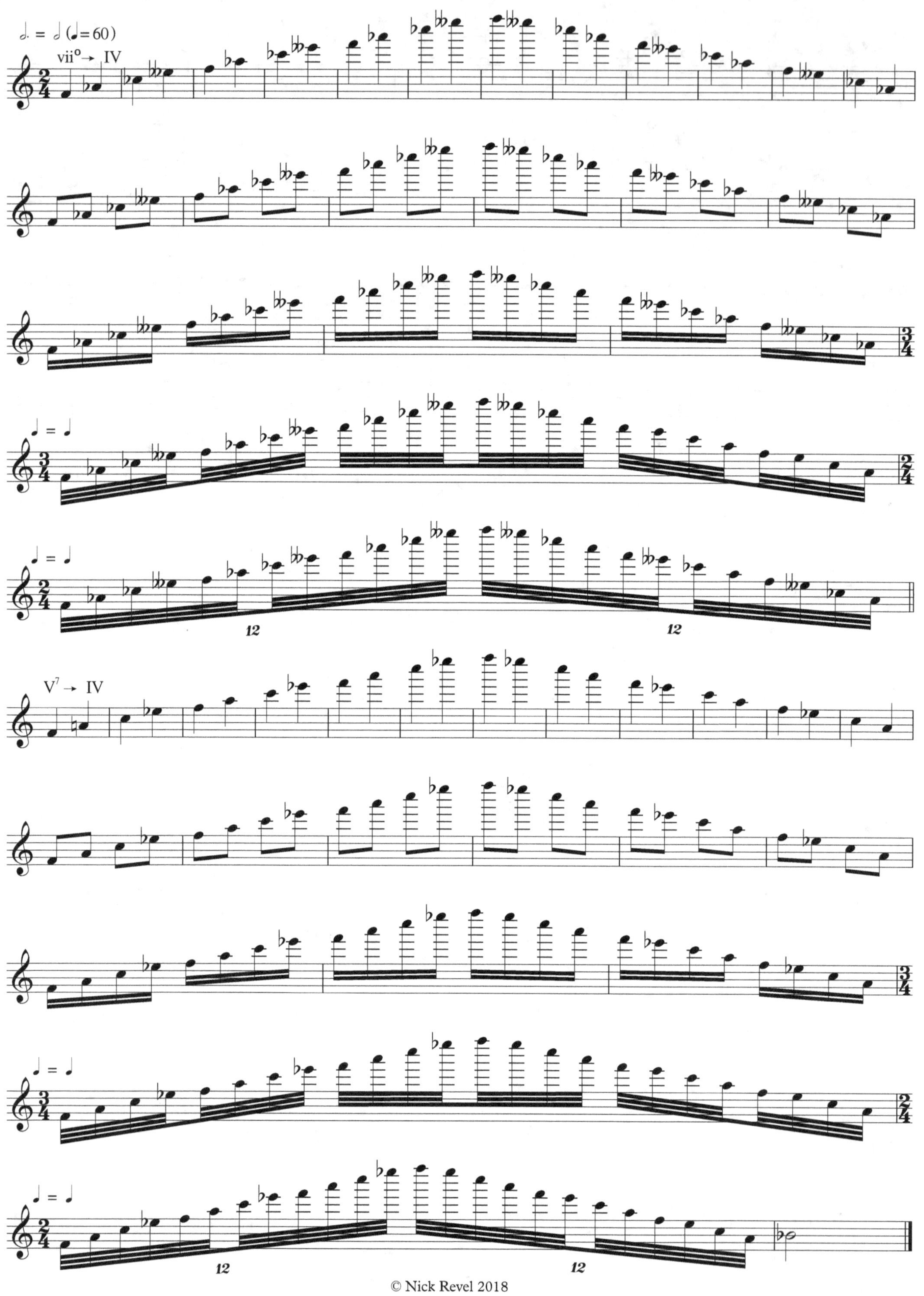


© Nick Revel 2018

# DRAGONSCALES

3-Octave Scales and Arpeggios
In Slow to Fast Rhythms
In All Keys

Nick Revel

# F#/Gb

# DragonScales
## The Complete Set in F#Gb

Nick Revel

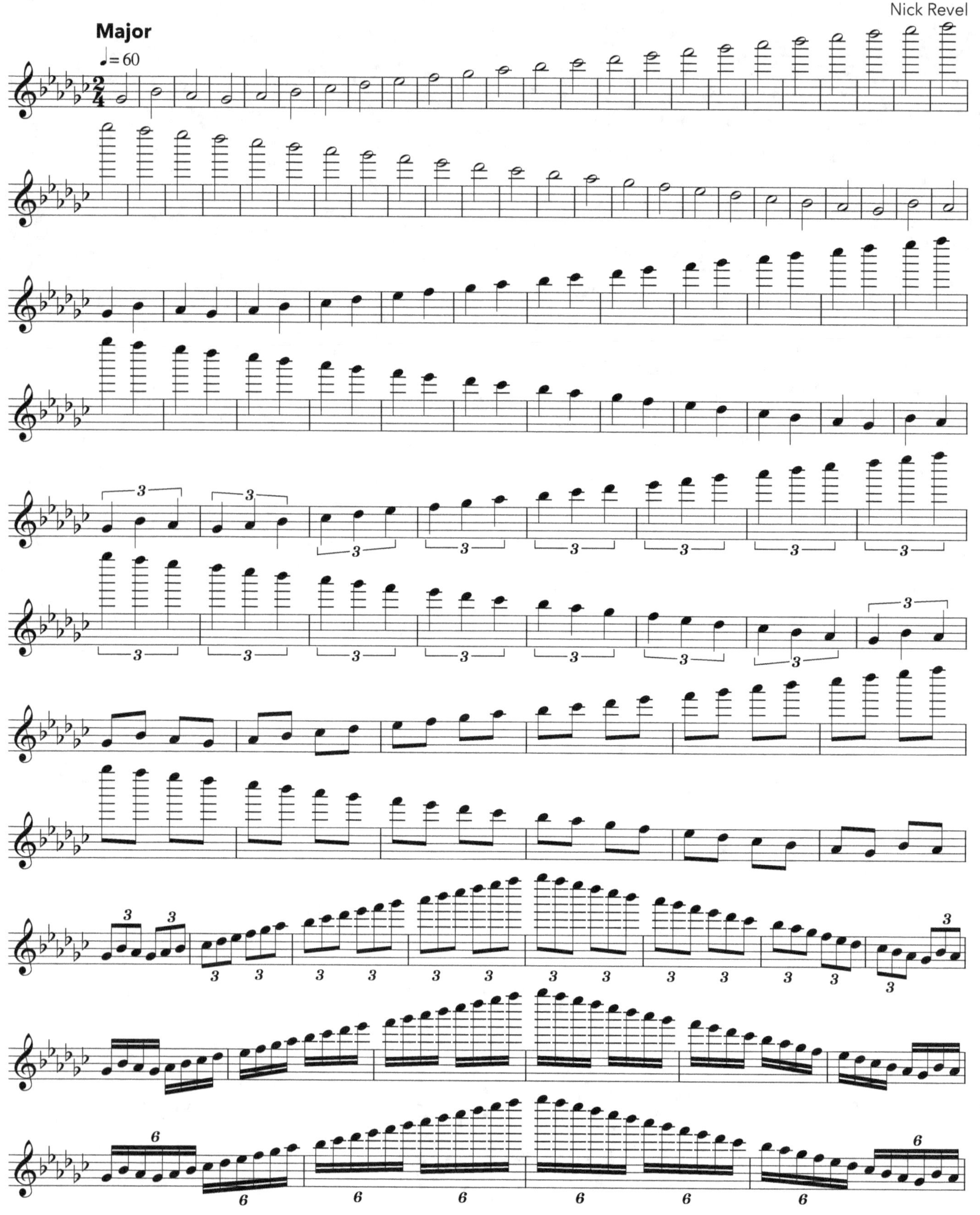


© Nick Revel 2018

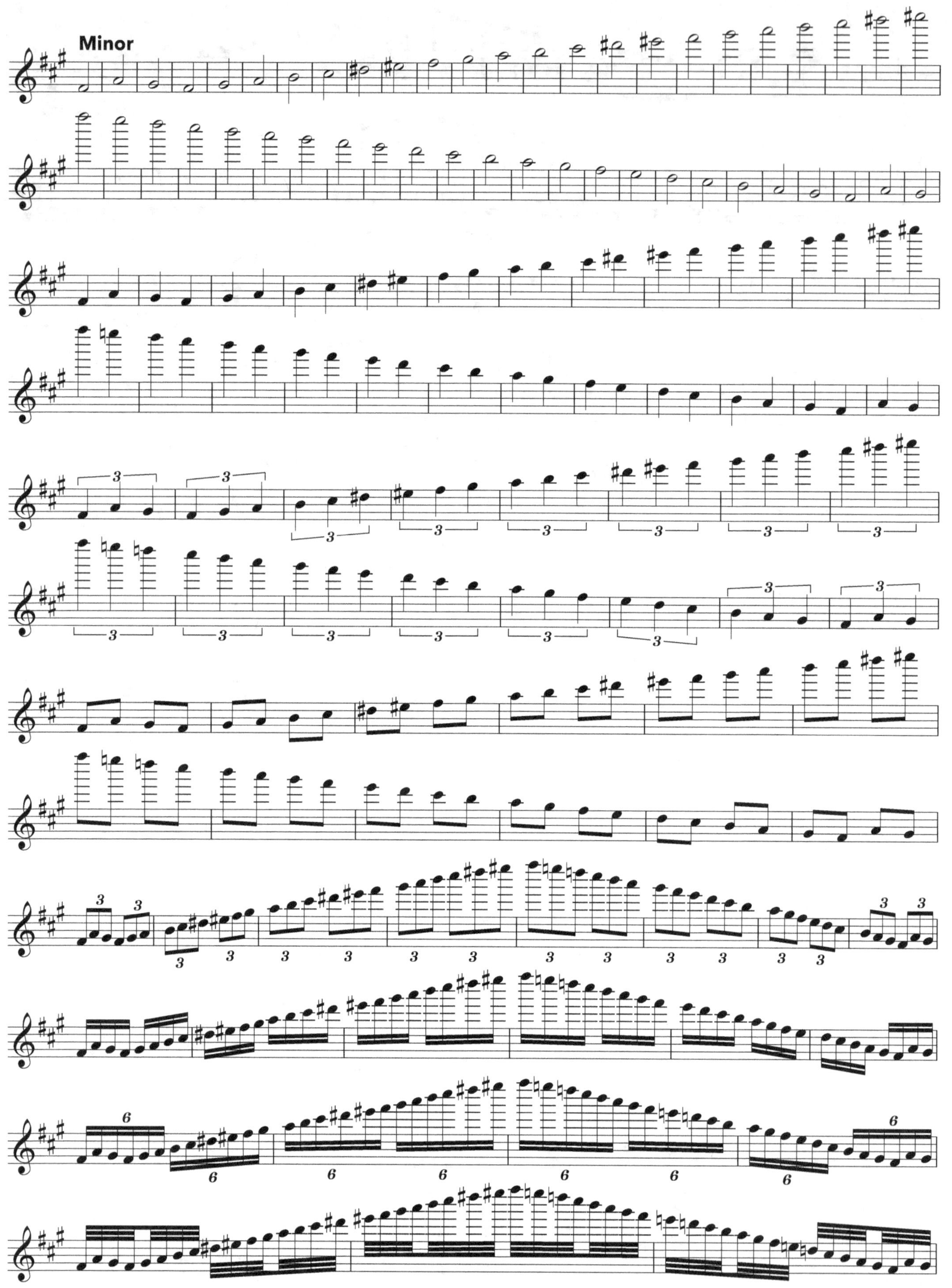
Minor

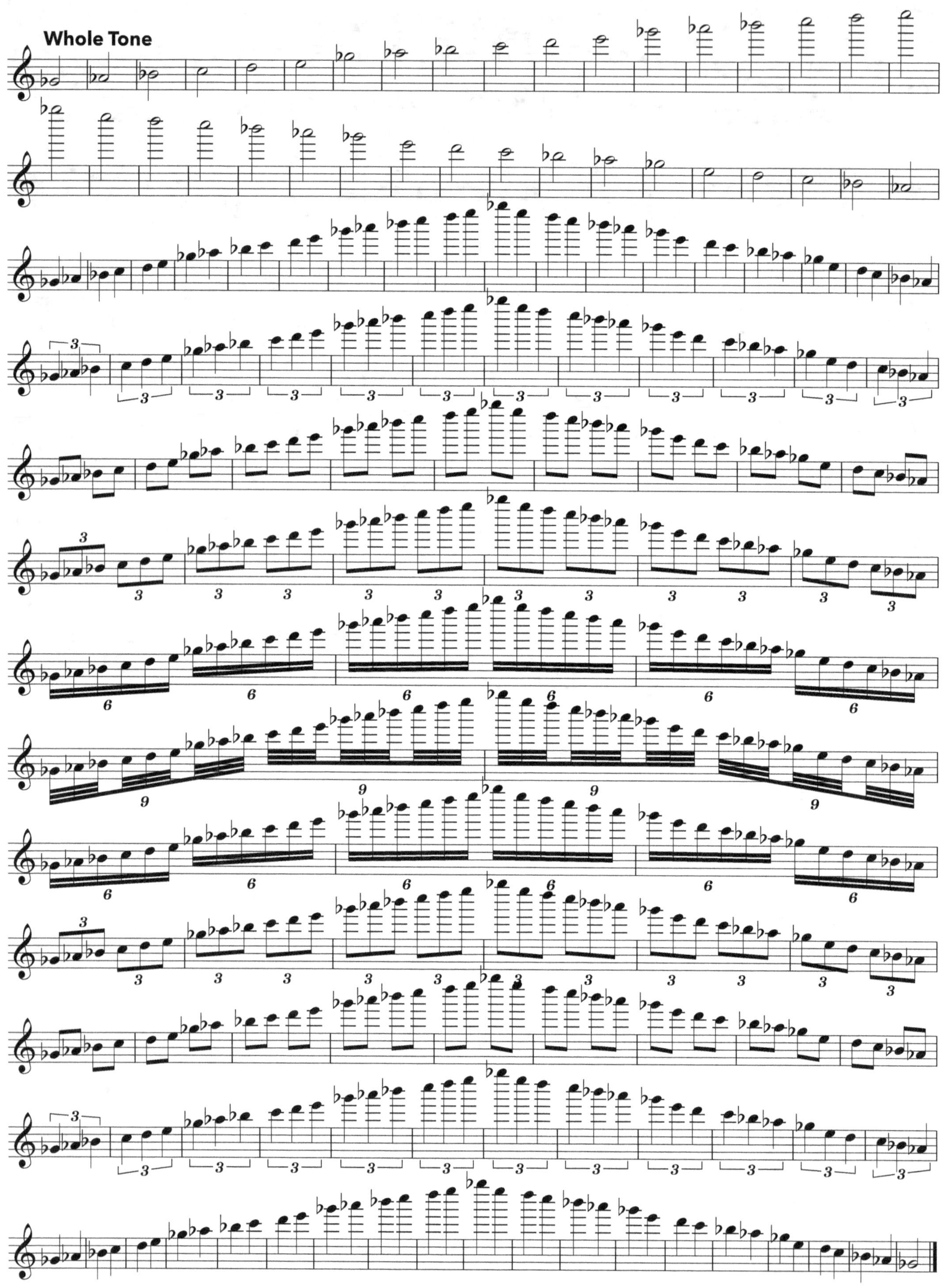


© Nick Revel 2018

226   DRAGONSCALES – VIOLIN

*This page left intentionally blank.*

Diminished Scale Version 1

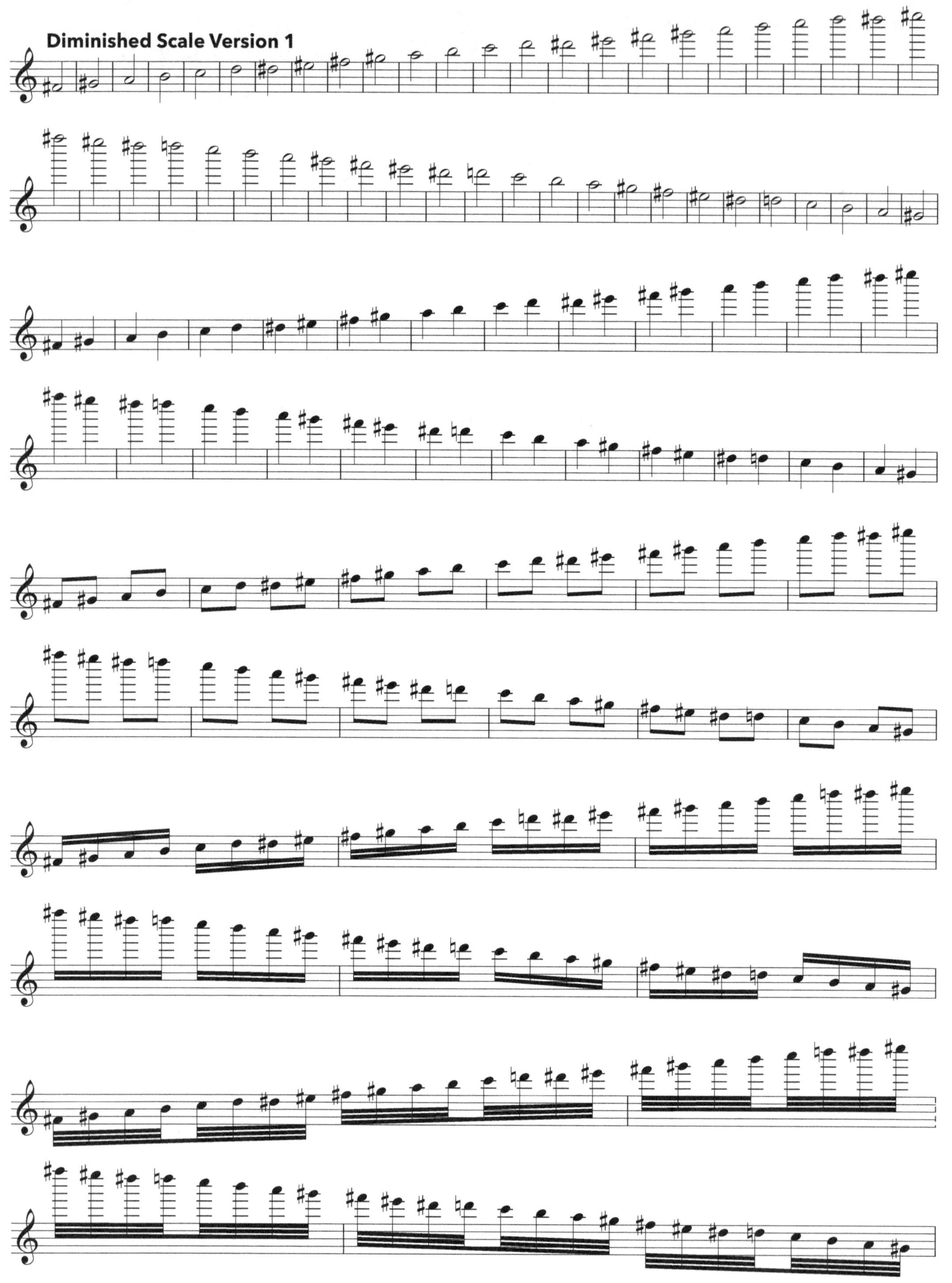

© Nick Revel 2018

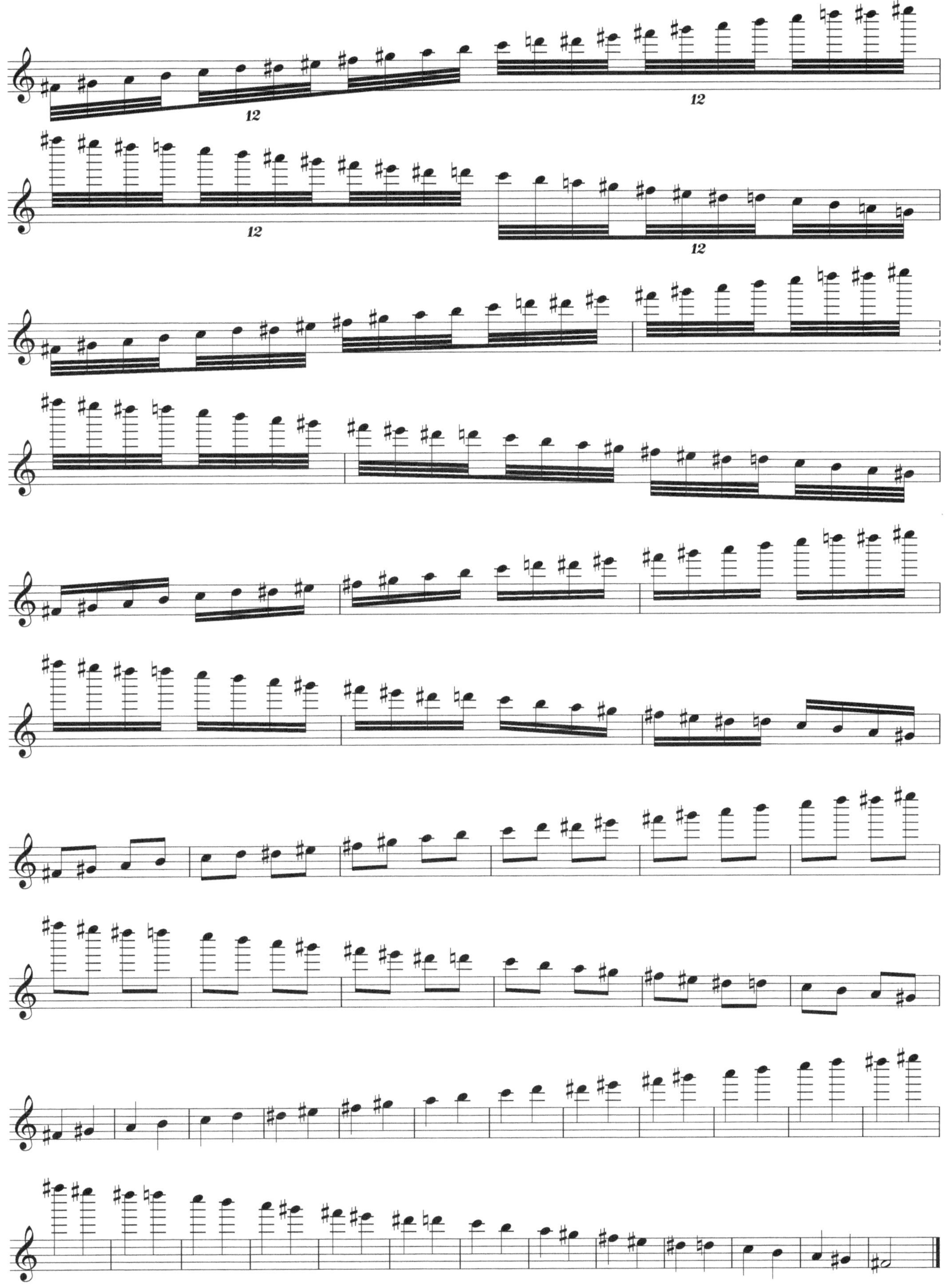

12
12
12
12

Diminished Scale Version 2

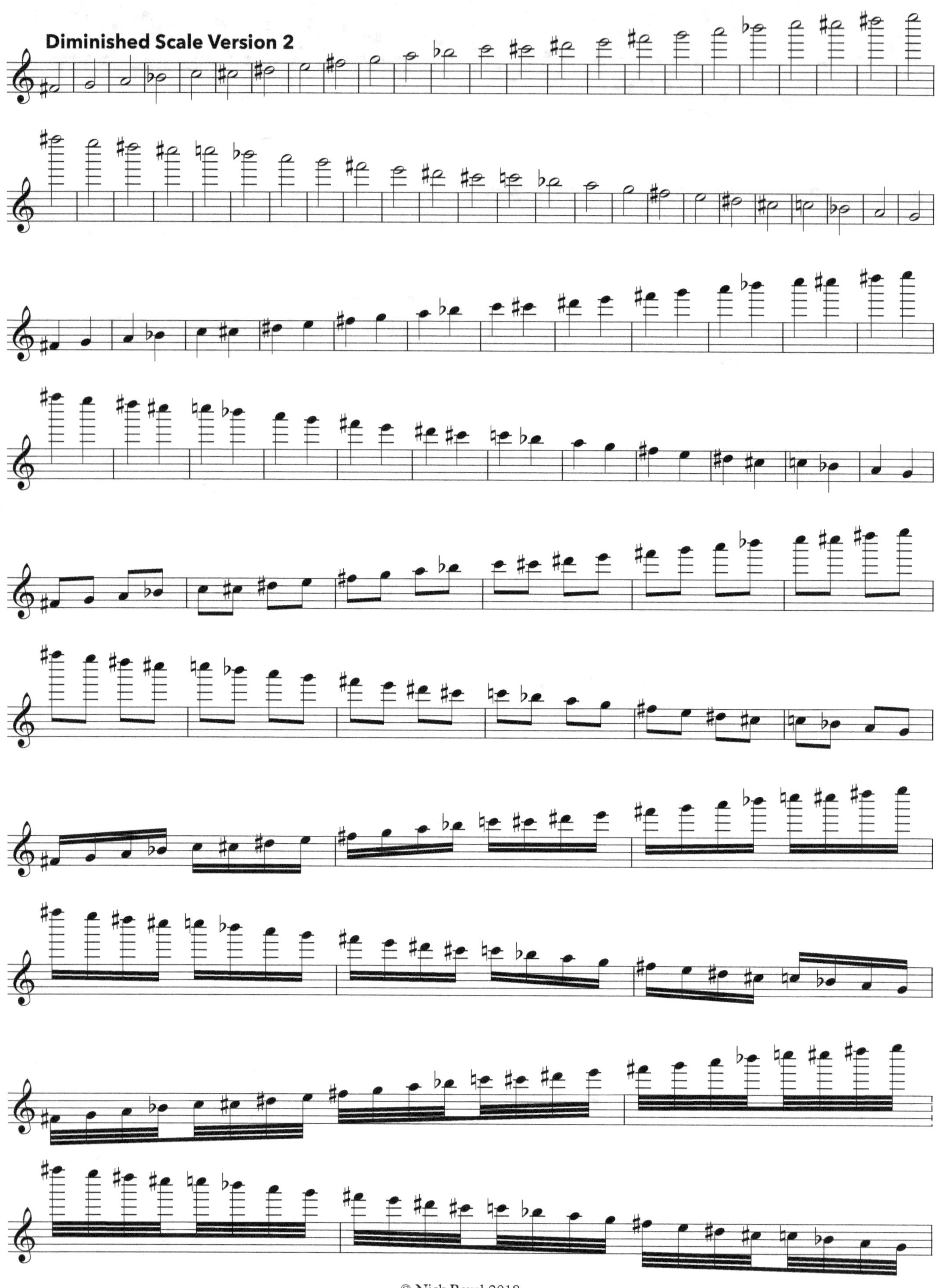

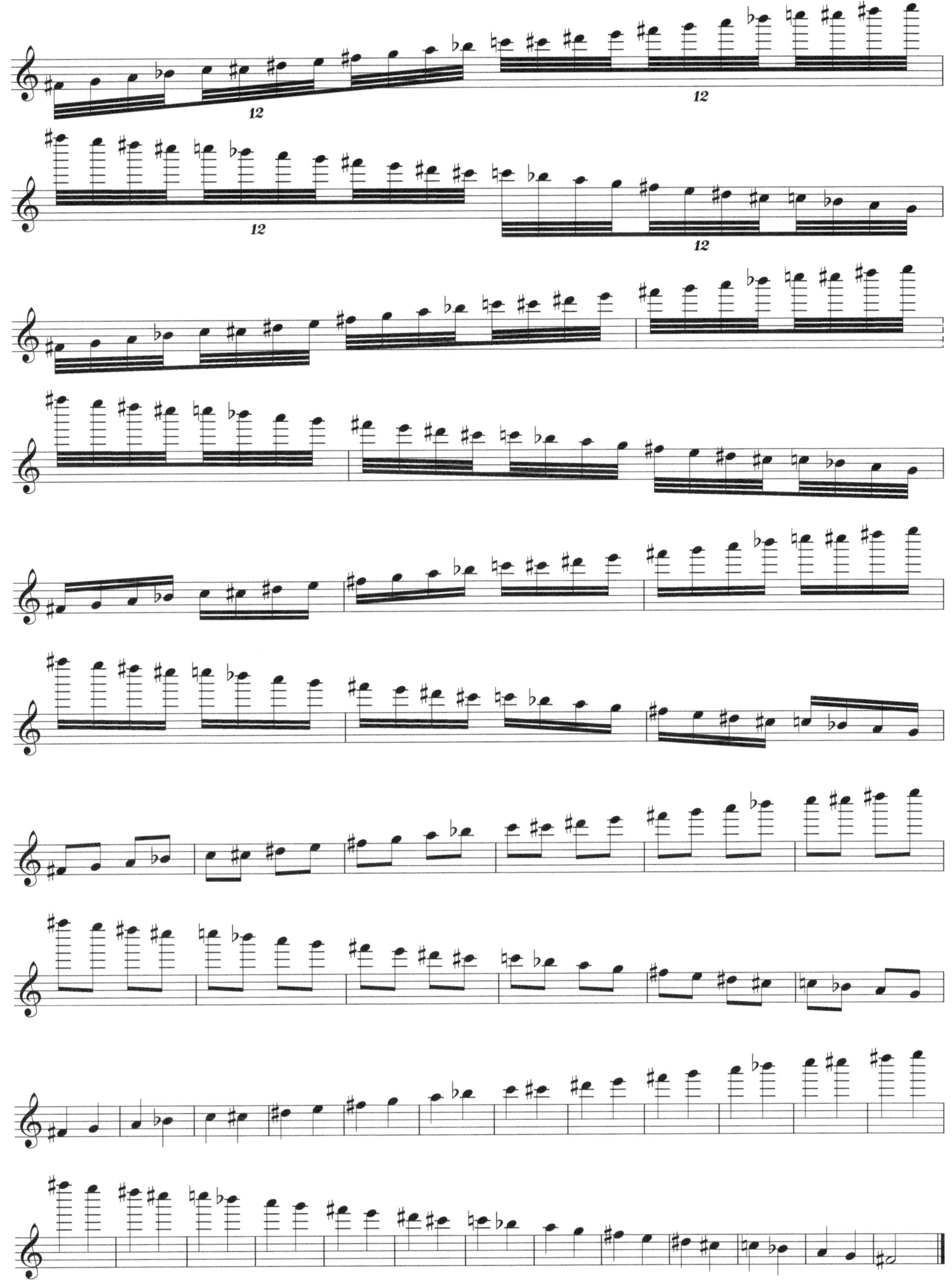


12
12
12
12

# Chromatic

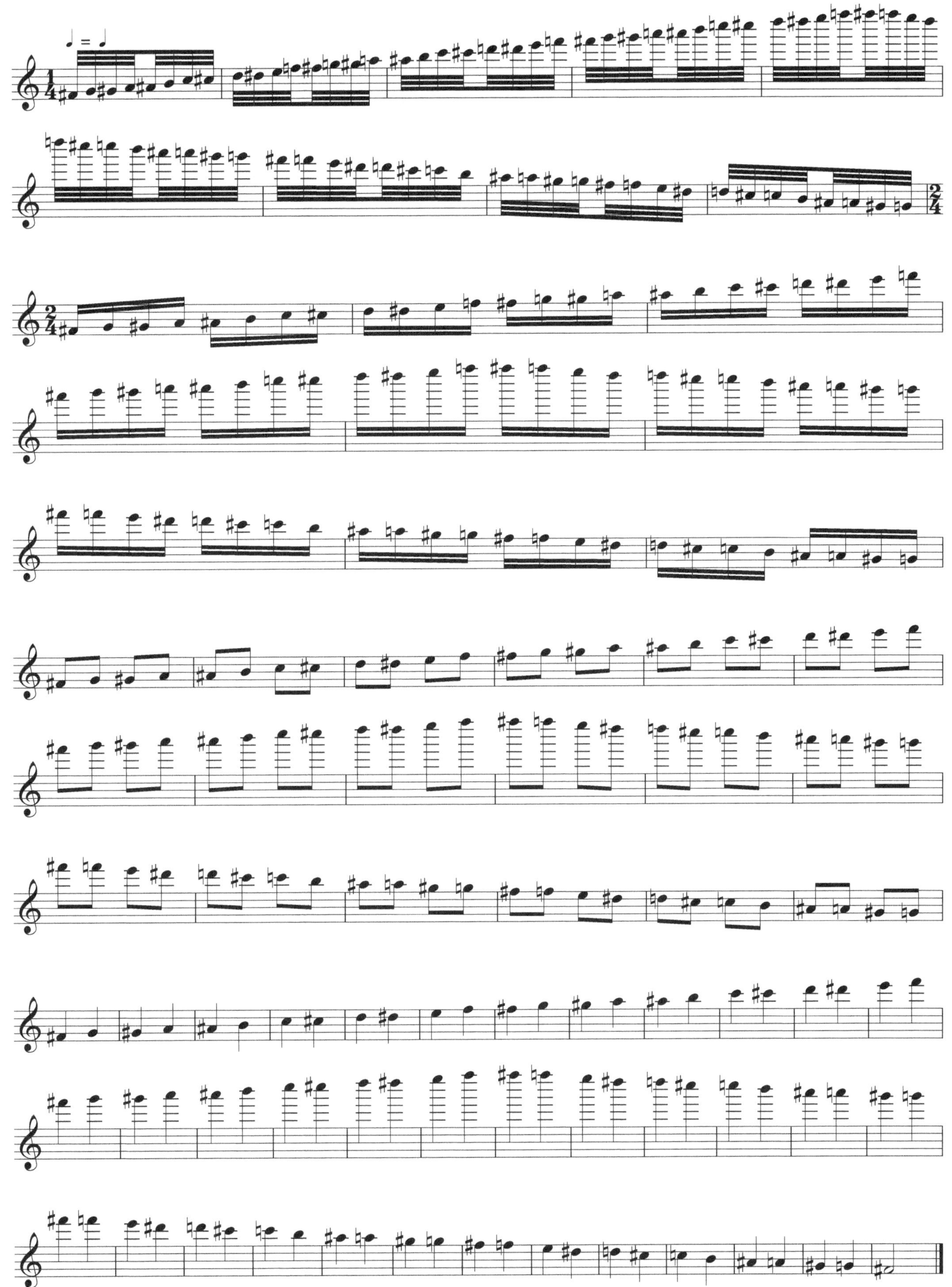


♩ = ♩
© Nick Revel 2018
DRAGONSCALES – VIOLIN   233

# Arpeggios Version 1

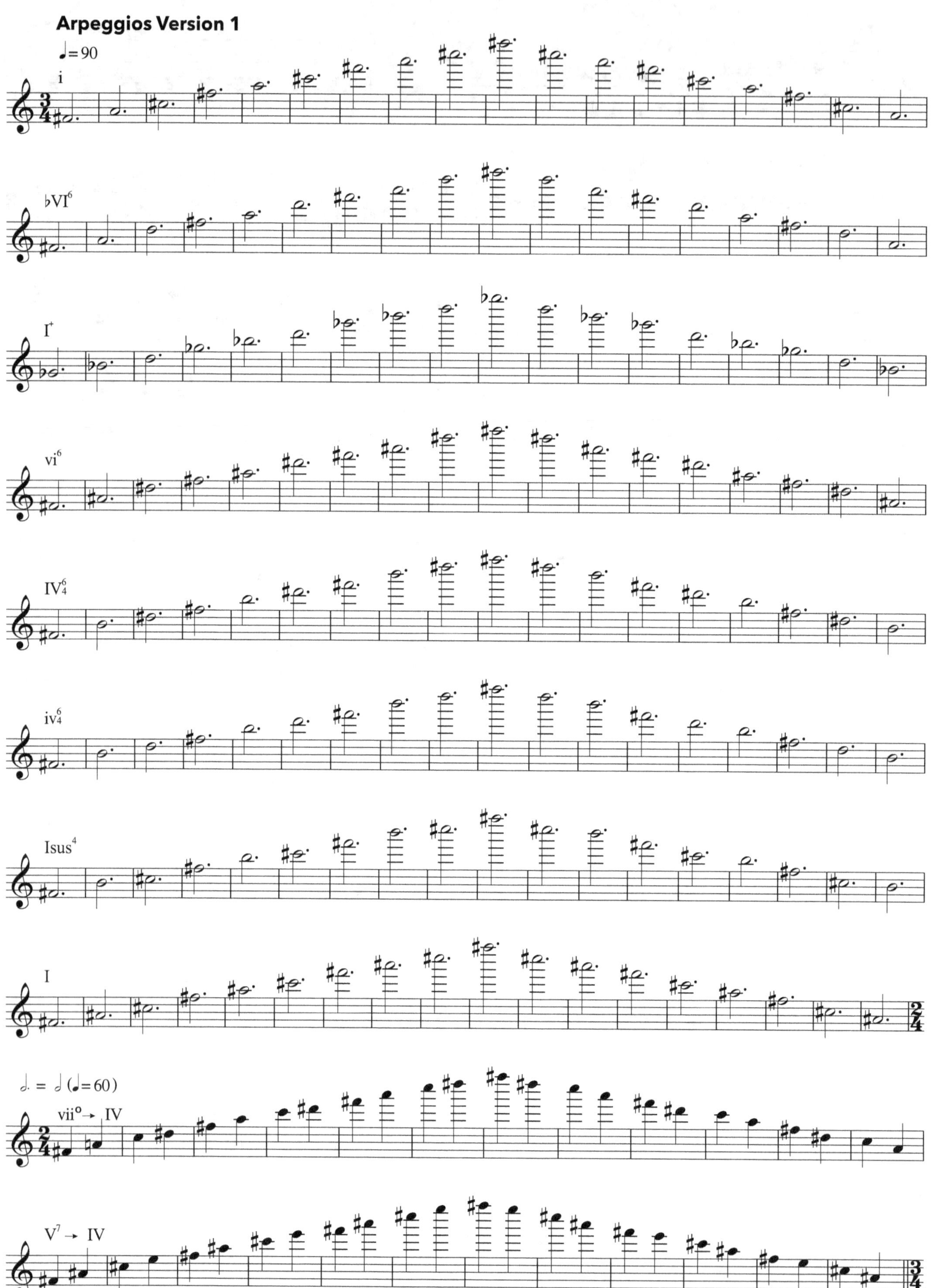

© Nick Revel 2018

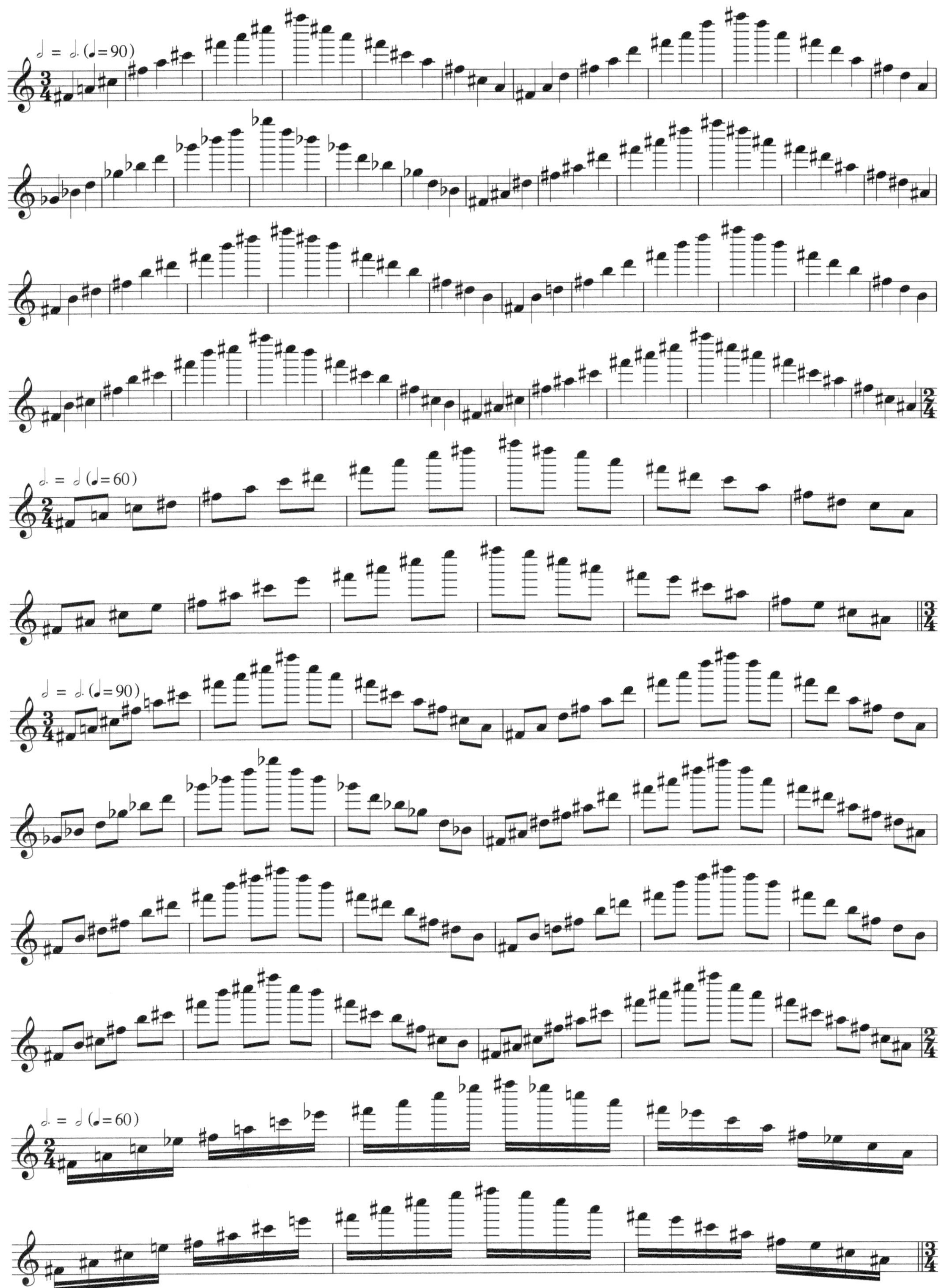

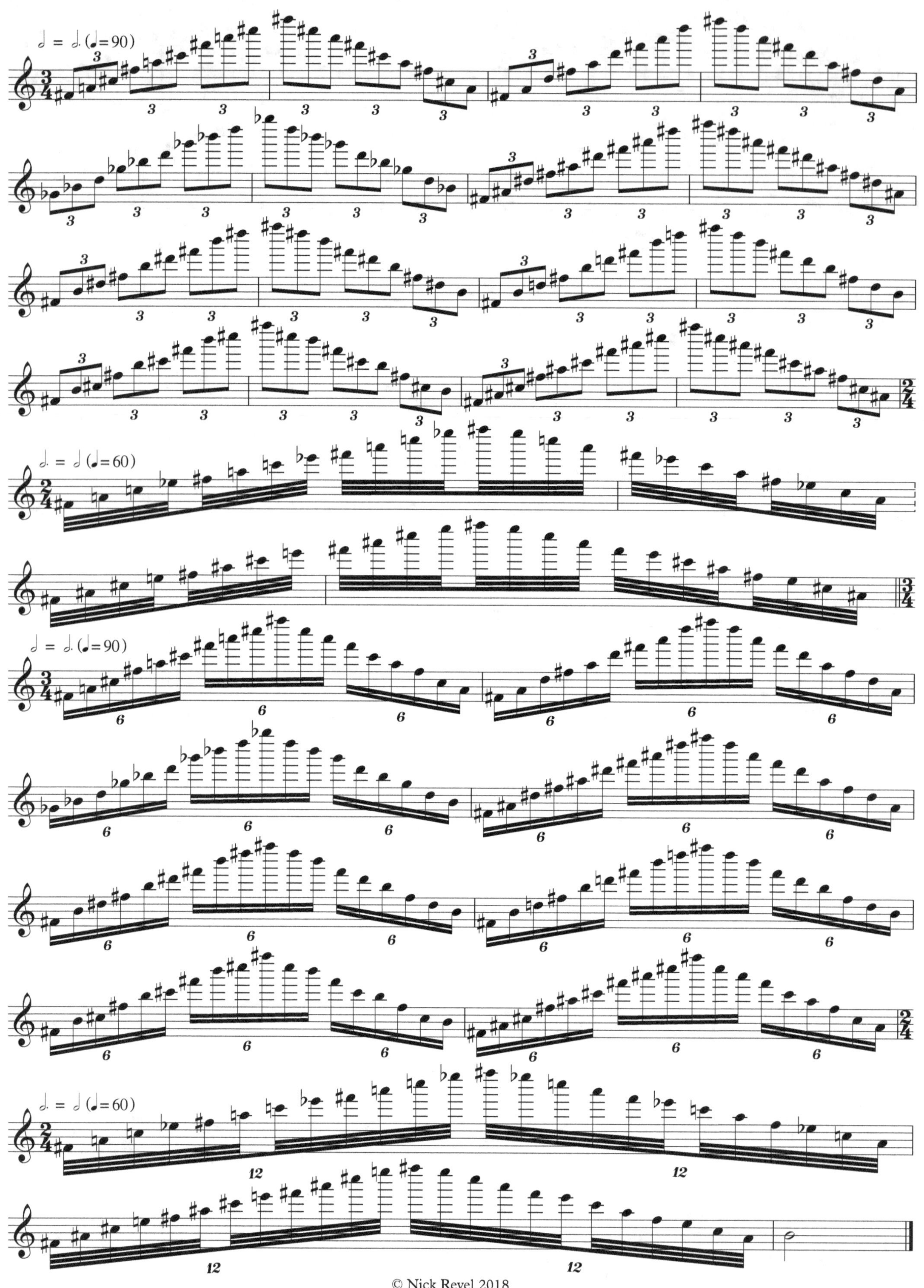

© Nick Revel 2018

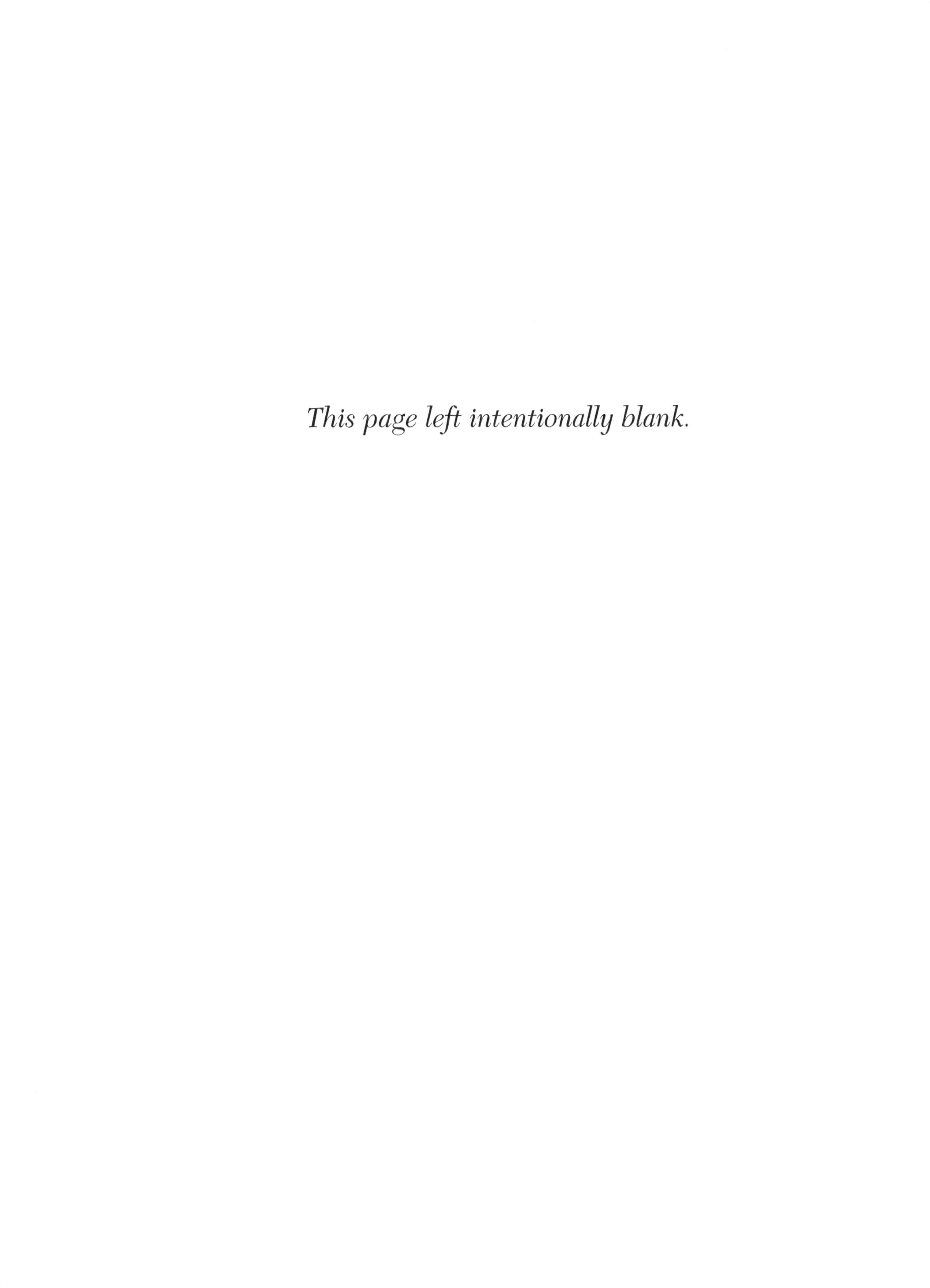

*This page left intentionally blank.*

Arpeggios Version 2

Arpeggios Version 2
♩=90

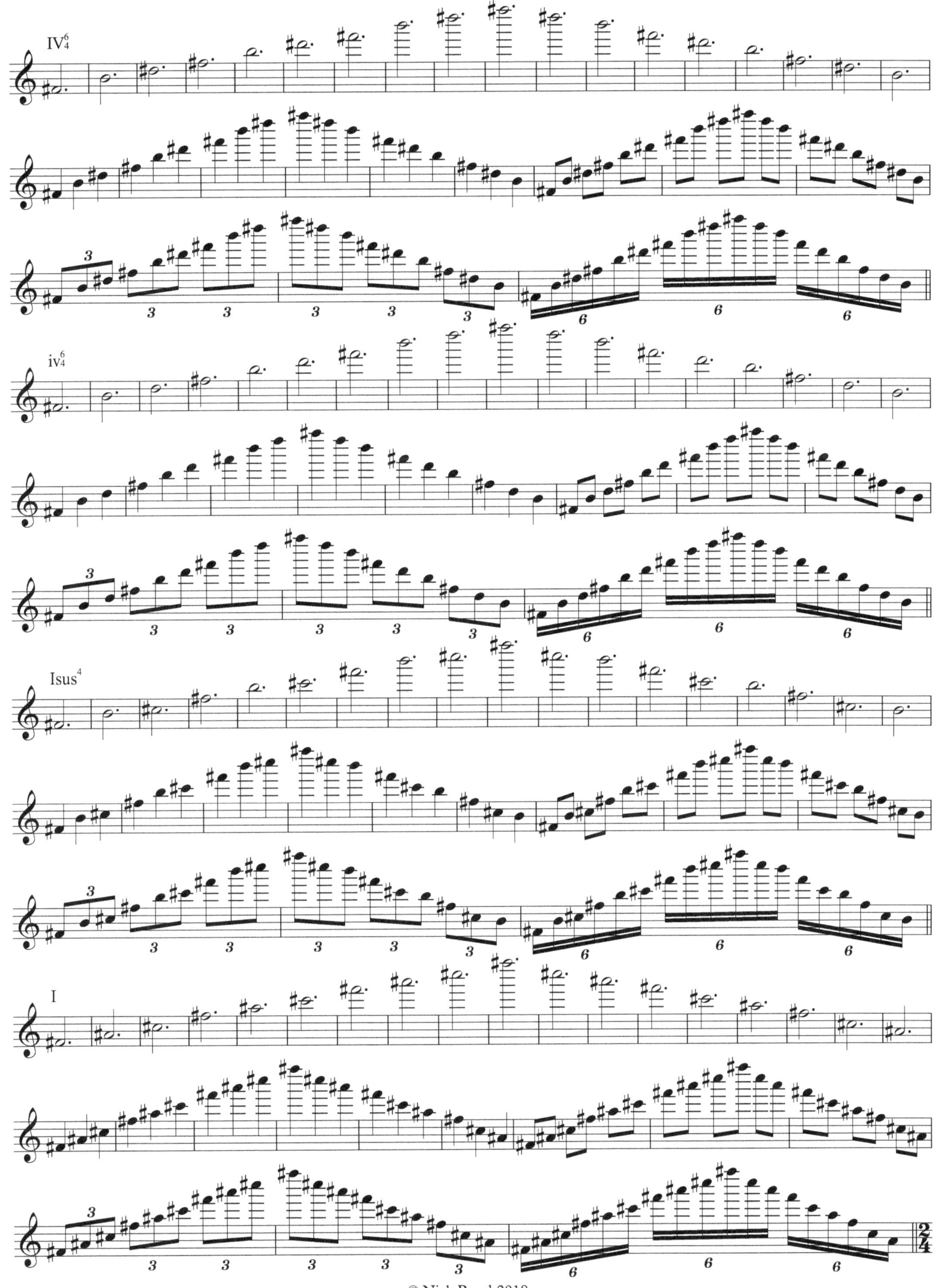


© Nick Revel 2018

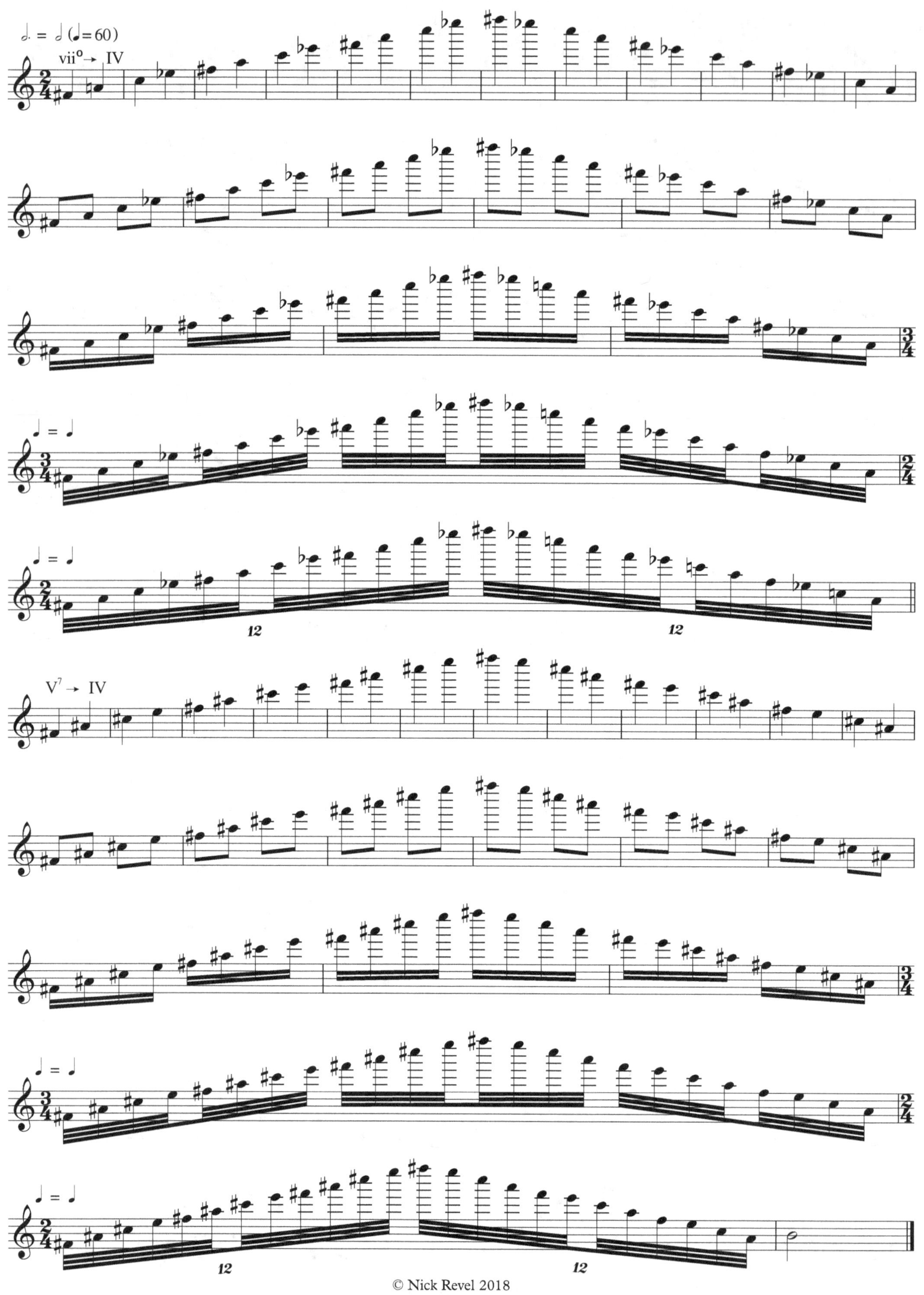

♩. = ♩ (♩=60)
vii° → IV
V⁷ → IV
12
12
12
12
© Nick Revel 2018